GLOBAL MARKETS AND NATIONAL INTERESTS

the new geopolitics of energy, capital, and information

Significant Issues Series
Timely books presenting current CSIS research and analysis of interest to the academic, business, government, and policy communities.
Managing editor: Roberta L. Howard

For four decades, the **Center for Strategic and International Studies (CSIS)** has been dedicated to providing world leaders with strategic insights on—and policy solutions to—current and emerging global issues.

CSIS is led by John J. Hamre, formerly deputy secretary of defense, who has been president and CEO since April 2000. It is guided by a board of trustees chaired by former senator Sam Nunn and consisting of prominent individuals from both the public and private sectors.

The CSIS staff of 190 researchers and support staff focus primarily on three subject areas. First, CSIS addresses the full spectrum of new challenges to national and international security. Second, it maintains resident experts on all of the world's major geographical regions. Third, it is committed to helping to develop new methods of governance for the global age; to this end, CSIS has programs on technology and public policy, international trade and finance, and energy.

Headquartered in Washington, D.C., CSIS is private, bipartisan, and tax-exempt. CSIS does not take specific policy positions; accordingly, all views expressed herein should be understood to be solely those of the authors.

The CSIS Press
Center for Strategic and International Studies
1800 K Street, N.W., Washington, D.C. 20006
Telephone: (202) 887-0200   Fax: (202) 775-3199

GLOBAL MARKETS AND NATIONAL INTERESTS

the new geopolitics of energy, capital, and information

edited by lincoln p. bloomfield jr. · foreword by james a. kelly

THE CSIS PRESS

**Center for Strategic
and International Studies**

Washington, D.C.

Significant Issues Series, Volume 24, Number 3
© 2002 by Center for Strategic and International Studies
Washington, D.C. 20006

The views expressed herein should be understood to be solely the personal views of the individual contributors and not the views of the government of the United States or any other country, or of any U.S. or foreign agency or official, or of any organization, whether public, private, for profit, or nonprofit.

06 05 04 03 02   5 4 3 2 1

ISSN 0736-7136
ISBN 0-89206-404-8

Library of Congress Cataloging-in-Publication Data
Global markets and national interests : the new geopolitics of energy, capital, and information / Lincoln P. Bloomfield Jr., editor ; foreword by James A. Kelly.
      p. cm. — (Significant issues series ; v. 24, no.3)
    Includes bibliographical references and index.
    ISBN 0-89206-404-8 (pb : alk. paper)
    1. Petroleum industry and trade—Political aspects. 2. Energy industries—Political aspects. 3. Capital movements—Political aspects. 4. Globalization. 5. Security, International.   I. Bloomfield, Lincoln P. Jr.   II. Series.
HD9560.6 .G55 2001
338.2'7282—dc21

                                                      2001004283

CONTENTS

FOREWORD

James A. Kelly

PUBLICATION OF THIS BOOK BY THE CSIS PRESS CULMINATES A ONE-year project undertaken by the Pacific Forum CSIS of Honolulu, Hawaii, in collaboration with Armitage Associates L.C. of Arlington, Virginia. The study project was conceived, and the participation of contributing authors arranged and coordinated, by Lincoln P. Bloomfield Jr., who also edited this volume. The work was performed under a grant from the Center for International Political Economy (CIPE) in New York.

For several years, CIPE has supported original research in three distinct areas of importance to U.S. policy and to the United States' political and economic partners on the Pacific Rim, notably Japan. Under the guidance of Ambassador Edward P. Djerejian and Senior Energy Adviser Amy Myers Jaffe, the James A. Baker III Institute for Public Policy at Rice University in Houston, Texas, conducted a range of very useful energy studies. The National Bureau of Economic Research in Cambridge, Massachusetts, led by Dr. Martin Feldstein, conducted several macroeconomic studies. Finally, a wide-ranging series of foreign policy issue seminars and study papers about the economic and military future of Asia was organized by Dr. Paul Wolfowitz, then dean of the Paul Nitze School of Advanced International Studies (SAIS) at the Johns Hopkins University in Washington, D.C., and Dr. Karl Jackson, also of SAIS.

Inspired by these bodies of original research on developments in the international energy, financial, and security arenas, respectively,

Pacific Forum CSIS and Armitage Associates combined to undertake an intellectually ambitious effort—a single study with roots in all three areas. The basic point of departure was to recognize that twentieth-century sensibilities about the U.S. national interest are inadequate as a guide in the twenty-first-century world. To fulfill U.S. leadership potential, a generation of U.S. and allied policymakers with core beliefs and expertise honed in the Cold War era needs to reexamine, revalidate, and, above all, broaden and deepen its grasp of the new geopolitical realities. To be effective, national security analysis must account for the fundamental transformations being effected by the information technology revolution, the globalization of national economic systems, and the emergence of distinctly post–Cold War priorities and linkages throughout the international community of nations.

Thus, our concept was to fuse into a single analysis key perspectives drawn from the ordinarily specialized and compartmented fields of energy, international economics, and national security policy. Such an analysis, informed by the past, would take stock of present trends, examine future possibilities, and divine their significance for larger foreign policy equities. We hoped that the resulting insights would suggest the new contours of a contemporary national interest formulation that is relevant to policymakers in Washington and other capitals, as well as instructive to students of foreign policy.

In pursuit of this objective, we incorporated into our work two novel variations on the traditional approach to such study projects. First, we engaged experts in the fields of energy and international economics to research changing market dynamics and examine future extreme oil price scenarios and asked them to present their findings in lay terms rather than in the language they commonly use among their professional peers. We chose this approach because our primary intended audience is the serious foreign policy generalist, who we assume does not have advanced professional experience with all of the concepts or methodologies involved. This approach required patient indulgence on the part of all of the contributing experts.

The second variation from common practice was to make this study a sequential rather than simultaneous process. In other words, we chose not to treat each piece of work as an autonomous product to be prepared in isolation and grouped with the other contributions for publication only at the conclusion of the project. Instead, each chapter of this book was developed with full cognizance of the work preceding it.

Peter Fusaro commenced the process by profiling the changing oil economy and international energy sector. We asked him to help us assess how much havoc extreme oil price trends could create a decade from now. Mr. Fusaro created a set of extreme high and low oil price scenarios, set against a normal or base case, for the year 2010. He projected global levels of production and consumption in each case, with enough regional and country-specific data to help us visualize the map of the world oil economy in each case. Dr. Herman Franssen served as an expert reader to Mr. Fusaro's study and contributed a chapter highlighting the enduring significance of Western access to Persian/Arabian Gulf oil supplies in the coming decade.

Much as Mr. Fusaro had done with the energy economy, Dr. Catherine Mann profiled the rapidly changing shape and dynamics of the international financial system. We wanted to anticipate the scale and significance of any major oil price distortions in the global economy of 2010. Working from Mr. Fusaro's oil scenarios, Dr. Mann estimated resulting capital flows and generated a fresh, contemporary model and analysis of the oil economy as it relates to overall capital movements in the global economy today and in the future.

Tokyo-based financial writer R. Taggart Murphy served as an expert reader of Dr. Mann's study. He also contributed a chapter describing the potential for serious disruptions of the U.S. and Japanese economies in particular, and the global energy economy generally, should Tokyo's practices in managing the yen-dollar relationship lead to a crisis of currency instability.

We then convened a panel of noted foreign policy experts to review these studies, hear from the principal researchers directly, and consider the evolving relationship of oil and international economics to national interests and national security planning in the new century.

Our intent was to draw from the energy economics and international capital flow analysis as a basis for probing the core foreign policy issues elaborated in Ambassador Richard Armitage's introduction (chapter 1).

At a conference at CSIS in Washington, D.C., on March 1, 2000, our foreign policy experts' panel received briefings that highlighted key insights from the energy and international economic studies. Peter Fusaro's discussion of the oil and energy sector was followed by comments from Adam Sieminski of Deutsche Bank Securities on the issues raised by Mr. Fusaro's work. Catherine Mann discussed the main findings of her international economic study, and Kevin Nealer of the Scowcroft Group offered insights inspired by her work. Several noted experts in these fields participated in the general discussion of future dynamics in the international energy and financial sectors.

Thus briefed, the foreign policy panel presented its insights. The panel consisted of Robert Zoellick, Yukio Okamoto, Janne Nolan, Robert Manning, and Paul Wolfowitz; it was moderated by Ambassador Armitage. The panelists' perspectives were the basis for the concluding chapter by Ambassador Armitage, Lincoln Bloomfield Jr., and myself.

Our expectation from the beginning was not to produce a definitive formulation of U.S. national interests or strategic imperatives in the twenty-first century. Indeed, a reader looking for solutions to all of the challenges raised here will surely be disappointed. Instead, our goal was and is to stimulate original thinking and invite further debate about fundamental national policy precepts at a time of technologically driven transformation throughout the world. We sincerely hope our readers will take us up on the invitation.

PREFACE

Lincoln P. Bloomfield Jr.

THIS BOOK IS NOT FOR THE INTELLECTUALLY FAINT-HEARTED. IT traverses the fields of energy, finance, and national security. Each field comprises a society of experts—academics, journalists, and policy practitioners—whose analytic domains do not routinely intersect. Each domain uses a unique language, vocabulary, and body of assumed knowledge. In these pages, we invited experts in all three areas to join in a common conversation about, essentially, the ways in which globalization is affecting foreign policy.

The impetus for this project was a belief that a world that will be shaped less by twentieth-century political dynamics and more by the digital revolution demands national leaders with a broad and sophisticated understanding of the new forces affecting people and nations. As James Kelly notes in the foreword, the goal from the outset of our study was to break free of the predictive or policy prescriptive trains of analysis that, for example, energy experts would deem of interest to the oil sector, or international economists to financial and economic officialdom.

Instead, we asked recognized experts in these areas to respond to concerns and priorities that were alien to their accustomed patterns of analysis. The foreign policy specialists leading the effort fulfilled a desire to learn more about how oil, international finance, and the information superhighway are connected today, as well as how their interplay in the global economy may give rise to future national security concerns. Our hope is that the same benefit will accrue to students, policy planners, journalists, government decisionmakers, and legislators with similar interests in foreign policy and national security.

At the initial stages of this study project in the fall of 1999, the question arose regarding what figure (in current dollars) would be an appropriate threshold for an "extreme" high price for crude oil for the year 2010 (as described in the scenarios in chapter 2). A benchmark crude oil price of $25 per barrel appeared to be a reasonable high-price figure because it certainly was higher than prices had been for a few years. The idea of $30-oil seemed so high in 1999 to some observers as to strain credulity.

In the end, we chose $30 as the threshold figure for our extreme high-price scenario. By the time this book went to print, benchmark prices had surged into the mid- and upper $30s for sustained periods, and our high-price scenario no longer seemed unrealistic. Neither, for that matter, did the notion that governments can be spurred into a crisis-response mode by extreme oil prices, pressured to answer political demands for action without triggering unanticipated adverse market effects. Indeed, recent energy sector developments suggest that the time is ripe for a fresh look at how things have changed since oil staked its claim to geopolitical eminence more than a quarter-century ago.

I speak for Pacific Forum CSIS and Armitage Associates in expressing deep appreciation to many individuals who have contributed to this effort. We are grateful to the participating authors and commentators whose research and ideas appear here.

The directors of this project, James A. Kelly and Richard L. Armitage, are responsible for launching an ambitious effort, assuring the cooperation and participation of key institutions and individuals, and providing the leadership that inspired the fresh thinking reflected on these pages.

Richard A. Nelson of Armitage Associates, Jane Skanderup of Pacific Forum CSIS, and Tom Kuhn and Catherine Wilkins of the Center for International Political Economy deserve particular acknowledgment for their central role in managing and administering the project. Lisa Bonner and Dahlia Astifo assisted in the administrative aspects of the study, as well as the March 2000 conference at CSIS. Leila Monroe skillfully transcribed the recording of the conference proceedings into typed text.

Frederic C. Hof and Michael P. C. Carns provided valuable input at various stages of the project. We thank the International Energy Agency in Paris for helping to meet our energy data requirements. Robert Ebel, director of the CSIS Energy and National Security Program, and Professor Dennis O'Brien of the University of Oklahoma provided expert perspective and critical suggestions as the manuscript was taking shape; to the extent that this work exhibits overall consistency and coherence, much credit and gratitude are due to them.

Our thanks also to many professional colleagues in the United States, the Middle East, and Asia who expressed interest in this work as it progressed. Their perspectives have helped us ask the questions and frame the issues for study in a way that will, we hope, have the most salience to policymakers, scholars, and private-sector analysts alike.

Roberta Howard, senior editor at CSIS, provided invaluable service in converting a project manuscript into a finished book. Responsibility for any and all editorial shortcomings, however, is mine alone.

PART ONE

THE NEW GEOPOLITICS

CHAPTER ONE

INTRODUCTION

Richard L. Armitage

To U.S. FOREIGN POLICY PRACTITIONERS OF LONG EXPERIENCE, THE idea that oil is a strategic resource is an article of faith, borne out repeatedly during the twentieth century. From the time of the earliest oil concessions in the late 1800s, American technology and know-how has tied U.S. commercial interests in some measure to the Middle East. Yet only after World War II did the United States come to view its interests as giving rise to enduring and wide-ranging international responsibilities in peacetime as well as war.

The spate of post-colonial nationalizations of various oil operations beginning in the 1950s was an early warning that U.S. and Western economic involvement in the oil-rich Middle East also was a central foreign policy interest and a trigger for foreign intervention. Washington's well-founded concern that the Soviet Union coveted influence, economic power, and, ultimately, control over an ever-greater swath of the world's geography heightened the policy connection between access to oil resources and national security. When the British withdrew from their longstanding great-power role "east of Suez," the United States assumed the mantle as the West's principal guarantor of stability throughout the Middle East.

And yet, the economic importance of oil was not fully understood until it was subjected to a severe disruption: the sudden scarcity imposed by the Arab oil embargo of 1973. As world prices for crude oil and retail prices for gasoline shot upward, the United States, Europe, and Japan realized that they were vulnerable as never before to the economic decisions of the major oil-producing countries. The 1979 crude oil shortages again produced lines for gasoline in the United States and helped push inflation and interest rates to crisis proportions, from which it took years to recover.

The several-fold increase in the price of crude oil during the 1970s led to a significant phenomenon in the international economy: the transfer of wealth from consuming to producing countries. Suddenly, key producers such as Saudi Arabia were generating foreign exchange income far exceeding their accustomed standard of living. This windfall of "petrodollars" could not all be absorbed domestically, and reinvestment of these capital flows overseas was so significant that the process became commonly known as "petrodollar recycling."

Economists familiar with the crisis that unfolded as U.S. banks loaned this capital to developing countries, notably Brazil, that later could not meet repayment obligations will agree that oil was a very significant driver of international capital flows in the 1970s. It also was an important commodity in its own right for the industrial manufacturing sectors of the United States and its allies in Europe and Japan. Oil price increases translated directly into inflation within the industrialized nations.

Thus did oil, and the principal oil-exporting countries of the Middle East, come to achieve a special global status in the latter part of the twentieth century. An area of the world that had been recognized after World War II as a focus of geopolitical competition between the Communist East and the Free World emerged, from 1973 onward, as a veritable jugular vein for the Western economies.

National security planners from the late 1970s to the 1990s required no specialized expertise to grasp the connection between oil and the national interest. The world's major oil supply was located in the strategic Persian/Arabian Gulf region. The transit of that oil, through pipelines and across the high seas, was recognized as a potential locus of risk to the consuming countries. Political stability throughout the so-called Arc of Crisis spanning from north Africa through Southwest and Central Asia became a major concern for U.S. foreign policy.

The end of the 1970s was a formative time for contemporary U.S. security policy. The United States, its civic morale damaged by Watergate and its appetite for foreign military intervention blunted by the recent pullout under fire from Vietnam, was not looking for trouble in the Gulf region. Perhaps that is why trouble occurred, and in spades, as externally supported security threats appeared within Saudi Arabia, revolution in Iran turned what Washington had hoped would become an American client state into a bitterly hostile adversary, and 140,000 Soviet military forces rolled southward to occupy neighboring Afghanistan.

In the face of a deteriorating strategic outlook, the United States' imperative to preserve access to the world's main oil supply became an explicit declaratory policy. President Jimmy Carter announced that access to the world's main crude oil supply was a "vital interest" of the United States, and he vowed that the United States would repel efforts "by any outside force to gain control of the Persian Gulf region." Thereafter, this policy was known as the Carter Doctrine.

The concept of a "rapid deployment force" to back up this national commitment moved quickly from Pentagon drawing boards to become a reality. Agreements to pre-position military stocks and to permit access by U.S. forces were made with sympathetic governments in the Middle East, including Oman and Egypt. A new unified military command, U.S. Central Command, took geographic responsibility for the Arab and Islamic Middle East region.

Throughout the 1980s, the task of promoting stability and maintaining positive influence in the Middle East was daunting for the United States, as Arab-Israeli, Arab-Arab, and inter-Islamic tensions of a political, social, and religious nature polarized and unsettled the peoples and governments of the area. The Gulf itself was consumed with the Iraq-Iran war. Maryland's respected internationalist, Senator Charles McC. Mathias Jr., writing in *Foreign Policy* in 1986—as the United States absorbed the impact of an ill-fated military intervention in Lebanon and an epidemic of bombings, hijackings, and hostage-takings—pleaded the case for continued American engagement in the Middle East as follows:

The U.S. need for Persian Gulf oil may be less today than a decade ago, but does anyone want to gamble that this will be true in the 1990s? Even if American needs remain low, America's closest allies are likely to remain dependent. Japan today imports 60 percent of its oil from the Middle East and Western Europe, 20 to 25 percent, and the United States has agreed to share petroleum in the event of a shortage.[1]

Senator Mathias' prescription turned out to be prescient. Within a year the U.S. Navy was called on to counter a serious security challenge in the Gulf. Operation Earnest Will involved re-flagging Kuwaiti oil tankers under the U.S. flag, clearing Iranian mines, and defending merchant traffic against attack from Iranian vessels.

Iraq's invasion of Kuwait in August 1990 raised the specter of a reckless and unprincipled regime in Baghdad gaining effective control over the oil reserves of not only Iraq and Kuwait but potentially the largest of all—Saudi Arabia. Saddam Hussein already had gravely transgressed international norms by using chemical weapons to attack his own citizens, at Halabja, and suspicions that Iraq in 1990 was close to achieving an operational nuclear weapons capability were confirmed later by U.N. inspectors.

In response to the Iraqi aggression, President George Bush, his advisers, and many members of Congress concluded that ceding to this regime a large measure of control over the world's daily oil supply and the price of crude oil would create untold instability and peril to U.S. interests. President Bush's decision to resist Iraq's seizure of Kuwait, notwithstanding Secretary of State James A. Baker III's rhetoric about "jobs," was rooted in geopolitics. U.S. political, economic, and military interests, along with U.S. influence in the world, were on the line. The United Nations Security Council, united as never before in authorizing the use of force under Chapter 7 of the UN Charter, reflected broad international recognition of the interests at stake.

After the Gulf War—with the Soviet Union dissolved and succeeded by 12 newly independent states, including Russia and the three liberated Baltic nations—the strategic landscape changed radically. American voters brought to power a new, post-World War II generation of Democratic and Republican representatives in the executive and legislative branches. The national political agenda shifted away from the fight to secure the Free World against Communist tyranny and took up the uniquely domestic concerns of American citizens.

Preservation of access to Middle Eastern oil lost a measure of prominence as a U.S. national priority during the 1990s, for several reasons. Within the United States, digital technology grew in economic importance as petroleum-intensive heavy industry, supplanted by lower-cost operations offshore, declined. Western Hemisphere oil producers such as Mexico, Venezuela, and Canada became more significant suppliers to the American market relative to Middle East producers, benefiting from shorter shipping times and costs. Progress in Israel's peace negotiations with its Arab neighbors, notably the Oslo Accord with the Palestinians and the Jordan-Israel peace treaty, fed optimism that a half-century of destabilizing tension in the Arab and Islamic world over the existence of Israel might be nearing an end.

As the U.S. defense budget after the Gulf War continued the downward trend that had begun in the latter part of the 1980s, the focus of national security efforts shifted from large-scale war planning to new categories of concerns. These new concerns included humanitarian crises within failing states, intrastate ethnic conflicts, proliferation of weapons of mass destruction and delivery systems to irresponsible actors, and terrorism, often carried out in the name of religion. Significant Middle East oil producers—including Libya, Iran, and Iraq—were among Washington's primary countries of concern relative to such threats.

By the 1990s, the gasoline shortages and steep oil price hikes of the 1970s were distant memories for members of Congress and Clinton administration officials alike, as they discovered a shared affection for the use of sanctions as an all-purpose foreign policy tool. Sanctioning a foreign country was seen as a convenient way to signal America's moral disapproval and make at least a pretense of exerting some suasion, without having to commit military forces or even expend foreign assistance funds. Between 1993 and 1996 alone, the U.S. government applied sanctions to no fewer than 61 countries.[2]

By the end of the 1990s, oil-producing countries under U.S. or UN sanctions included Iran, Iraq, Libya Azerbaijan, and Burma/Myanmar, and U.S. political relations with other energy states, such as Algeria and Indonesia, were strained. Even Saudi Arabia found surprisingly few congressional defenders when its cooperation with U.S. investigators was called into question after the second of two terrorist bombing attacks in five months killed 19 U.S. airmen at Khobar Towers in Dhahran in April 1996.

In early 2000, as benchmark oil prices climbed above $30, U.S. officials entreated the oil ministers of Mexico, Norway, Saudi Arabia, and Kuwait, among others, to pump more crude oil. The irony was not lost on many observers that unlike the 1970s, this time the shortfall in world oil supply relative to demand arguably owed something to U.S. government policies—namely, sanctions aimed at constricting the hydrocarbon sector in major producing countries—along with the production cutbacks by the Organization of Petroleum Exporting Countries (OPEC).

As the twenty-first century began, the U.S. military's Central Command and the U.S. Navy's Fifth Fleet, based in the Gulf, retained a keen appreciation that American interests, as well as those of the United States' European and Pacific allies, remained at risk in a geopolitically sensitive region. But at the same time, the world had changed in the two decades since the Carter Doctrine proclaimed the Gulf an area of "vital interest" to the United States.

The question is, how much has the world changed and in what sense has it remained the same? The U.S. policy community today doubtless believes that the oil reserves and daily production of the Persian/Arabian Gulf region continue to be strategically significant to U.S. national interests. How significant are they in the 2000s, however—and will they remain so a decade hence?

Whereas other studies may predict whether oil will be plentiful or scarce, expensive or cheap, heavily or lightly utilized in the years to come, our goal has been to discern whether oil will be as important to the United States and other countries in the future as it has been in the past. We want to know whether "security of oil supply" means the same thing today as it did 25 years ago, and whether it will long remain a central concern of national security planning.

The start of the twenty-first century is an opportune moment to revisit some of the fundamental geopolitical underpinnings of the U.S. national interest that have guided the foreign and defense policies of the United States and its allies for a generation or more. By asking anew some basic questions, we imply no lack of enthusiasm for enduring American responsibilities in the world. Instead, we hope to help illuminate the path ahead for U.S. and allied policymakers, who will carry the burden of explaining and defending their future commitments before legislative bodies and public opinion.

Among these questions are the following:

- Will the defense of the Persian/Arabian Gulf remain a vital interest of the United States in the year 2010 and beyond? Will the security of oil supplies from the Gulf be significantly more important to other major actors in the world than to the United States? How does this outlook affect U.S. policy considerations?

- In the same vein, will the defense of the Asia-Pacific region remain a vital interest of the United States in 2010 and beyond? If so, to what extent will that interest derive from our allies' need for access to imported oil supplies? And if oil from the Gulf is of declining importance to the U.S. economy, what is the twenty-first century basis for such a U.S. strategic commitment?

- What circumstances in the modern global oil economy should national security planners consider most threatening to U.S. and allied interests? What are the indicators of crisis? And are existing policies and capabilities adequate to guard against such contingencies?

- Are there national interest—and even national security—aspects of the emerging digitally driven global economy that were not clearly discernible through the Cold War lens of the last half of the twentieth century? What dynamics do tomorrow's foreign policy practitioners need to master to be conversant with the geopolitics of the twenty-first-century energy economy and the global financial system?

To pose such questions is by no means to presume that good answers exist. Nor do we call into question the expectation of an engaged, energetic American role in the world. We assume that the elected and appointed officials entrusted with conducting U.S. foreign policy in the years ahead will treasure and seek to preserve this country's special role of international leadership.

There can be no doubt, however, that the national interests of the United States and other countries, and the risks to those interests, are being redefined by the explosion of applied technology across the globe. We need to take stock of the changes occurring all around us, touching almost every field of endeavor, and look critically into the future.

Experience tells us that energy trends are not linear. Economic trends lately have defied cyclical interpretations. National security plans informed by previous conflicts can never fully anticipate new threats that often do the most harm. Challenging though the task may be, however, we must try to anticipate and prepare for future crises.

Success in U.S. policy planning, including sustained cultivation of strong and vibrant international cooperation backed by political support at home, will be assured only to the extent that we can grasp these transformative developments in the international environment. To that end, and with all due modesty for its obvious shortcomings, we offer this study as a first look at the new century's new geopolitics.

Notes

[1] Charles McC. Mathias Jr., "Dateline Middle East: the Dangers of Disengagement," *Foreign Policy* no. 63 (Summer 1986): 172.

[2] Stuart E. Eizenstat, under secretary of state for economic, agricultural, and business affairs, remarks before the North American Committee of the National Policy Association, Washington, D.C., January 7, 1998.

PART TWO

OIL AND ENERGY MARKETS
FROM NOW TO 2010

CHAPTER TWO

THE FUTURE IMPORTANCE OF OIL
GEOPOLITICAL LYNCHPIN OR COMMON COMMODITY?

Peter C. Fusaro

THIS CHAPTER EXAMINES THE RAPIDLY CHANGING NATURE OF ENERGY
markets. The first part of the chapter notes some of the future implications of those changes. The second part tests the extremes in the behavior of the oil markets in 2010 by positing artificial scenarios:
extended very high and low oil prices, set against a reference normal
set of conditions. The global, regional, and country-specific consequences of these alternative extreme market scenarios form the basis
for the analysis in succeeding chapters.

THE CHANGING CHARACTERISTICS OF ENERGY
MARKETS AND THE ROLE OF OIL IN THE 2010 GLOBAL
ECONOMY

The energy industry is in the midst of fundamental change driven by
consolidation, continuous technology improvements, commodity
market price volatility, environmental imperatives, and new market
fundamentals. Oil, extracted and consumed in so many parts of the
world, has been the most global of commodities for much of the past
century. The new regime of market forces, however, has begun to
render obsolete the supply management techniques that oil producers have used successfully, including in the recent past. Their continued effectiveness in restraining supply will be short-lived. The
capability to see oil prices on a screen and to trade oil and its products 24 hours a day has introduced global price transparency, such

that short-term price swings even out over time, while reductions in operating costs since the price crash of 1986 already have changed the relationship between oil suppliers and consumers.

Today's energy industry is more driven by technology, efficiency gains, environmental imperatives, and competition than it was previously. New forms of integration and strategic alliances are emerging. Privatization and deregulation trends in energy have accelerated this process. The overall trend is toward consolidation.

As oil and gas companies today continue the late 1990s trend to restructure and merge, they face the challenge of how to maximize the productivity of their fixed assets, such as production and manufacturing assets, in an era of relentless and accelerating market evolution. These assets typically have operated in 20- to 30-year life cycles and are modified continuously. Challenges to asset performance are now more pronounced, and more consequential, because of the new market dynamics. Because the ability to predict market movements is problematic if not impossible, a preferred way to protect future capital investments in this sector is to anticipate the life cycle of the investment and build in additional capacity that can later add efficiency.

The emerging global energy economy, therefore, is not like it was in the past. North American and European private companies will continue to merge, reorganize, and develop strategic alliances, while government-directed national oil companies will become more regional in outlook and some may privatize. Japanese and Korean refiners will continue to consolidate, and some will move from being domestic companies to become regional and even global players. Energy service companies will expand and offer more kinds of services, such as outsourcing, project finance, and technology transfer.

The role of technology in this equation is to influence and even reshape the basic structure of the oil and gas industry, particularly on the production side. Improvements in technology such as three-dimensional seismic and horizontal drilling already have demonstrated their significance by reducing production costs to $5 per barrel by the mid-1990s. Continuous technology advances such as four-dimensional seismic, three-phase pumps, and rotary drilling will further reduce costs; equally important, these technologies will accelerate the depletion of existing private reserves as they raise recovery rates.

In other words, one significant effect of technology is that lower-cost, more easily accessible oil is being depleted more efficiently, thoroughly, and quickly, putting off and thereby raising the eventual cost of exploiting most untapped reserves in the world. This situation has some interesting implications.

Based on the current higher cost spiral for finding and exploiting new reserves, we anticipate that recovery costs will grow in the future because most of the easily accessible oil will already have been found. The point to remember for private oil companies is that rising costs may follow rising prices. Thus, if market incentives dictate that easily recovered reserves are to be depleted even more quickly with the benefit of the new technologies, the future balance of oil productive capacity will shift to the OPEC producers.[1]

For most producers at least, their need and desire for foreign capital investment and expertise to increase exploitation of their known reserves will accelerate. Such was the case with Venezuela until changes under the Chavez government, as the major oil companies invested capital and expertise to support development of existing and new reserves in that country's newly liberalized and privatized energy sector.

Increased efficiency in oil production is but one side of the energy equation that is coming into focus. Commercializing technologies now entering the marketplace are beginning to reshape the entire industry from the wellhead right up to the wires behind the consumer's home usage meter. This global reintegration of the energy industry affects all segments of the energy value chain, from production to refining to power generation to transportation to consumption.

The key insight is that the impact of enhanced energy efficiency gains on energy consumption is not a straight-line function. Restructuring and consolidation fostered by financial and technological innovation will include further developments in how energy is produced, transported, and consumed. Breakthroughs in fuel cell and microturbine technology, on-site generation of power, hybrid electric vehicles, and influences of the Internet on commercial practices will determine how the future energy industry is structured and functions.

All of this analysis begs the question of oil's strategic importance in the twenty-first century—its patterns of availability and usage, as well as its salience as an economic and political factor. Attempts by OPEC and other producers to manage oil markets and prices seem destined over time to fall by the wayside because price hikes of any duration will only provoke increasingly efficient responses in the form of new investment and production that will alleviate pressure on global supplies. Technological shifts are driving this market adaptability further than before. The only question is how soon supply management efforts will become ineffective.

This study aims to provoke a new strategic appreciation of this emerging twenty-first-century energy equation. Whereas at one time a few governments acting as a cartel and a handful of major international oil companies determined what oil supplies were available, and where, and at what price, the market drivers from this point on are many and pervasive. Technologically driven change is occurring across the energy value chain. Moreover, beyond these developments, still other new factors are at work.

Environmental considerations now play a meaningful global role because of international concerns over greenhouse gas emissions and because cleaner fuel and conservation technologies are becoming more available and price-competitive at the retail level. The recent surge in use of natural gas for power generation in single- and combined-cycle turbines, and the emergence of a liquefied natural gas (LNG) trading market, are far more important elements in the overall global energy market equation than in the past. Growing electricity consumption across the globe—particularly in the major developing markets of China and India, among others—is a crucial market factor for the future.

The Internet economy is driving the dispersal and application of new processes, technologies, and ideas with unprecedented immediacy. Already, equipment procurement for upstream project development is commonly handled via electronic commerce (e-commerce) for the best price and "just-in-time" delivery. Retail functions for oil companies are utilizing integrated pricing, billing, and settlement through electronic applications. Efficiency, already a key focus in achieving oil company profitability in recent years, has been affected profoundly by such agents of change.

Specific aspects in the ongoing transformation of the global oil economy, and the energy sector as a whole, merit elaboration.

Oil Becomes an Increasingly "Commoditized" Commodity

Security of oil supplies has been regarded, at least since World War II, as a basic national interest for many nations, particularly the advanced industrial economies and the leading military powers. The United States, Europe, and Japan have long regarded the maintenance of energy security as key to their national strategies, even when oil was low-priced.

From the time of the Arab oil embargo in 1973–1974, when controlled scarcity forced much higher prices, oil has reigned as a central consideration in international economics, politics, and security. The threat of oil supply and price disruptions has guided national security policy planning in the United States and many other countries. The large-scale transfer of economic resources from the consuming countries to the producing countries and the reinvestment of windfall oil revenues internationally have made a large impact on the world economy in the past quarter-century. Predicting price movements in the global oil market has become as necessary as it has been frustrating.

Now comes the information technology revolution and its accelerating insinuation into every aspect of the oil trade. As in so many other sectors, the impact of this revolution not only is affecting the marketplace; it is creating structural changes of a higher order in the energy sector. When we ask, therefore, what to expect a decade hence in the global oil market, the answer might begin with an appreciation of the traditional logic of oil price movements.

By far the more significant insight, however, concerns the rapid transformation of the international energy economy from a fairly discrete equation among oligopolistic producers, refiners, and consumers to a much bigger, more complex, and speculative economy, one whose drivers henceforth will include global investment activity involving oil market securities instruments and a more ready ability to access alternative means of satisfying energy demand.

The latest elevation in oil prices, which began in 1999, represents a transitory phenomenon brought on first by the rebound in Asian oil demand following the region's economic crisis in 1997–1998. A second factor has been coordinated production restraint on the part of oil producers, which removed about 5 million barrels per day of the global supply. The sustained rise in prices from 1999 to 2001 also is indicative, however, of longer-term uncertainty about whether Central Asian oil will ever come to the world market.

In effect, this oil price buoyancy has been caused more by a cutback in supply than by increases in demand and reflects a growing concern over future supply choices. While the sustainability of oil prices at high levels is a matter of speculation, there is no reason to expect that prices will descend to the price lows of December 1998 very soon.

Previous oil-driven economic recessions were sparked by political events that posed a clear prospect of creating a significant oil supply disruption, such as the Soviet invasion of Afghanistan and the fall of the Shah of Iran, both in 1979, and the Gulf War crisis of 1990–1991. These events led to sustained higher oil prices—and war always has the potential to produce this effect. But the role of oil in many consuming country economies is now less prominent than in the past, as evidenced by relatively lower energy prices today compared to 1973. The reasons for this are several. The most important, however, is what one might term the "commoditization" of oil.

Energy trading began after the end of Official Selling Price (OSP) programs by the major oil companies and the OPEC nations following the 1973–1974 oil embargo; it coincided with the development of a spot market for crude oil and petroleum products.[2] In 1978, the changing structure nature of the physical spot market for oil presaged the development of energy futures with the successful launch of the New York Mercantile Exchange (NYMEX) heating oil futures contract, which was tied to its physical delivery in New York Harbor.[3]

Successive oil futures contracts and the development of an active over-the-counter (OTC) market for forward oil trading in the early 1980s significantly increased price transparency, and thereby boosted both physical and financial trading of crude oil and petroleum products globally.[4]

Oil's commoditization also has influenced the broader energy economy. Today, the price of oil on a forward curve for NYMEX or London's International Petroleum Exchange (IPE) affects drilling activity more profoundly than may be commonly realized. The markets react to continuous price volatility, which is a function of commodity markets in a situation of supply/demand imbalance. The influence of commodity markets is undeniable, no matter how reluctant OPEC producers are to become actively involved with either exchange-traded futures contracts or OTC financial oil price swaps.[5] Producers of oil are evidencing a newfound appreciation of the significance of price volatility and the role of hedging in their own short-term strategies.

Commodity markets for energy are growing, and rapidly. NYMEX open interest (an indicator of contract liquidity) for its benchmark West Texas Intermediate (WTI) crude oil contract grew 50 percent in 1999 alone, and similar trends have been seen on the IPE's Brent crude oil contract as well as the OTC oil markers, which are deeper and longer term.[6] Oil price risk management has come to be regarded as a survival skill within energy companies.

The point is that oil has broken out of the semi-cartelized market paradigm of the past quarter-century and become, over the past decade, a significant financial commodity. The driving force of markets today is no longer the fundamentals, but the speculators, hedge funds, and traders.[7] The next wave of this technology-driven oil market revolution will be further securitization of the physical asset—oilfields—into monetized trusts, funds, or equities that can be traded worldwide. This development builds on the initial steps represented by the Mexican Petrobonds of the early 1980s and the BP Royalty Trust of 1989. What we are witnessing, in effect, is the transfer of what economists would call the "commodity price risk of oil" to the capital markets at large.

The Emergence of Electronic Energy Trading

During the 1990s, financial transactions grew exponentially faster than global industrial output. Several web-based exchanges have been launched recently, and others are being readied, to trade the financial energy complex. The move to electronic energy trading on the Internet will alter commodity trading of oil and accelerate the process and rate of change in the value of assets.

Price assessment panels and index trading, which failed in the late 1980s, began to succeed in the 1990s.[8] Electronic index construction and screen trading are leading the new global trend, in which electronic brokerage and trading platforms will continue to displace the traditional patterns and structures of energy commerce, notably in the area of energy futures trading.

We can already see the effects of this emerging global energy trading market on the traditionally capital-intensive and conservative oil industry. The energy industry as a whole is responding to the proliferation of electronic trading platforms in all energy markets.[9] Companies such as Altra Energy Technologies, Houston Street, Swapnet, and Bloomberg, among others, are leading the way.

For their part, the futures exchanges also are beginning to adapt to this global challenge out of necessity because the energy business has been consolidating, restructuring, and concentrating as never before. Because profit margins have become razor-thin compared to the past, volume is now the key variable of profitability, and the need to move more barrels, molecules, or electrons is paramount.

Energy hedging is still in its infancy today; most producers and consumers are not hedging against price movements. Yet the trend toward energy sector deregulation in many countries shifts risk from governments to companies, such that more trading and hedging is virtually inevitable. Looking a mere decade forward, it is fair to project that the technological drivers of electronic trading and the Internet will enhance market liquidity across the energy complex and around the world.

Business-to-business e-commerce already has found ready applications in global energy trading markets. It has been estimated that electronic trading of natural gas, which has been active over the past five years, already accounts for about one-fourth of the entire U.S. Internet economy today. Electronic trading of gas, power, crude oil, coal, and natural gas liquids is well under way and allows efficient selection of creditworthy counterparties—a major concern in energy markets because many energy companies have lesser credit. It also reduces transaction costs through greater economies of scale—an advantage over both futures exchanges and brokers. In time, electronic energy trading will be integrated into a robust price risk and transaction management system so that real-time trading operations are integrated into a company's front-to-back office.

Larger, higher-capacity, and more prevalent electronic exchanges are the next phase in the shift of the energy industry toward an e-commerce base. Energy deregulation created the need for information systems that will support competitive global markets. The Internet has demonstrated itself to be the tool required for this higher-speed, higher-volume environment.

Key to setting the pace of change in energy markets worldwide is the spread of deregulation and liberalization schemes for oil, gas, and power. Such policy adjustments, coupled with the general rise of competition around the world, are intersecting with technological enhancements. The proliferation of electronic news dissemination, greater volumes of available data, and the perceived need for more real-time price discovery are all driving the move to electronic trading.

The e-commerce infrastructure being developed for the international energy industry will be scalable, and not every segment will be an instant success. Creation of this new infrastructure, however, will bring other tangible changes to the industry: it will decrease time to market, open new market channels, increase productivity, and lower sales costs.

It also will accelerate the focus of the industry to the downstream—to its customers, who will now have more, and more readily accessible, supply-side choices. In all of these developments one sees a common denominator of changing relationships between oil producers and their consumers in a world in which supply outpaces demand. American consumers—be they drivers of energy-inefficient trucks and sport utility vehicles objecting to high gasoline prices or lower-income residents of northern states clamoring for affordable home heating oil during a hard winter—are exercising political influence on their elected officials.

The media can magnify consumer power by fanning public anxieties over rising prices or dwindling supplies. Nor is this phenomenon limited to the United States; from Iran to the Philippines, popular sentiment in favor of continuing subsidization of artificially low gasoline prices will be ignored by governments at their peril.

Impact of Information Technology on the Shape of the Energy Sector

The shift from a heavy industrial society to a network-based society will have severe ramifications for the global energy industry, almost in the manner of a creative destruction model. This change will be in the direction of monetizing the value of assets in the ground and throughout the energy value chain—a departure from the old paradigm in which companies have pursued price competition globally through mass production, hardware, and economies of scale.

The new factors of success are information, ideas, relationships, and adaptability. Maintaining a competitive position will require continuous innovation as products and even services are "commoditized." The ongoing restructuring and consolidation of the energy industry worldwide is effectively destroying the old oil industry as we knew it in the twentieth century and recreating a new energy world with more supply-side choices dictated by the preferences and needs of customers rather than by the oligopolistic advantages of producers, notwithstanding OPEC's recent success in restricting global oil supplies.

Although size matters, as demonstrated by the recent emergence of larger competitors such as BP Amoco Arco, Exxon Mobil, and TotalFina Elf through mega mergers, the value of underlying assets is being redefined in the age of information. Having one's asset base sited in long molecules of oil and gas rather than in the marketplace is not where private or state-owned oil companies will want to be in the future.[10] They already recognize the need to diversify their energy supply portfolios and thereby spread their risks.

The focus of major oil companies after the recent spate of mergers has been acquiring assets rather than drilling for more reserves. The major companies already know where the physical assets are; they are waiting to see how sustainable higher prices will be before they invest substantially in new production. What these companies are finding is that the world has changed. The vertical integration of energy markets in the future, driven by electronic forces, will involve a mix and match of large and small energy players, with assets and markets finding efficient and transitory linkages. The key to survival and success in this new energy economy will be the flexibility of the large companies to react quickly and intelligently to this continuous process of optimization.

The Environment as a Market Driver

The importance of environmental considerations in the global energy market, already high, promises to grow further in this decade. Initially, the thrust was on the elimination of lead in gasoline, beginning in the United States during the 1970s. The effort then widened during the 1990s to global fuel reformulation, which means removing lead, sulfur, and volatile organic compounds from gasoline and diesel fuel. From fuel reformulation, the impetus has now shifted to stationary sources of pollution, beginning with a tightening of the Clean Air Act Amendment and extending to the requirements of the Kyoto Protocol of 1997, with its focus on greenhouse gas reductions.[11] The purposes of Kyoto remain salient to the energy industry, notwithstanding official U.S. misgivings over the terms of the protocol itself.[12]

What had been a peripheral economic externality for the energy industry—compliance with environmental regulation—is becoming a major challenge in how the industry does business throughout the world. Looking at the shape of the future market, the environmental factor will be a significant cost of doing business in the global energy arena.

Greenhouse gas reduction efforts now focus on stationary sources of pollution—primarily oil and gas production, refining, petrochemicals, and the power industry, as well as numerous other industrial processes. The priority of reducing carbon dioxide (CO_2) emissions, as well as sulfur dioxide and nitrous oxides (SO_2 and NO_X), feeds a predisposition against burning fossil fuels such as oil, gas, and coal.

The movement to reduce carbon emissions will force change, some of it painful, in the energy industry by directing the world's industrial base toward increasingly systemic energy efficiency, renewable energy, and the use of natural gas as a transition fuel for international environmental compliance. Emissions trading schemes are already being developed in the United States, the European Union (EU), Australia, and Japan to lower overall greenhouse gas emissions; the result is a greater role for more environmentally benign technologies in the generation and utilization of energy.

This trend poses a challenge to oil producers who are sitting on substantial unrealized resources that may lose much of their value if they are not brought to market in the next few decades; Saudi Arabia comes to mind in this regard. The coal industry is experiencing this loss of value, as all major oil companies have divested coal—a commodity whose sole function is power generation. Coal's share in the energy market today is in peril, and its value continues to decline because of increasing environmental concerns about global warming.

The longer-term impact of these environmental considerations on oil and gas producers is that they now feel more pressure to bring reserves to market as quickly as possible—a strategy that is diametrically opposed to the supply containment strategies that had, until now, formed the basic operating concept of the industry. The carbon world is vulnerable to being undermined by newer, cleaner, and greener technologies and a tidal wave of energy-efficient devices that will change the fabric of industrial infrastructure in the more advanced economies.

The cost of seeking greater environmental compliance will be particularly onerous in countries that already have made first-order adjustments—for example, Japan, which already is energy-efficient as a result of its concerted response to the oil price shocks of the 1970s. The bottom line, however, is that a price signal for carbon reduction will impose high costs in many countries.

Future environmentally driven price shocks will be international in scope; they will be regarded as a cost of doing business and, for some countries, a trade issue as well. The environmental issue will gain visibility during this decade as developing countries grapple with their own concerns, costs, and benefits on the road to sustainable development.

The Other Major Energy Trend—The Emerging Gas World

Global demand for natural gas as a source of power appears set to expand dramatically. The only near-term impediment is the shortage of combined-cycle turbines available from ABB, Siemens, and GE, which are sold out through 2003. Even in the United States, gas consumption has surpassed 1970s consumption levels only very recently as a result of fuel-use restrictions and fuel-switching capacity constraints of the past two decades. Natural gas consumption in the United States will likely increase four- to fivefold, however, relative to current usage for power generation over the next two decades, according to the Gas Research Institute. Already, all power stations burning oil in the United States have dual-fuel burning capability with gas.

In Europe, the Electricity Directive on Competition of February 1999 drove down prices, and the EU Gas Directive of August 2000 compounded the downward pressure on prices, with more gas-on-gas competition expected in that market. The Asia-Pacific region has myriad gas needs, including the need for liquefied natural gas in Japan, South Korea, Taiwan, India, and possibly China for power generation. Gas pipeline projects currently planned for the ASEAN region of Southeast Asia, China, and Australasia will intensify gas usage in power generation.[13] Improved gasification technology using coal, petroleum coke, Orimulsion, and residual fuel oil will further develop gas-fired power.[14]

In the Middle East, Saudi Arabia is stepping up gas production for domestic use, while Iran and Qatar, which together have the largest gas reserves in the region, are accelerating gas exploration and production. Iran should become an important exporter in the future, as development of the South Pars Field and the newly constructed gas pipeline into Turkey are realized. Qatar, whose 8.5 billion cubic meters of reserves are the third largest globally, has co-invested heavily in LNG technology with foreign partners (notably Japan), and plans exist for a local pipeline network to serve the states along the southern Arabian Gulf. Oman also is expected to become a prominent gas exporter among the Middle East states, possibly developing an underwater pipeline to Pakistan for the South Asia market.

The obvious outlets for either piped gas or LNG will be the Asia-Pacific and European power markets. Table 2.1 (page 53) illustrates the anticipated rapid rise of gas consumption across all regions.

The Changing Nature of Oil Production Economics

Oil production finding costs, which are the per barrel cost of adding new oil and gas reserves by exploration and development, have declined significantly since the early 1980s, when oil prices and drilling activities hit all-time peaks. These benefits appear to have plateaued, however; most of the more than $10 (per barrel) drop in finding and development occurred during the 1980s. Since 1995, finding costs have risen again to a level that erased the declines of the early 1990s, and they continue to increase. These increases are associated with drilling, acreage acquisition, equipment leasing, and other overhead costs.

The implementation of new seismic technologies for oil and gas production also has contributed to decreasing finding rates, measured as the quantity of resources found per dollar expended, because greater costs usually accompany initial implementation of such new technologies. One major advance in new exploration and drilling technologies was the increased use of three-dimensional (3-D) seismic data acquisition and interpretation. Commercialization of this process was hindered by large data processing requirements, but these added costs have been eliminated due to increased capacity and reliability of microprocessing.

Trends spurred by technological advances can be dramatic, as evidenced by the share of wells drilled in the U.S. Gulf of Mexico using 3-D seismic technology, which increased from 5 percent in 1989 to 80 percent in 1996. Application of this and other technologies such as horizontal drilling, three-phase pumps, coiled tubing, sub-sea completions, and separation should have an even more pronounced impact on the exploration success rate. The net effect is to increase oil production while drilling fewer wells. In fact, because of these advances in technology, most of the oil produced in this decade may come from existing oilfields—a trend that is fraught with implications for future oil price dynamics as those existing fields become depleted.

Contemplating the Energy Map of the World in 2010

Charting the historic and revolutionary changes in the energy marketplace as they are occurring is a challenge in and of itself. Projecting the shape of the not-too-distant future is even more challenging. Conventional wisdom among oil market analysts posits temporary conditions of normality in the global supply-demand equilibrium, giving way inevitably to the influences of rising demand from ascendant economies in China, India, Indonesia, and other developing countries, mostly in Asia.

Although one may acknowledge the validity of these broad economic assumptions, prudence dictates that we ask whether other factors and trends might mitigate or even override the impact of rising Asian demand on the future oil price equation. The thesis here is that the transformative market trends will have price effects that are at least as significant and enduring as that of the projected rise of energy demand in the world.

Regardless of which forces weigh most heavily on the future price of oil, however, the key concern for policymakers in the United States, Europe, Japan, and other countries is not so much predicting the specific movements of the future oil market, but grasping the importance—and potential disruptive impact—of that market on national and international interests, be they economic, political, or security.

To help address that question, we have composed projections that seek less to predict the future than to test its properties. Any specific oil price projection in 2010 must be regarded as very tenuous at best, for reasons elucidated throughout this chapter. Although the political leadership of the United States and other major economies must consider estimated future energy price trends, their efforts would be better directed toward seeking an appreciation of where oil fits into the global economy of the future and the strategic implications stemming therefrom. It is important for them to consider questions such as the following:

- Do anticipated trends in oil consumption point to significant economic linkages between major producers and future major consumers that could shape the international political environment?

- Does oil hold the potential in 2010, under any credible circumstances, to arrest or severely impede the functioning of the international economy and thereby generate serious economic, social, or even military disruptions?

- What would the world look like under extreme oil price conditions, high or low? And whose interests would be most profoundly affected, directly or indirectly?

What follows are three scenarios, two of which represent circumstances intended to posit "extreme" oil price conditions in the world. One is an extended low-price scenario, the other a high-price scenario, both set against a third set of data representing notional "normal" market conditions. The underlying premise of this exercise is the belief that by simulating the outer boundaries of energy market conditions a decade or so in the future, it will be possible to perceive the essential dynamics of economic and political activity brought about by such disruptions. The larger purpose is to test the durability of fundamental assumptions that have served as the underpinning for U.S. national security policy and the respective geopolitical outlooks, policies, and strategies of many U.S. allies and adversaries, dating back at least to the 1970s, if not before.

EXTREME OIL PRICE SCENARIOS IN 2010—EXPLORING THE SHAPE, SCOPE, AND IMPACT OF A FUTURE OIL "CRISIS"

Setting the Stage: Current Indicators of Future Market Characteristics

One does not have to engage in flights of fantasy to envision circumstances in the 2010 global energy markets that mark a significant departure from the experiences of the latter part of the twentieth century. The year 1999 presaged many of the new trends whose influence is likely to grow rapidly from now on.

Using West Texas Intermediate (WTI) crude oil, which is traded on the New York Mercantile Exchange, as the oil price benchmark, 1999 saw WTI prices move from a low of $12 per barrel to more than $27 per barrel—an increase of more than 100 percent. Although 1999 could not be considered a "normal" year for oil prices, by any recent standard of market behavior it did illustrate the price volatility of oil as a commodity and offered insights into the newer factors that underlie its commodity price movements.

In effect, political or economic factors are now translated instantaneously into price movements on trading screens in world oil markets, thus affecting crude oil and product cargo movements, which are increasingly based on arbitrage opportunities—price variances for the same commodity—between different regions of the world. The 1999 high and low prices offer an analytical point of departure in exploring low and high oil price scenarios a decade hence. In particular, oil price behavior now has a direct bearing on industry expenditures and strategies.

The lower oil prices during much of the 1990s before the 1999 price rally certainly were a factor behind industry consolidation and restructuring, although the industry megamergers of the late 1990s were driven primarily by a broader need to enhance performance and profitability in a changed marketplace. The cost-cutting efficiencies of reducing duplicative payrolls in the merged oil giants tell only a part of the story.

The main rationale of the 1998–2000 merger trend was to achieve global geographical diversity, economies of scale, and better focus on the core competencies of energy production, processing, and retail distribution. In going through this often-painful reorganization, the energy industry by necessity has improved its adaptability in order to be able to respond to changing market conditions and underlying price signals. In the new, bigger, faster, and more complex global energy economy, size matters and risk must be diversified for an oil company to remain productive and profitable.

The "extreme" low and high oil price scenarios delineated in this chapter and discussed throughout this book are intended to demonstrate the maximum impact of sustained abnormal market conditions on the industry and the global economic system. Although this study offers no prediction that either scenario will come to pass—indeed, our analysis suggests the improbability of that occurring—these scenarios depict the range of supply and demand conditions within which the global oil economy is likely to be operating in 2010.

For our scenarios, we define "low" oil prices as less than $10 per barrel in 1997 dollars and "high" oil prices as more than $30 per barrel in 1997 dollars, on a sustained basis of three years or longer. As a baseline for comparison, we define as "normal" oil market conditions the range, in 1997 dollars, between $15 and $25 per barrel. That said, what will be understood as "normal" conditions in 2010 inevitably will reflect differences from today's market. Some of these differences are likely to derive from the following circumstances.

Asian Oil Developments

Over a period of two decades until the onset of the Asian economic crisis in late 1997, Asian energy market growth was the most robust in the world. The extra boost in oil consumption during this growth period shortened the recovery time within the oil sector from the huge excess capacities accumulated in the early 1980s at a time of higher oil prices. The rapid growth in Asian energy consumption also focused attention on energy investment in this region; however, larger-scale oil reserves have not been located in Asia, with the exception of the Russian Far East.

Growth in Asia's energy consumption early in the twenty-first century is still widely projected to exceed that of the rest of the world. The prospect that China's energy consumption, in particular, will grow faster than that of the rest of the region has important energy security ramifications. China's policies on oil imports also will have an important influence on its overall foreign investment and balance of trade.

Security-of-supply issues have long dominated Asian oil market concerns, heightened by the region's heavy dependency on Middle Eastern supplies. These concerns, which have been perennial among Japanese policy planners since the 1970s, have now extended to China, India, and South Korea and may lead to the adoption of any of several energy security measures for Asian countries. These strategies may include further emergency stockpiling of oil, acquisition of greater equity interests in Middle East production, increased political and commercial ties between the major Asian consumer countries and Middle East producers, and adoption of governmental policies to restrain domestic oil demand and consumption.

Increased oil dependency also may lead to expanded use of natural gas to enhance energy security in the region and to respond to awakening popular environmental concerns. Both the development of a gas pipeline infrastructure and increased use of LNG are important supply-side options for Asian economies.

Gulf/OPEC Dominance of World Oil and Gas Reserves

Tables 2.2, 2.3, and 2.4 list the known reserves of oil and gas around the world. Worth noting are the vast oil and gas quantities held by the Organization of Petroleum Exporting Countries as its reserve base. Almost 65 percent—nearly two-thirds—of the world's proven oil reserves are located in the Middle East, with OPEC controlling 75 percent of the world's oil reserve base. Predictions vary about how much of this reserve base will reach the market in the coming decades.

A number of OPEC producers—notably Venezuela, Saudi Arabia, and Kuwait—have made significant investments in the downstream oil markets, including substantial refining and marketing assets in the United States and Europe. In recent years, these major producers have been pursuing downstream investments in important consumer countries to the east, notably China and India, as well as South Korea, the Philippines, Thailand, and Pakistan. These developments weigh against the possibility that OPEC producers would ever again engineer a cutoff of supply to key consumer markets, as happened in 1973.

2010 OIL PRICE SCENARIOS

Base or "Normal" Case Scenario

Because of the many uncertainties in predicting actual changes in the oil markets due to OPEC supply management, Asian demand, potential environmental policy impacts of the Kyoto Protocol and the like, we have chosen to use as a base, or "normal," case the very credible U.S. Department of Energy's (Energy Information Administration) 2010 Reference Case forecast, with modifications to show individual OPEC producers. Table 2.5 shows world production and consumption for this case.

Use of this reference case is not intended to imply endorsement of these data as a forecast of the future, even though the Department of Energy itself uses this database for its own projections. Because our study is neither a modeling exercise nor a forecasting exercise, the DOE data serve here only to provide an existing, authoritative set of 2010-era projections that facilitate our purposes of defining each end of the price spectrum. These data provide a benchmark against which our two extreme scenarios for extended low ($10 per barrel or less) and high ($30 per barrel or higher) oil prices can be compared. Because the DOE 2010 forecast assumes an oil price of $21.30 in 1997 dollars, our own 2010 low- and high-price scenarios also are posited in 1997 dollars. We have used a blend of the DOE's forecasts for supply, demand, and price as a means to create our low- and high-price scenarios.

With this "policy neutral" base case as our point of departure, we now turn to the extreme price scenarios. It bears repeating that although our purpose here is not to predict the actual state of global oil prices in 2010, the burden remains of explaining how the market could settle at either the extreme low or extreme high end of the spectrum and remain in the extreme range for three years or more.

In fact, many of the factors in this analysis suggest that movement of oil prices to either extreme would stimulate countervailing pressures on the price level, tending back toward a more normal range. Moreover, although the magnitude of each price collapse or spike and subsequent rebound or retreat may be greater in the future, the duration of these movements will be shorter because of commodity market influences, fuel switching, and technological and environmental imperatives.

Notwithstanding these evolving market phenomena and their overall counterbalancing nature, extremes do occur, and unexpectedly. The foregoing analysis cites many elements that contribute to future price uncertainty, including technological change, continued commoditization trends, environmental imperatives, and a switch to alternative fuels such as natural gas. One certainty in 2010 is that there will be no shortage of fossil fuels. The U.S. Geological Survey (USGS) has estimated worldwide recoverable oil resources at more than 1.6 trillion barrels, and this figure does not fully account for the rather dramatically increasing technical recoverability of oil from existing reservoirs.[15]

Thus, any oil "shortage" in the 2010 timeframe, other than a very transitory circumstance, should be understood as, in all likelihood, a by-product of political factors rather than physical constraints. The key underlying factor to grasp is that OPEC's share of global supply will continue to grow during the first decade of the twenty-first century.

Extreme Scenario One—Extended Low Oil Prices in 2010

A global energy market gripped by extended low oil prices will stimulate several existing trends within the industry, beyond the important movements toward corporate consolidation and convergence into the power industry that already are well under way. These trends include the scaling back of funding for exploration and production, refinery and petrochemical expansion, and a retrenchment in all segments of the business.

Key among the attributes of these trends is the overall movement to a customer-driven industry. A factor often overlooked in policy planning circles is that world oil markets today offer supply choices in sourcing material that did not exist two decades ago. Part of the explanation for new cargo movements is found in the increasingly interconnected world oil market and its responsiveness to price signals. This has demonstrably affected global trade patterns for crude oil, petroleum products, and LNG during the past several years. Some of these changes were influenced by environmental considerations, but all were market-driven as a result of the transparency of oil prices worldwide.

The key point is that with the world market becoming more globalized, countries or companies are losing whatever latitude they might have had to insulate themselves from disruptive external trends. Increased competition is a direct by-product of market liberalization and global reach on the part of large and small players alike. Competitive forces increase efficiency and drive down costs. Consumers have more market power and political influence. Thus, when we explore the question of how oil prices could decline and remain extremely low for three years or more, the answer must begin with the modernizing factors that have a downward effect on oil prices.

The onset of a low oil price market usually is unanticipated. Price movement does not give the industry time to earmark sufficient funds to invest in future production. Accordingly, the downward price movement tends to shift the balance of reserve capacity to the OPEC countries, where production costs are lowest. However, a 2010 price collapse will not necessarily resemble that of 1986, when most of the OPEC producers already had in hand financial surpluses from the higher oil prices of the early 1980s.

The effects of a future price collapse could well be more negative because almost all OPEC oil producers have been running budget deficits, even during the present-day price rally. A severe, extended lower-price scenario could even be taken to be the last major "play" for global market share among the OPEC oil producers. The vast reserve base shown in table 2.3 suggests that the central tenet of such an endgame would very likely be to develop and exploit commercially as much reserve capacity as quickly as possible. In such a situation, prices could remain low for an extended time as the lowest-cost producers aggressively consolidated their market shares.

Oil is still a political weapon, and its prices are still affected by the collusion of major producers to withhold supply from the market, as they have done effectively since March 1999. This action has succeeded in sustaining higher oil prices for more than two years, but higher prices ultimately have several price-dampening effects, including fuel switching to cheaper sources of energy such as natural gas or coal. More vigorous energy conservation is inevitable if higher prices are sustained. Already, industry is adapting the next wave of energy efficiency devices as a result of electricity restructuring; such technologies are adopted more readily in a high-price environment.

Economic recessions also soften energy demand brought on by higher prices. Cheating by OPEC members on their agreed production quotas, which has been rampant in the past when prices were higher, is another factor pushing prices downward. Spurred by these stimuli and coupled with increased production by non-OPEC suppliers, the market ordinarily would head for a price crash after a price run up. In any case, many of the market influences and dynamics that are evident today render a future low oil price scenario such as ours credible, if not predictable.

Table 2.6 presents projections regarding the global consumption and production of oil in 2010 in the third year of prices below $10 per barrel (1997 dollars). The first-order impacts of the low oil price scenario include a major increase in Saudi oil production to more than 17.3 million barrels per day and an increase in OPEC market share to more than one-half of world supply. The second key change is that U.S., Japanese, Latin American, and, particularly, Chinese oil demand grows dramatically, increasing those countries' overall dependence on imported oil, mainly from OPEC sources of oil production.

Lower prices will delay the development of promising but speculative areas such as the Caspian region, and they also will delay or cancel other promising developments that require significant capital investment. They do not affect deepwater exploration and development that should be sustainable worldwide for additional supplies. Their impact is immediate, and negative, on U.S. and Canadian exploration and production, which are higher-cost centers, and ultimately delay their movement to world markets. They also delay offshore Gulf of Mexico production, Latin American deepwater products, and increased Alaskan production, as well as Chinese, Thai, and Vietnamese deepwater projects. Their overall impact on the Caspian region is to slow the much-anticipated increase of oil supply to world markets from this area.

The dominant effect of persistently low oil prices on global patterns of oil production is to shift market share to lower-cost producers—notably, Persian/Arabian Gulf producers. Although non-OPEC supply, particularly from the North Sea, played a major role in the erosion of OPEC's global market share during the 1980s, OPEC's large reserves and low production costs are capable of accommodating most of the projected increase in oil demand a decade into the future. About two-thirds of new oil supply in the world will come from OPEC production increases in this decade.

Although OPEC's share of the world's oil markets is projected to increase in coming years, residual competitive forces among global producers should frustrate any concerted effort by OPEC to escalate prices significantly for sustained periods of time in a low-price environment. These competitive forces may reside within OPEC as well as between OPEC members and non-OPEC suppliers. In addition, there is the ever-present and growing competitive threat posed by alternative sources of energy, particularly natural gas, for power generation.

Oil supply dynamics aside, while we would expect Persian/Arabian Gulf exports to industrialized countries to be elevated in this scenario, the more salient fact is that these exports are falling dramatically as a percentage of overall energy dependency in the advanced economies. The key factor in sustaining OPEC's global market power, therefore, will be its petroleum exports to developing countries, which are expected to increase significantly, with fully half going to Asia. China alone is projected to become a significant oil importer, with most of that oil coming from the Persian/Arabian Gulf.

In this event, it seems likely that more participation by international oil companies (IOCs) will be needed to achieve the huge production increases required in these Middle Eastern countries. IOCs can offer advanced technologies for efficient oilfield exploration and management. This foreign participation could take the form of direct equity investment or, at a minimum, oil services for production and distribution.

One development of strategic significance, based on oil producer-consumer linkages under this scenario, is the inevitable Saudi Arabian-Chinese linkage, binding the world's largest oil producer with its fastest-growing major consumer. Although the Chinese oil industry has been active in upstream projects around the world, including in Venezuela and the Caspian region, Saudi Arabia's vast resource base and comparatively easy means to ramp up low-cost production would suggest that Saudi Arabia (along with other Gulf producers) holds the key to ensuring the adequacy of China's future energy supply.

The voracious demand anticipated in China under almost any future price scenario makes this an important new reality in world oil markets. While China forges this key linkage, Japan's consumer relationships in the Persian/Arabian Gulf would be expected to continue more in a business-as-usual mode. South Korea also would have an interest in developing deeper linkages to the low-cost Gulf producers.

Other OPEC suppliers that probably would be stimulated to higher production under our extreme low oil price scenario include Iraq, Kuwait, Iran, and Venezuela, all of which would secure increased market share even as OPEC price discipline would have collapsed. Most likely, Venezuela would further solidify its position as the key regional supplier to the United States. On the consuming side, China, India, the United States, Japan, and the EU would all derive some economic benefit from lower oil prices, as would the developing world at large.

Other ramifications of lower oil prices would include a cutting off of much capital investment in alternative energy, further undermining international environmental imperatives. Oil would capture more market share for transportation—its dominant niche—but probably not much more for power generation because much of the planned global capacity calls for gas-fired combined-cycle turbines (unless these generators were dual fuel-capable for oil and gas). The net effect on economies around the world would be to lessen inflation, as oil imports would require less foreign exchange.

The most negative effects of an extreme low-price scenario would be to further consolidate the oil industry, including the services sector, into a handful of global players working in a low-value commodity market. Much industry expertise might leave the industry, as has happened before. High-risk, high-cost projects such as extended Caspian and deep-sea development would be put off, perhaps never to be pursued. To the extent that Russia's economy in 2010 still rose or fell with world oil prices, it would be negatively affected. Thus, alongside the favorable impacts of low prices, there would be clear losers; indeed, even the "winners"—the leading OPEC producers—would much prefer higher prices.

Extreme Scenario Two—Extended High Oil Prices in 2010

Higher oil prices also can be a double-edged sword for the oil industry because they tend to stifle demand and spur energy-consuming countries to take decisive action to diversify sources of energy and reduce energy import dependency. Persistent higher prices accelerate substitution for oil and adoption of cleaner fuel technology. Although such changes take time, they are inevitable.

Normal conditions in oil markets would be contemplated when supply and demand are relatively in balance and price volatility is more muted than we have seen since 1999 on. Because oil demand is still tied to economic growth, the steady rise in demand tends to keep pace with supply increases. Artificially holding supply off the market—as has been the case from OPEC's inception to the present day—will have the intended effect of increasing prices, but this effect must be regarded as unsustainable, at least at very high price levels.

High-priced oil creates pressure to exploit known reserves and exhaust mature fields using newer technologies such as horizontal drilling that can squeeze more production out of existing capillaries. The application of such technology is the fastest way to increase production—far more efficient and risk-averse than investing in infrastructure for new production. This choice is more natural than financing and arranging for new exploration insofar as it involves proven, productive fields whose ownership is already settled. This effect is evident today in the mature oilfields of Texas and Oklahoma, which have been producing for most of the twentieth century and continue to be productive.

Intensified utilization of the newer, more efficient drilling and production technologies, while it will extend the productivity of existing fields, will ultimately deplete these fields faster as it increases production. One interesting side effect, evident since mid-1999, is that major oil companies have hesitated to commit more capital to their drilling programs out of concern that the current price rally might abruptly end. Having suffered damage to their financial balance sheets in the past, companies are concentrating instead on buying "paper" reserves—that is, acquiring other companies with existing productive assets, rather than drilling for more hydrocarbons.

The effect of extreme high prices, therefore, at least initially, is more rapid and comprehensive depletion of existing producing oilfields. This pattern suggests the potential for more severe disruption later if companies continue to be slow to invest in new production.

Extreme high oil prices also radically shift the inventory patterns of the industry to the building of oil stockpiles. Although there is an ongoing need by the oil industry to have a working inventory of oil stocks for refiners to run through their facilities and store as petroleum products, crude oil and petroleum products in storage bear a "cost of carry," which means that there is an expense to holding oil, particularly oil products, in storage. These storage costs, paid on a monthly basis, are incorporated into the sales price of the fuel.

The advent of greater efficiencies made possible by information technology permits the industry to operate on a more "just-in-time" basis, with lower working inventories. This greater efficiency brings with it an element of greater sensitivity to market disruptions—an ironic flip side to the stability that a more efficient global oil and oil products market otherwise will produce.

Many refiners and oil traders actually arbitrage their storage costs with futures and OTC financial contracts. When prices are high, inventories are built up, and when prices are low as a result of a supply glut, inventory is drawn down because supply balancing can be achieved easily on the spot market. Already, inventory management by oil producers and refiners plays a noticeable role in price determination in world oil markets, and this will only continue.

A number of consuming country governments are obligated by international agreements to hold oil stockpiles in anticipation of future supply disruptions. These oil reserves were developed in response to the first oil price shock and embargo of 1973. In a perfect world, governments would build inventory in periods of high supply and low oil prices. This behavior pattern has rarely been the case, however; much of the oil in storage actually is high-priced oil, filled during the late 1970s and early 1980s. Although contemplated, petroleum product storage was never a serious consideration because products could not be stored indefinitely and would need to be turned over continuously through sales and purchases.

The U.S. Strategic Petroleum Reserve (SPR) could be used to dampen higher prices that might be detrimental to the U.S. economy, although that was not the purpose of the reserve. The reserve's purpose was to respond to an oil supply crisis such as an embargo in which the United States would be cut off from oil supplies. The SPR holds 575 million barrels of crude oil, or enough supply for 55 days of imports (as of late 1999). The oil is stored in sites along the Texas and Louisiana coastline where it can easily be drawn out and shipped to refiners.

This supply management technique was used as a symbolic measure during the Gulf crisis of 1990–1991, illustrating its potential to be used to calm oil markets in a high-price situation by releasing quantities of government-owned oil for sale in the market. During the summer of 2000, President Clinton decided to use the reserve to supply heating oil stocks for the northeastern United States, and in September 2000 he authorized the release of 30 million barrels from the reserve at a time when prices were approaching $40 per barrel. Other major consuming countries, including Japan, also have strategic reserves. EU requirements are for 90 days' supply.

The insight for the future is that greater efficiency in the global oil marketplace means less utilization of inventories on a commercial basis. Only in a very high price environment will significant incentives exist for investment in crude oil and product inventories. While the market continues to become ever more efficient, it becomes inherently more susceptible to any factor, real or anticipated, that could perturb the smooth flow of goods from the source of production to the eventual point of consumption. The watchword for the new oil economy is "volatility."

Low-Cost vs. High-Cost Production

It is well known that Venezuela, Saudi Arabia, the United Arab Emirates, Iraq, Kuwait, and Iran have significant unexploited oil production potential. The fact that these and other producers have held production off the market beginning in 1999 despite higher oil prices suggests that sustainable higher prices are necessarily a phenomenon of finite duration.

At some point in a high-price rally, some or all of these producers recognize the opportunity, as well as the need, to bring more of their reserves into production. In the first instance, such a step is regarded as profitable because global market demand will have demonstrated the value of new production.

Beyond this factor is the negative calculation that unless production rises to meet this demand, there will be shifts away from petroleum production in long-time consumer markets. It is probably an immutable fact within the most developed economies that once an energy infrastructure investment is made in order to shift away from utilization of costly petroleum, there will be no going back to using oil—ever. An extreme, extended high oil price scenario, however lucrative to the Gulf countries while it lasted, would be a calamity of historic proportions for those producers if it turned American policy, technology, and investment in the direction of a concerted switch to alternative energy sources and maximum conservation.

Finally, there is always the underlying element of competition between major oil-producing countries, notably Saudi Arabia, Iraq, Iran, and Kuwait, among others. Beneath the superstructure of cooperation between these states rests the certainty that when it comes to claiming production shares, "possession is nine-tenths of the law," so to speak. It is far more difficult to envision an OPEC member being prevailed on by its neighbors to scale back its production unilaterally than to accept common restraints, along with fellow OPEC members, that are proportional to existing production.

All of these considerations would impel oil producers to make the investments and bring additional capacity into production in an extended period of extreme high prices. These factors, along with the commoditization and financial maturation of the global energy market described earlier in this chapter, only underscore how rare and unlikely an extreme high oil price condition that lasted three years or more would be. In fact, future oil price cycles may turn out to be more severe and of shorter duration than experience to date.

Table 2.7 provides projections regarding the global consumption and production of oil in 2010 in the third year of prices above $30 per barrel (1997 dollars). Spiking of oil prices to more than $30 per barrel for a sustained period of three years would have immediate as well as longer-term impacts on energy markets. Higher real oil prices deter consumption and encourage significant competition for marginal and unconventional supplies of energy, including non-oil supplies; lower oil prices have the opposite effect. Therefore, one rapidly evident effect is that consumers who cannot afford the higher price do not buy as much, so that worldwide levels of consumption—and production—are reduced.

The high oil price scenario shows a dramatically different oil picture than the other extreme. In this case, Saudi production is still the dominant supply choice, but the rest of OPEC loses relative influence in world oil markets. The dampening of demand can lead to a surplus in supply. As long as prices remain very high, however, the world switches more quickly to alternative fuels, driven by price, technology, and environmental imperatives. This trend would accelerate the downward spiral of oil's role in world energy markets.

The limiting factors on long-term oil price spikes during the 2010 timeframe include fuel substitution (in particular, switching to natural gas), marginal sources of conventional oil coming to the market and thereby eroding the oligopolistic advantage of the low-cost producers, and the development and production of unconventional sources of oil. Further advances in exploration and production technologies also are likely to make new contributions to downward pressure on prices as additional oil resources become part of the global reserve base. Natural gas production and market share have been rising since the late 1990s. This is primarily because of mounting environmental concerns in the electric power generation segment, but it is also a reflection of a strategic thrust by multinational oil companies to develop their gas portfolios—which they regard as a high-growth area compared to transportation fuels.

Higher prices diversify supply sources and unleash more drilling activity and more competitors. At a price greater than $25 per barrel (1997 dollars), sources that are considered "unconventional supplies" become commercially viable, such as tar sands in Venezuela and Canada and oil shale in the United States. With greater production being brought to bear, the net result is more supply and lower prices. The trend of declining U.S. production, for example, is expected to be compensated in some measure by technological advances as well as increases in offshore Gulf of Mexico drilling and Alaskan production. The most obvious "winner" in this high-price scenario is Caspian Basin production (see below).

Similarly, deepwater oil production technology requires only a normal price level of $18 to $20 (1997 dollars) to be fully viable commercially, but there is significant production potential at the higher price level. Areas of exploration and production of deepwater projects include not only the United States but also the North Sea, West Africa (particularly Angola), Brazil, Colombia, the South China Sea, and the Caspian Basin. Lower prices, conversely, delay or inhibit the consummation of these projects, as in the two-year period before the price rally started in 1999.

Renewable technologies will experience accelerated market penetration in the event of extreme high oil prices because the search for alternate fuels increases and more of these technologies become price-competitive with oil. Politically driven environmental imperatives to control or reduce emissions also accelerate growth in renewable technology deployment.

Higher oil prices materially affect the balance of trade of Asian countries most directly. Because Japan, South Korea, China, India, and Indonesia will all become (and already are) significant importers of Middle Eastern oil, extreme high prices may lead to more oil substitution, particularly in the highly developed Japanese market. Mass-produced hybrid gasoline/electric vehicles already have been introduced into that market (and subsequently in the United States), and fully electric vehicles are not that far off in the future.

U.S. economic and political interests are affected in dramatically different ways by higher oil prices. The U.S. oil industry obviously benefits, but American consumers do not, as in 2000–2001. U.S. industry, particularly energy-intensive sectors, is negatively affected. The U.S. balance of trade also is negatively affected under either extreme price scenario, but particularly in the high-price case (the balance of trade suffers in the low-price scenario because imports would rise while more domestic production would be shut in).

Turning to the Persian/Arabian Gulf, notwithstanding higher short-term revenue gains under the high-price scenario, the lower-price scenario arguably could benefit Saudi Arabia in the long term because the Kingdom's vast resource base would be developed and exploited rather than becoming a stranded oil reserve, never to be produced. With low oil prices, the Saudis would securitize their reserve base by getting more of their oil to market, while delaying the entry of alternative fuels on a larger scale to the same market.

One Constant in Either Extreme Price Scenario: OPEC Supply Goes Up

Regardless of the price scenario, we assume that OPEC members with large reserves and low production costs will expand capacity easily and that capacity utilization also will increase sharply. This effect is centered primarily in the Persian/Arabian Gulf nations of OPEC, which have production costs of less than $1.75 per barrel, according to the Department of Energy's Energy Information Administration. A conservative estimate is that these Gulf producers have an oil reserve-to-production ratio of 80 years, and this estimate does not take into account the area's vast natural gas reserves.

Other OPEC producers, such as Nigeria and Venezuela, have higher developmental costs but also will be able to increase their oil production platforms between now and 2010. In fact, of the non-Persian/Arabian Gulf OPEC producers, Venezuela has the greatest potential to increase production, predicated on its ability to continue to attract foreign capital.

Iraq's steady increase in functioning production capacity in recent years was inhibited only by Baghdad's interplay with the United Nations Security Council regarding the sanctions regulating its exports. It is known that Iraq plans to claim a major role for itself in the regional and global oil economy by increasing production to 6 million barrels per day within a decade once UN sanctions are lifted. An increase of this magnitude in Iraqi supply on world oil markets would tend to dampen long-term global price prospects.

Prior to August 1990, Iraq was producing 3 million barrels per day and exporting 2.8 million barrels per day. By 1999, it was producing as much as 2.6–2.8 million barrels per day. Thus, it is entirely credible that Iraqi production capacity could well surpass the 3.8 million barrels per day posited in EIA's 2010 Base Case projection, assuming that UN sanctions are lifted in the intervening years.

Because of Asia's growing oil dependency, the economic bonds between Asian markets and the Middle East are expected to be strengthened in 2010, with foreign policy implications as well for the concerned countries. China, India, Japan, and South Korea will become increasingly dependent on Middle Eastern oil and gas supplies. China, in particular, will become more dependent on Middle Eastern oil to fuel domestic transportation as it continues to industrialize.

Under either a low or high extreme price scenario, oil productive capacity shifts to the Middle East producers, with Saudi Arabia providing the dominant supply role. It could produce from 12.9 to 17.3 million barrels per day by 2010, according to EIA forecasts. In effect, Saudi Arabia is regarded once again as being able to play the market-balancing role as global "swing producer." Secondarily, Iran and Iraq can add the bulk of incremental supply because their oil is cheap to produce and geographically accessible to markets. Thus, in most circumstances of 2010, the marginal barrel becomes a Persian/Arabian Gulf barrel, and the destination of that barrel is most likely to be developing Asia.

Non-OPEC Supply

Non-OPEC supply increased throughout the 1990s despite a relatively low price environment for much of the time, adding more than 4 million barrels per day of supply. Non-OPEC supply has been driven by the advantages of new exploration and production technology, cost reductions by the major oil companies, and encouragement of foreign investment by producer governments. It is expected that these trends will continue to support added global production between now and 2010.

Non-OPEC production is predicted to continue to rise, mainly due to technology improvements in the recovery of oil, particularly in offshore production. There will be a further effect from the transference and diffusion of these improvements globally (see below). The more economically viable fields will be brought on line much more quickly than in the past; the traditional seven-year process of exploration and delivery already is being compressed to about 18 months. Indeed, the entire oil supply chain is changing and becoming more responsive to market opportunities. Among non-OPEC producers, this trend amounts to a dilution of OPEC's power to control supply and sustain higher prices. Low prices would be a disincentive, however, for non-OPEC producers to supply more oil to the market because their production costs are higher.

Implications for Caspian Basin Production

Although continued exploitation in the North Sea and offshore West Africa will add supply in the next few years, it is development of the Caspian Basin that has been the focal point of interest in world markets, with several proposed exploration and pipeline projects under development. The key question is when and how much Caspian oil will reach world markets.

It is thought that the 1998 price collapse delayed a major ramping up of production (meaning onshore and offshore Azerbaijan and Kazakhstan production) from the 1999 combined level of 800,000 barrels per day to the 2 million per day target level. It is now widely believed that projections for full Caspian production of as much as 6 million barrels per day may have been overly optimistic.[16] The key question remains, however: what will production be, and under what price conditions?

Under the extreme low-price scenario, it is fair to question how much Caspian oil actually will be produced and reach the market. This issue is important because much of the anticipated Caspian oil carries with it both a relatively high cost of exploration and production and—the critical impediment—a high cost of conveying the oil from Central Asia and the Caucasus to the world market. These very real cost factors aside, the very existence of this new source of oil supply also is a psychological factor in the behavior of the markets. In essence, it acts as an effective overhang of supply on world markets and may lead to a discernible price-dampening effect when more of this supply becomes available.

Political uncertainty in the Caucasus region—both within these fragile post-Soviet political systems and between these newly independent countries and their ambitious neighbors, Russia and Iran—obviously remains a potential barrier to development of these resources. In considering the future importance of the Caspian Basin to the world of 2010, one also should remember that production in the former Soviet Union was 11.4 million barrels per day in 1990—an aggregate level that Russia and its Caspian neighbors may not attain for the next 20 years.

The extreme low-price scenario will push back exploitation of the Caspian region substantially. Part of the reason is that one barrel of every three barrels of anticipated production must come from fields not yet discovered. Political uncertainties as well as economic and transportation risk will only further reduce and delay the expected increase in production. Oil discoveries and exploitation also are constrained by capital, despite the openness of foreign participants in Azerbaijan, Kazakhstan, and Turkmenistan. Thus, lower prices postpone future development because of the steep investment requirements for ramping up oil production.

High prices, in contrast, would enable Caspian production to come to market earlier. Capital investment will determine the level of oil production in the Caspian, which places this region in competition with other regions for upstream investment. The necessity of having a revenue stream from active producing fields will hasten investment to ramp up production. Long-term capital commitments will require a large base of producing fields.

The two most advanced major development projects at present are the Tengiz field in Kazakhstan and the offshore Azeri-Guneshli-Chirag complex in Azerbaijan, which together will provide one of every three barrels of new production in the Caspian region. These fields were producing more than 200,000 barrels per day as of 2001; production should rise further by 2010. Overall, however, the lack of infrastructure, pipeline transportation uncertainties, and political risk may not delay or prevent the large quantity of Caspian production from coming to market that has always been touted.

The Effect of Technological Improvements on Oil Prices

Technological improvements in hydrocarbon production will contribute to greater worldwide recovery rates of 50–70 percent, up from the present level of 35 percent (exclusive of the United States and the North Sea), according to industry sources. The overall impact of these developments will be to add to conventional reserves. Moreover, unconventional reserves such as oil shale and gas-to-liquids (GTL) technology can add significantly to supply, particularly as prices rise well above the normal range.

New-generation intelligent technology will bring about real-time management of reserves and like efficiencies. In time, most or all of these advances will be dispersed among all oil-producing regions. Improved data acquisition, data processing, and integration of other geologic data, combined with lower-cost computing power, will place downward pressure on the costs of exploration and production even as they significantly improve finding and success rates. The effects of this double efficiency will be particularly evident in unconventional and deepwater fields.

However, while the direction of this trend is apparent, extreme higher and lower oil price scenarios would influence the pace of technological adaptation. In sum, continuous technology improvements for the production and consumption of fossil fuels will add a countervailing pressure on high prices, making an extreme high-price scenario even less sustainable in 2010 and beyond than it would be today.

Another Constant: Natural Gas' Market Share Rising

Under any price scenario—normal, low, or high—the market share for natural gas continues to increase, particularly for electric power generation, such that it should surpass coal consumption within the present decade. Natural gas will be a choice alternative to the use of oil, both because of its clean burning and low carbon content and because of its abundant and highly diversified global supply. It has been estimated that the commercial potential of gas-to-liquids technology could reach 150 billion barrels of liquids. Its role obviously continues to grow as a supply choice driven by growing global environmental concerns.

CONCLUSION: CHANGING PERCEPTIONS ABOUT ENERGY RESOURCES

International oil markets are undergoing major structural changes that will continue to challenge existing notions of oil dependency vis-à-vis consuming countries. Oil's run-up in prices starting in 1999 has been far less of a drag on the U.S. economy that it would have been 25 years ago. Fundamentally, the acknowledged quantity of proven oil reserves in the world continues to rise as a result of technological innovation. The era of real shortage is over, even as an artificially engineered shortage temporarily pushes up current prices. The long-term movement to zero-carbon energy is under way and gaining, driven by global environmental imperatives.

Energy will be used more efficiently and benignly in the future. The Western Hemisphere could conceivably become, in effect, energy self-sufficient over the long term. The shift in oil dependency is moving steadily to the Asia Pacific region, with supply from the Persian/Arabian Gulf states. Finally, commodity markets do work, and they set international oil prices, investment decisions, and resource allocation. The past is not prologue, and U.S. energy policy, such as it is, can be said to be at a crossroads.

A changing global economy, diversification of oil supplies, oil market transparency, the ability to lay off risk on futures markets, and International Energy Agency (IEA) stock requirements have all contributed to changing perceptions about oil supply security.[17] The world has not experienced a major contraction of the global economy caused directly or indirectly by oil price developments since the early 1980s, and the $15-to-$20 per barrel price range has been generally comfortable for producers and consumers alike.

If developments in the world economy and the world oil market are in the process of making serious oil shocks and extended periods of extremely high oil prices a concern of the past, this process has implications not only for U.S. energy policy, but also for U.S. policy perspectives on major Middle East producers and the role of OPEC.

The future is coming. The writing is on the wall. Oil's importance is waning.

Notes

[1] The Organization of the Petroleum Exporting Countries (OPEC), founded in 1960 and headquartered in Vienna, Austria, now has 11 member states: Algeria, Indonesia, Iran, Iraq, Kuwait, Libya, Nigeria, Qatar, Saudi Arabia, United Arab Emirates, and Venezuela.

[2] Energy trading involves both the physical wet barrel trading of crude oil and petroleum products as well as the financial trading of oil on futures exchanges and on the over-the-counter (OTC) derivatives markets. The spot market is the physical daily market to buy and sell oil that is not under a long-term contract.

[3] Energy futures are commodity contracts for oil, gas, and electricity that are traded on regulated exchanges. They are used to discover the future price

of the commodity. The heating oil futures contract was the first successful oil futures contract, in 1978.

[4] Over-the-counter is the unregulated market for energy derivatives (estimated at about $2 trillion for the worldwide energy complex). Forward oil trading is the future price of oil on which traders agree for future delivery of the commodity.

[5] An oil price swap is a financial instrument that is used to hedge oil. It involves two parties that enter into an agreement to pay one another the difference between a fixed price and a floating price (the market price at an agreed future time). Two parties will enter into such an agreement when each has different price expectations.

[6] Open interest is the number of outstanding futures contracts that have not settled or been netted out.

[7] Hedge funds are pooled investments that are used by investors to speculate on the price of oil or any commodity.

[8] Indexes or price assessments allow the energy trader to determine prices on a transaction basis rather than through oil price reporters. These indexes are now migrating to the Internet in addition to being posted on Reuters, Bloomberg, or Dow Jones monitors.

[9] This is particularly the case with Internet-based electronic trading, which is not part of a physical exchange but exists in cyberspace. It is presently unregulated.

[10] *Long molecules* refers to oil and gas assets that are still in the ground and thus have not been produced.

[11] The December 1997 international environmental summit hosted by Japan, known as the Kyoto Conference, established a Protocol to the United Nations Framework Convention on Climate Change, according to which developed countries would be required to reduce emissions of six designated "greenhouse gases" by a total of about 5 percent below 1990 levels by the years 2008–2012 (International Energy Agency, OECD).

[12] Soon after taking office, the administration of President George W. Bush made clear its objection to what it regarded as an unreasonable apportionment of compliance obligations on the advanced economies relative to the developing economies in the Kyoto Protocol.

[13] The Association of Southeast Asian Nations (ASEAN), founded in 1967, has 10 member states: Brunei Darussalam, Cambodia, Indonesia, Laos, Myanmar (Burma), Malaysia, the Philippines, Singapore, Thailand, and Vietnam.

[14] Orimulsion is the Venezuelan-produced boiler fuel that is an emulsion of water and oil. It is produced from the heavy oil reserves of Venezuela's Orinoco oil belt.

[15] This refers to the U.S. Geological Survey's year 2000 survey estimate of technically recoverable oil reserves worldwide. World Energy Assessment Team, U.S. Geological Survey Digital Data Services. series 60, World Undiscovered Assessment Results Summary.

[16] New finds in the Caspian are promising, however: The Kashagan discovery offshore Kazakhstan may be one of the most significant finds in decades, and the Karachaganak gas condensate deposit, also in Kazakhstan, reportedly could be the world's largest.

[17] The International Energy Agency (IEA), created in 1974 and based in Paris, is an autonomous agency linked with the OECD. Its member governments are committed to taking joint measures to meet oil supply emergencies. IEA members are Australia, Austria, Belgium, Canada, the Czech Republic, Denmark, Finland, France, Germany, Greece, Hungary, Ireland, Italy, Japan, Luxembourg, the Netherlands, New Zealand, Norway, Portugal, Spain, Sweden, Switzerland, Turkey, the United Kingdom, and the United States. The European Commission also has a role in the work of the IEA.

Table 2.1
Global Natural Gas Consumption Outlook
(in billion cubic feet)

Region	1997	2000	2010	2020
Asia Pacific	8,901	9,171	11,740	16,243
Middle East	5,660	6,367	10,371	16,894
North America	26,118	27,232	35,227	43,381
Latin America	2,930	3,382	6,349	13,086
Western Europe	14,263	15,360	20,642	30,263
Eastern Europe/FSU*	22,221	22,696	27,396	35,069
Africa	1,844	2,015	3,129	5,603
World total	81,409	86,223	114,954	160,539

Sources: Data for 1997 from U.S. Department of Energy, Energy Information Administration
(EIA), Annual Energy Outlook, World Dry Gas Consumption (1990–1999). Data from 2000,
2010, and 2020 from Enron Corporation forecasts.
*FSU refers to the independent states of the former Soviet Union.

Table 2.2
Proven Oil Reserves (at end 2000)
(in billion barrels)

Middle East	683.6
Latin America	95.2
North America	64.4
Africa	74.8
Former Soviet Union	65.3
Asia Pacific	44.0
Europe	19.1
Total	1,046.4

Source: BP Amoco Statistical Review of World Energy 1999.

Table 2.3
Distribution of Oil Reserves (at end 2000)

	Barrels (billions)	Share of world supply (%)
Non-OPEC		
OECD	84.8	8.1
FSU	65.3	6.4
Other non-OPEC	81.9	7.7
Total non-OPEC	232.0	22.2
OPEC		
Iran	89.7	8.6
Iraq	112.5	10.8
Kuwait	96.5	9.2
Saudi Arabia	261.7	25.0
United Arab Emirates	97.8	9.3
Other OPEC	156.2	14.9
Total OPEC	**814.4**	**77.8**

Source: BP Statistical Review of World Energy 2001.

Table 2.4
Proven Natural Gas Reserves (end of 1998)
(in trillion cubic meters)

FSU	56.7
Middle East	49.5
Africa	10.2
Asia Pacific	10.2
North America	8.4
Latin America	6.2
Europe	5.2

Source: BP Statistical Review of World Energy 1999.

Table 2.5
2010 Base Case—"Normal" Conditions
(in million barrels per day)

	Production	Consumption
OPEC		
Saudi Arabia	14.1	
Venezuela	5.1	
Iran	4.5	
Iraq	3.8	
UAE	3.4	
Kuwait	3.2	
Nigeria	3.2	
Total OPEC	**43.3**	
Non-OPEC		
United States	9.0	22.7
Canada	3.2	2.1
Mexico	4.0	2.6
China	3.5	6.4
FSU	10.1	4.7
Japan	–	6.0
South Korea	–	3.4
India	–	3.1
Latin America (including Brazil)	4.4	7.4
Total non-OPEC	**51.7**	**58.4**
World totals	**95.0**	**93.5**

Source: U.S. Energy Information Agency, "International Energy Outlook 1999," including reference cases for "World Oil Production Capacity by Region and Country, Reference Case, 1990-2020" (Table D1), "World Oil Production by Region and Country, Reference Case, 1990–2020" (Table D6), and "World Oil Consumption by Region, Reference Case, 1990–2020" (Table A4). EIA reference case assumes oil prices at $21.30 in 1997 dollars.

Table 2.6
2010 Extreme Low Oil Price Scenario
(World price below $10 per barrel for 3 years)
(in million barrels per day)

	Production	Consumption
OPEC		
Saudi Arabia	17.3	
Iran	5.3	
Iraq	6.0	
UAE	4.0	
Kuwait	3.7	
Venezuela	6.3	
Nigeria	3.5	
Total OPEC	**52.6**	
Non-OPEC		
United States	8.1	23.7
Canada	3.2	2.3
Mexico	3.9	2.8
China	3.4	7.3
FSU	9.8	5.7
Japan	—	6.7
South Korea	—	4.0
India	—	3.6
Latin America (including Brazil)	4.3	9.4
Total non-OPEC	**49.6**	**65.5**
World totals	**102.2**	**99.4**

Source: EIA, "International Energy Outlook 1999," "Table D2, World Oil Production Capacity by region and Country, Low Oil Price Case, 1990–2020," and "Table B4, World Oil Consumption by Region, High Economic Growth Case, 1990–2020," with adjustment upward to 6 million barrels per day (mmb/d) for Iraqi production.

Table 2.7
2010 Extreme High Oil Price Scenario
(World price above $30 per barrel for 3 years)
(in million barrels per day)

	Production	Consumption
OPEC		
Saudi Arabia	12.9	
Iran	4.2	
Iraq	3.2	
UAE	3.1	
Kuwait	3.1	
Venezuela	4.9	
Nigeria	2.8	
Total OPEC	**39.9**	
Non-OPEC		
United States	9.5	21.6
Canada	3.3	2.0
Mexico	4.1	2.3
China	3.6	4.9
FSU	10.3	4.3
Japan	—	5.4
South Korea	—	2.8
India	—	2.6
Latin America (including Brazil)	4.5	5.8
Total non-OPEC		**53.1**
World totals	**93.0**	**83.1**

Source: EIA, "International Energy Outlook 1999," "Table D8, World Oil Production Capacity by region and Country, Low Oil Price Case, 1990–2020," and "Table C4, World Oil Consumption by Region, Low Economic Growth Case, 1990–2020."

CHAPTER THREE

OIL SUPPLY SECURITY THROUGH 2010

Herman T. Franssen

THE TWO OIL SHOCKS OF THE 1970S HAD A DEVASTATING IMPACT ON the global economy, and the aftershocks were apparent well after the initial damage done by the price increases at that time. The oil embargo of 1973–1974 and the 1979 Iranian revolution led to sharp oil price increases that contributed significantly to galloping inflation, followed by serious recessions. Following the Iranian revolution, the oil market survived the 1980–1988 Iran-Iraq war, the oil price crash of 1986, the 1990–1991 Gulf War crisis, and, most recently, the oil price collapse of 1998 and the price spike of 1999–2001. In fact, ever since OPEC moved to market pricing in late 1985, oil prices generally have moved within a band of $15 to $20 per barrel, only occasionally moving above or below this range.[1]

The world has not experienced a major contraction of the global economy caused directly or indirectly by oil price developments since the early 1980s, and the $15–$20 per barrel price range since 1986 generally has been comfortable for producers and consumers alike. Oil economists have been asking whether developments in the global economy and the world oil market have changed so fundamentally that oil shocks and extended periods of high oil prices are becoming an issue of the past.

In the mid-1970s, when OPEC controlled more than 60 percent of global oil production, the OPEC member countries were able to take advantage of developments in the oil market by raising prices, taking full control over their upstream assets, and, after 1980, managing supply through production quotas. At that time, the Organization for Economic Cooperation and Development (OECD) economies depended on oil for more than 50 percent of their energy use.[2] There were no strategic stocks, and oil markets were not as diversified and transparent as they are today. Hence, oil prices overshot their medium- and long-term equilibrium, and insiders and outsiders alike in the oil industry generally were unaware of this dynamic at the time. Only a few academics consistently promoted the view that high oil prices were not sustainable.

By contrast, the oil industry, banks, governments, and international organizations all appeared to agree with OPEC that oil demand and supply were fairly inelastic and that oil prices could only rise further, along with ever-growing demand. For a few years between the two oil shocks of the 1970s, it appeared that the oil industry would be proved right: global oil demand continued to rise, and the supply response initially was rather slow, particularly outside the United States.

Even when OECD countries' oil demand began to drop sharply in the early 1980s—as a result of conservation and fuel switching to gas, coal, and nuclear-powered electricity—and non-OPEC crude oil production began to rise, OPEC ignored the signals and continued its policy of supply management at $30 plus per barrel (1980 dollars), expecting an early turnaround. By the time OPEC recognized the new realities, its market share had dropped from 64 percent in 1973 to 30 percent in 1985. By 1998—13 years after OPEC moved to market pricing and prices in real terms had returned to levels prevailing prior to the 1970s oil shocks—OPEC's market share still had only rebounded to 38 percent of world production.

Policymakers in International Energy Agency (IEA) countries—the world's leading industrial economies—have paid very little attention to oil supply security issues since the end of the Gulf War in 1991. The prime focus of the IEA secretariat instead has been environmental issues. Most member countries have appeared to believe that the chances of another major oil supply interruption, with serious adverse consequences for the global economy, were remote. In fact, on a few occasions the United States and some other member countries have sold off some of their emergency stocks that exceeded the IEA requirements.

The OECD economies had changed by the 1990s; dependence on oil, expressed in an oil-to-gross domestic product (GDP) ratio, had been reduced;[3] and the political use of the oil weapon by OPEC was considered highly unlikely. Instead, the largest IEA member state, the United States, increasingly resorted to its own version of the oil weapon by imposing unilateral sanctions against major OPEC oil-producing countries.

And yet, by the fall of 2000, oil markets had become very tight and global spare capacity had been reduced to the lowest level since the early 1970s. Events in October 2000 once again confronted the West with the possibility of another major explosion in the Middle East. Unchecked confrontation amid a stalled peace process held the potential to create a climate of anger throughout the region that could turn against ruling regimes. In such an atmosphere, the West's friends in the Gulf can find it difficult to accommodate consuming countries further by easing oil market conditions. The tight oil market conditions prevailing as the winter of 2000–2001 approached were vulnerable to potential further tightening in the event that governments in the region felt compelled by internal political pressures to be less than fully cooperative on oil supply issues.

In the case of Iraq—a country with an oil resource base second only to that of Saudi Arabia—production has been interrupted for long periods, first during the Iran-Iraq war of the 1980s and later during and after the 1991 Gulf War. Fortunately, when supplies were cut off from Iran and Iraq, there was ample spare capacity in other OPEC countries, particularly in the Gulf Cooperation Council (GCC) states.[4]

The situation was different in the fall of 2000, however. Spare capacity had shrunk to such an extent that if Iraq alone were to stop exporting oil under the United Nations-authorized oil-for-food program, no group of countries could make up for the lost Iraqi oil in the short run. A complete supply interruption by Iraq at that time would have caused another oil price spike, and probably led to a further U.S. Strategic Petroleum Reserve release, either within or outside the context of an overall IEA emergency stock release. That situation represented perhaps the most serious threat to the global oil market since the Gulf War. The circumstances included a tight oil market, an angry Iraq in a strong bargaining position to up the ante as the December 5 deadline approached for the next phase of the oil-for-food program, and the beginning of a new phase of the Palestinian *intifada*.[5]

In addition to weighing the risks posed by regional conflict and its attendant political tensions, it is worth considering the potential for disruption in oil production resulting from changes in the governing regimes of major producing countries. Many oil analysts argue that regardless of whether revolutions or peaceful regime changes occur, the new leadership will continue to produce as much oil as the previous one. Few seem to remember that Iran's production fell sharply from close to 6 million barrels per day before the 1979 revolution; 20 years later, the country's productive capacity is still only 3.8 million barrels per day.

In short, a changing global economy, diversification of oil supplies, oil market transparency, the ability to lay off risks in futures markets, and IEA stockpile requirements have all contributed to changing perceptions about oil supply security over the past two decades. Have policymakers become too complacent about the prospects of another major oil shock with a correspondingly major adverse impact on the global economy?

At a U.S. government workshop on oil supply security in Washington, D.C. in 1999, almost all participants believed that an oil supply interruption, triggered by either a regional war or internal upheaval, was likely to occur at some point in the next decade. When asked when and how large this disruption would be, however, the majority predicted that it would happen later rather than sooner and that it would involve no more than 5 percent of global supply. Only a small group believed that it was prudent to plan on a 10–15 percent supply interruption during the decade of the 2000s.

A number of developments, however, could reduce oil supply security in the coming decade.

1. *Declining global commercial stocks.* IEA countries are required to hold 90 days of commercial stocks in days of forward

consumption. Many IEA countries used to hold larger stock-piles but have reduced stocks in recent years for budgetary reasons. Non-IEA members bear no requirements to hold strategic stocks, and, with a few exceptions, most non-IEA countries hold no strategic stocks. When the IEA was established, non-IEA oil consumption was 38 percent of global oil consumption; today it is 44 percent, and by 2010 it could increase still further to perhaps 50 percent. Hence, in a future major oil supply interruption, panic buying by non-IEA members could be substantial enough to offset positive actions (including strategic draw-downs of these stocks) by the IEA countries.[6]

2. *The switch away from secure to less secure non-OPEC supply.* In the past two decades, much of the incremental non-OPEC production has come from Alaska and the North Sea. Alaskan production has long since peaked,[7] and the North Sea is very close to peaking and may show a decline sometime later in the decade. Most long-term oil market forecasts project that Russia and the Caspian will become the largest incremental non-OPEC oil exporters in this decade. Whatever one's view of future exports from the former Soviet republics, all are far less secure sources of supply than the North Sea has been. In fact, the Caspian region and possibly Russia may be less secure supply sources than the Persian Gulf countries.

3. *Limited fuel substitution potential.* In the 1970s, when the share of oil in total energy consumption within the OECD countries was about 54 percent, higher prices led to rapid fuel switching away from oil to natural gas and coal in power plants and large industrial boilers. Currently, the share of oil in total OECD energy consumption is only 40 percent, and most of it is used in the transportation sector, where there are no ready substitutes in the short term.

4. *Increasing dependence on Gulf production.* Within OPEC, the share of non-Gulf oil producers has been relatively stable: about one-third of OPEC production. Most forecasts for 2010 project a rising share of Middle East oil production. The United

States, which in recent years had relied increasingly on oil from the Atlantic basin, is itself expected to become more dependent on Middle East oil imports, particularly in the latter half of the decade, as a result of stagnant oil production in the North Sea and much slower than initially projected growth in Latin American production.

5. *Looming challenges to Gulf internal stability.* Per capita income in Saudi Arabia has declined by as much as 75 percent since the late 1970s because of lower oil prices, demographic factors, and inability to shift from oil to a more diversified economy. Half of the population in the Gulf states is younger than 15 years old, and a few years from now huge numbers of young people, ill prepared by local educational systems, will be looking for jobs. Several governments in the region may face potentially serious challenges to the status quo, with unknown political consequences.

6. *Regional tensions surrounding the Gulf.* These tensions include continued geopolitical uncertainty in a region with many territorial disputes; the unresolved Arab-Israeli problem; the introduction of weapons of mass destruction in some countries in the region; and the threat of radical fundamentalist Islamic forces taking advantage of regional and local socioeconomic and political problems. The response to the renewed 2000–2001 *intifada* could result in a regional conflict leading to an oil supply interruption. Even if this does not happen, the communications revolution, with its 24-hours-a-day coverage in Arabic of the Israeli-Palestinian violence, has had a dramatic impact on popular sentiment throughout the region. Unless the conflict can be brought to an end, it could undermine the governments of the conservative GCC states.

7. *Uncertainty about the Western security role.* There may be a growing perception in the region that the West may no longer be able to respond as positively to major external military threats as it did during the Gulf War. In the first place, it may become more difficult to reach a consensus among Western countries on any

future military action in the region. The Gulf War was paid for largely by Saudi Arabia, Kuwait, Japan, and Germany, while the United States and the UK provided most of the military forces. Although the United States and the UK still have meaningful forces in the area and technological military superiority, the ability and willingness of others to pay for a future war in the region are doubtful. Awareness of division within the Western alliance and financial constraints, combined with the regional introduction of weapons of mass destruction, could make some regimes more adventurous in attempting to achieve limited military or political objectives in the Gulf. Moreover, the terrorist attack on the American destroyer USS *Cole* in Aden harbor in October 2000 suggests that there are limits to the overwhelming technological power of the United States to counter the threat of terrorism.

8. *Decline of spare productive capacity.* The availability of spare productive capacity in the OPEC countries, particularly in Saudi Arabia and to a lesser extent in Kuwait and the UAE, has contributed greatly to avoiding or significantly reducing the impact of past oil supply interruptions—notably the Iran-Iraq War and the Gulf War. OPEC spare capacity fell from 11 million barrels per day in 1986 to perhaps as little as 1.0–1.5 million barrels per day in late 2000. OPEC's supply cuts in early 2001, combined with a modest increase in capacity in some countries, may have increased its overall spare capacity to a more comfortable 3.0 million barrels per day. Even 3.0 million barrels per day, however, is less than Iraq's current production capacity. Saudi Arabia (which holds roughly 80 percent of global spare capacity), Kuwait, and the UAE may well decide to allow spare capacity to decline in future years to save money. If they do, it will affect global oil supply security.

In sum, the threat of an oil supply interruption resulting from local or regional instability has not substantially abated since the oil shocks of the 1970s. Changing oil markets, the ability to lay off risks at futures exchanges, IEA policy, and the readiness of key consumer countries such as the United States to release strategic stocks will mitigate any future oil supply interruption. There is no doubt that the world today could cope better with an oil supply interruption of the magnitude and duration of the first or second oil shock.

Rising global reliance on Middle East oil in this decade, however, coupled with declining spare capacity and continued political instability in the region, suggests that security of supply should remain an issue of considerable concern for policymakers in the United States. The last time a major oil-producing country collapsed internally was the Iranian revolution. Fortunately for the world, declining oil consumption in the OECD countries and ample Saudi spare capacity saved the day. Are we adequately prepared for a supply interruption of a similar magnitude from the world's largest oil exporter, or extended supply interruptions caused by a major regional war? Are we prepared to cope with a nightmare scenario of a full oil embargo?

For the United States, the existence of the IEA and its own strategic reserve remain the best means to cope with a potential major oil supply interruption. The IEA should spearhead the move to persuade Asian countries to build strategic reserves of their own and establish a mechanism to coordinate a global stockdraw in case of a major oil supply interruption. In view of the probability that threats to Middle East oil supplies will continue, the U.S. role as the main protector of this vital resource undoubtedly will have to continue for the foreseeable future.

Notes

[1] World oil prices did fall sharply in 1998, providing an additional lift to the global economy as it was recovering from the Asian economic crisis. Despite a slowdown in the global economy by 2001, oil prices remained in the high twenties ($) as a result of OPEC's ability to manage crude supply and oil product supply tightness, particularly in the Atlantic basin. Although the future of the global economy remains uncertain, sustained high oil prices will adversely affect economic growth, predominantly in the developing, oil-importing countries.

[2] The Organization for Economic Cooperation and Development, originally created by 20 Western countries in Europe and North America, has since expanded to include 29 members comprising most of the world's wealthiest countries. The members share the principles of market economics, pluralist

democracy, and respect for human rights; headquartered in Paris, OECD promotes a range of policies and practices that are consistent with members' common political and economic philosophy and shared interests.

[3] The September 2000 "fuel riots" in European capitals were directed against high government taxes on transportation fuel, which in many countries accounted for as much as 70–80 percent of the price at the pump. Recent rises in crude oil prices, coupled with the sharp fall of the Euro, had put additional upward pressure on what were already very high gasoline and diesel fuel prices.

[4] The Gulf Cooperation Council, formed in 1981, is an organization aimed at coordination and harmonization of political, security, and economic policies and laws. Its member states are Kuwait, Saudi Arabia, Bahrain, Qatar, the United Arab Emirates (UAE), and Oman. At the time of the Iraq-Iran war, Saudi Arabia, Kuwait, and the UAE had millions of barrels of spare capacity, and several other OPEC countries had some shut-in capacity resulting from the major drop in OECD oil consumption after 1980.

[5] The *intifada* is the Palestinian "grassroots" protest against Israel's occupation of territories acquired in the 1967 War.

[6] Indeed, the overall trend here, if anything, is worsening. The Republic of Korea, an OECD member aspiring to become an IEA member country, admitted in 2000 that it allowed its crude oil stocks to decline to as little as 29 days of forward consumption.

[7] The Bush administration seeks to open federal lands in the eastern Gulf of Mexico, the Rocky Mountain area, and, most important, the naval petroleum reserve in Alaska—that is, the Alaskan National Wildlife Refuge (ANWAR)—for energy development. If political resistance to developing ANWAR can be overcome, it will take at least five years before any ANWAR oil will reach the lower 48 states. An optimistic view of ANWAR's supply potential suggests that full development could reduce U.S. oil imports by 10–15 percent by 2010.

PART THREE

OIL PRICE EFFECTS IN THE GLOBAL FINANCIAL SYSTEM

CHAPTER FOUR

OIL IN THE NEW GLOBAL ECONOMY
INTERNATIONAL CAPITAL MARKET INTEGRATION AND THE ECONOMIC EFFECTS OF OIL PRICE EXTREMES
Catherine L. Mann

IN CHAPTER 2 OF THIS VOLUME, PETER FUSARO PROVIDES AN OVERVIEW of the changing nature of world oil markets and analyzes the implications for production and consumption of oil at extreme high and low oil price levels (sustained for three years) as compared to a baseline oil price. This chapter investigates the implications of those oil price scenarios for international capital flows.

That the relationship between oil prices and international capital flows might warrant investigation has not always been obvious, but the experience of the 1970s shows that the links are quite strong. The surprise oil price increases by the OPEC cartel in 1973 and again in 1978 importantly affected U.S. and global economic activity in the 1970s and 1980s through two channels. The first channel is better understood and is incorporated into most macroeconomic models: higher oil prices affect economic activity directly.[1]

The higher oil prices of the 1970s and 1980s also changed the gross volume and international distribution of capital flows, however, as some countries became net lenders of international capital by running current account surpluses and others became net international borrowers by running current account deficits. The implications of this change in international capital flows were not (and perhaps are not to this day) well understood. The following section, entitled "Changing Characteristics of International Capital Flows over the Last Three Decades," starts on that path of understanding. It reviews how the gross volume, the international distribution, and the characteristics of how capital flows were intermediated changed during and following the 1970s and 1980s episodes. This review sets the stage for the analysis of the impact of the high and low oil price scenarios for global capital flows in the 2010 timeframe.

The next section, entitled "Economic Implications of Extreme Oil Price Scenarios in 2010," presents a contemporary model of net international financing sources and needs that links together the scenarios for oil prices (i.e., for production and consumption of oil) and the resulting international capital flows. This part traces the net financing sources and needs for countries, based on their energy intensities and the impact of high versus low oil prices on production and consumption.

It is essential to understand how the nature of financial intermediation has changed from the 1980s to the present because this factor affects our assessment of the ability of the international capital markets to intermediate effectively the sources of and needs for financing under high or low extreme oil prices. Some countries will be net suppliers of international capital, and some will be net borrowers. How the geographical distribution and financial characteristics of these financing needs interact with international capital markets will differ depending on the nature of a country's existing relationships with international capital market intermediaries.

For example, some countries are more diversified with regard to the types of financial intermediaries and financial instruments that they utilize; other countries are more dependent on certain types of financial flows, such as official aid,[2] bank capital, or foreign direct investment (FDI).[3] The implications of alternative oil price conditions for international capital markets will be affected by who is a net borrower and who is a net lender, as well as how the magnitude of these net positions changes.

Finally, there are several ways in which the markets might change in this decade that are important for the relationship between financial flows and oil flows. First, how economic value in a country is created has changed over the past 20 years. Information technology is a much more important source of value-creation in the economy of the United States and some other countries, replacing to some degree the more energy-intensive manufacturing sector for value-creation. Second, deregulation of some financial markets (and possibly re-regulation of others) is likely to be an important source of change in the characteristics and geographical distribution of international capital flows in the future. Third, the dependence on energy for the creation of economic value (the so-called energy intensity of production) of key large trading partners, such as Brazil, India, and China, could affect international financing requirements. Tracing the effects of these three elements of technological change, regulatory reform and energy intensity on international capital flows, and recognizing key conduits of economic pressure, are the subject of the section entitled "Extended Scenarios." The chapter concludes with an analysis of the implications of bigger, more evolved global capital markets.

CHANGING CHARACTERISTICS OF INTERNATIONAL CAPITAL FLOWS OVER THE PAST THREE DECADES

International capital flows have changed dramatically since the 1973 oil crisis. In the 1970s and early 1980s, international financial flows were made predominantly through international bank loans and mainly between industrial countries. Most were linked to trade relationships between corporations in the borrowing and lending countries. Countries tended to finance their investments internally, and current account positions were relatively small, both in dollar terms and as a share of their gross domestic product (GDP).

The 1973 and 1979 oil crises changed this environment in several ways. First, they created a wedge between trade and corporate relationships, on the one hand, and financial flows on the other. Current account positions widened, in surplus for the oil exporters and in deficit for the oil importers (see, on page 103, table 4.1, columns 1 and 2 for each year). Countries that were earning international foreign exchange (notably, OPEC members) were unable to absorb the tremendous inflows of funds into quality domestic investment projects and had to "invest" some of the proceeds abroad (see table 4.1, column 3). International banks took on the role of intermediating these financial flows using the financial instrument of the bank loan (see table 4.1, comparing column 4 in each year, where the share of flows intermediated by banks generally rises between 1970 and 1980).

The outcome of this intermediation process included an increase in the number of countries in international capital markets, but not in the types of financial instruments or intermediaries. At the time, what developed was not a web of international capital flows by many types of financial intermediaries and many types of financial instruments, but rather (particularly in hindsight) a unidirectional flow of earnings from the oil exporters to the oil importers through the single financial intermediary of international banks and the single financial instrument of international loans.[4]

Starting in the mid-1980s and rapidly gathering momentum throughout the 1990s, several factors have further separated financial flows from trade relationships and created much greater richness in terms of the set of countries participating in the international capital markets and the types of financial instruments available. First, economic growth has increased investable financial wealth in the industrial countries as well as in some developing countries. A desire for diversification of wealth portfolios and an ability to diversify internationally thanks to deregulation have further contributed to a developing web of international capital flows.

Second, a retrenchment in the activities of international banks, partly as a result of capital adequacy concerns and guidelines, has coincided with an increase in bond and stock market instruments to increase the range of financial instruments available to both investors and borrowers. Real-time computing power applied to financial market pricing formulas, against the backdrop of an environment of foreign exchange and interest rate variability (as well as sovereign risk), have encouraged the proliferation of derivative financial instruments.[5] Altogether, this trend implies a much more complex and interwoven international financial market in the first decade of the twenty-first century than in the 1970s or 1980s.

Because this increased complexity of international financial markets in the new global economy has implications for how oil price changes will affect many countries, including the United States, it bears closer examination. Several countries and regions of the world were selected for this study, based on their current or projected importance in terms of production or consumption of oil. The following section examines how these countries have become more integrated into the international financial markets and the extent to which they have used a wider range of financial instruments. The emerging patterns of financial development observed over the 1990s inform the subsequent analysis, which projects the (1) magnitude of capital flows, (2) the direction of capital flows, and (3) methods of financing capital flows under the three oil price scenarios for 2010.

Geography, Magnitude, and Type of Gross Flows of Finance

Since 1985, gross flows of international capital as measured by direct and portfolio investment of industrial and developing countries have increased nearly fivefold (see table 4.2).[6] Over that period, direct and portfolio investments have been undertaken both by and into industrial countries and developing countries. That is, the direction of investment is not simply North-to-North or North-to-South; some is South-to-North and some South-to-South. Thus, international capital flows have become much more extensive, and more countries have been participating as both investors and recipients of capital.

We can make some broad distinctions, however, about how much the gross flows have changed over the past 15 years. First, gross flows by the industrial countries have grown at a much slower rate (about 5-fold) than the gross flows by developing countries, which have grown nearly 23-fold. We would expect gross flows into and by developing countries to continue to grow faster than those for mature industrial countries, which have greater wealth and have been participants in the international financial markets for some time.

Moreover, the patterns of growth of portfolio and direct investment flows are somewhat different over this 15-year period. Gross outflows and inflows of direct investment by and into industrial countries increased about 10-fold, whereas for developing countries, the increase was about 20-fold. In contrast, the growth of gross portfolio flows by and into industrial countries increased just 4-fold, whereas gross flows of portfolio investment by and into developing countries increased 56-fold and, overall, are larger than the gross flows of direct investment for those countries. The relatively lower flow of direct investment is important because it often is the result of regulatory restrictions on ownership by foreigners of assets in some developing countries.

To some extent, these patterns of gross flows are reflected in the net flows. Industrial countries are net investors into developing countries through both forms of private investment. The industrial countries were net direct investors to developing countries of about $136 billion as of 1997, compared with only $24 billion in 1985. For portfolio investment, the net flow from industrial to developing countries was about $250 billion, compared with only about $10 billion in 1985.

All told, the developing countries are being incorporated relatively faster into the portfolio market than into the direct market. To some extent, the larger increase for portfolio flows reflects the small initial base. However, to a significant degree, the larger growth of portfolio flows reflects the fact that developing countries, as a general proposition, liberalized the types of financial investment into instruments that did not confer control to the purchaser (e.g., they liberalized portfolio financial investment but not direct financial investment).

Only very recently (and still to a limited degree) have these countries been willing to allow substantial foreign direct investment, which generally does give a higher share of ownership and control to the foreign purchaser. This trend may be changing in the aftermath of the Asian financial crisis, but the direction of change remains unclear. Will developing countries liberalize the FDI market more completely? Or will they try to reduce inflows of portfolio capital because of their concern about "hot" money flows?

Direction, Magnitude, and Composition of Net Flows to Specific Developing Countries

The direction, magnitude, and composition of net flows to specific developing countries have changed dramatically since the early

1980s. A broad-gauged look at the differences in types of flows distinguishes between private and official finance (see table 4.3). Official finance used to be almost equal to private finance as a net inflow (1980) and even exceeded private finance in the difficult year 1990. However, as private finance markets have increased their gross contribution to international financing (as discussed above), the role for official finance has fallen. In 1997, only about 12 percent of the net flows to developing countries were official finance. Even in 1998, as the Asian financial crisis was metastasizing amid large outflows of private capital, the ratio of private to official net flows was still about 2 to 1.

For the countries and regions of greatest interest for this study, differences in the types and magnitudes of flows are dramatic. Brazil, Mexico, and India have experienced net outflows of official finance. In contrast, China, Indonesia, Russia, and the Caspian Basin countries (defined here as Azerbaijan, Turkmenistan and Kazakhstan) have been net recipients.[7] Among these countries, China and Russia are major recipients of official finance—with ratios of private net inflows to official net inflows of about 2 to 1. By comparison, the Caspian area receives about three dollars of private finance for each dollar of official finance.

Increasingly, multilateral lenders (e.g., the World Bank) want to achieve poverty reduction rather than simply finance a country's external funding gap. In this vein, these official lenders are focusing on whether the money will be spent in a policy environment that is directed toward reducing poverty. A country such as India is more likely to receive multilateral official funding from this source going forward than might another country such as Russia, where (at least in the years leading up to 2001) the policy focus on poverty reduction has lacked commitment and the underlying policy environment has not inspired confidence.

In sum, whereas some developing countries are participating more fully in international capital markets, some of the countries targeted for more careful examination in our study resemble more the developing countries of the 1970s. These countries tend to be more dependent on official finance consisting of official development assistance through bilateral governmental arrangements and low-interest loans (so-called concessional lending) from multilateral development institutions. This dependency could become an issue in the future because the availability of such official resources on concessional terms has become much more constrained in the late 1990s and the early twenty-first century, with little prospect for change.

There also has been a dramatic change in the composition of private flows. In 1981–1982, bank- and trade-related finance represented about 80 percent of total net private capital flows to developing countries; FDI was about 15 percent; and portfolio investment in the form of bonds (as opposed to portfolio investment in the form of bank loans) accounted for the rest. By 1995–1996, in contrast, FDI represented about 45 percent, with bank- and trade-related lending, portfolio bonds, and portfolio equity each taking about equal shares. Thus, portfolio investment in the form of bonds and equity had risen to account for nearly 40 percent of financing.[8]

These aggregates conceal significant differences across countries and regions. Between 1992 and 1995, net resources flows into China were about 60 percent FDI and about 10 percent each official and private portfolio equity (the remainder was private debt—loans and bonds). In contrast, flows to India were about 10 percent FDI and about 30 percent each official and private equity portfolio. Flows to Indonesia were about 30 percent each official, FDI, and private portfolio equity. Flows to Brazil were about 50 percent private debt, and flows to Russia were about 40 percent each official and private debt.[9]

Overall, international banks played a less important role in the 1990s than in the 1970s and 1980s, particularly in financing of developing countries. Bank- and trade-related finance for developing countries fell from about 80 percent of total private flows in 1980–1982 to about 20 percent of total private flows in 1995–1996.[10] The most significant international banking players remain European and Japanese banks. U.S. banks have retreated substantially from the international banking market for developing countries; indeed, U.S. financial flows in general have been disintermediated from banks as other forms of capital intermediation have become much more prevalent in U.S. financial markets.

In contrast, continued de facto regulation within the European and Japanese financial markets generally has not supported development of a more diversified capital market. European and Japanese banks remain important sources of international bank financing, although Japanese bank financing trended downward during the 1990s as a result of structural problems within the banking system there.[11]

FDI is coming to play a very important role in financing, albeit much more for some countries than others. Direct investment in developing countries has increased 14-fold over this time period. This statistic leaves a somewhat skewed impression, however, given the overwhelming predominance of China in the global total. Between 1991 and 1995, China absorbed $114 billion of international FDI flows—ranking second behind the United States ($198 billion)! Although the trend of FDI into China has slowed somewhat since 1995, China remains the largest recipient among developing countries.

Among private financial investments that do not offer control (e.g., bank loans, portfolio equity, and bonds), there also has been an increase in the richness of choice in investment instrument (see table 4.4). Developing countries increasingly are participating in the international portfolio equity and direct investment markets. Some developing countries are FDI investors; South Korea is a notable example. In portfolio bonds, developing countries are issuing international debt securities to a greater extent, issuing $40 billion of international debt securities in 1997, compared with $634 billion issued by corporations in industrial countries. In portfolio equity, developing countries have been offering mutual funds (e.g., the Korea Fund) and, more recently, individual investments on domestic stock exchanges. Equity issues by all developing countries together accounted for $24.8 billion in 1997, up from $5.6 billion in 1991.[12]

Stock market turnover offers a mixed picture as to the participation of individual countries in the sample.[13] Higher stock turnover might indicate more participation in international markets, although it might not necessarily indicate deeper stock markets within those countries. That is, higher stock market turnover could derive simply from international investors churning through (e.g., buying and selling and buying) a limited set of available equity instruments.[14]

In India and Indonesia, turnover generally declined in the first half of the 1990s from 66 percent and 77 percent, respectively, to 9 percent and 25 percent in 1995 respectively, before rising a bit over the subsequent two years. Turnover in South Korea has been more than double or even three times that in those two countries—ranging from 114 percent in 1992 to 189 percent in 1997. In Mexico, turnover was relatively stable at about 40 percent for the 1990s, with a high of 50 percent in the crisis year of 1994 and a low of 31 percent in the following year. In China, where the data begin in 1993, turnover started at nearly double the percentage for these other examples, and has since risen still further, from 131 percent in 1992 to 329 percent in 1996. (Comparable turnover statistics for all equity markets worldwide ranged from 44 percent in 1992 to 83 percent in 1997.)

Some of the differences in stock market turnover derive from changes in investor sentiment. The generally lower turnover levels in Indonesia and India probably can be explained by limitations on foreign participation in the stock market. Looking forward, a key question will be the extent to which countries will alter their attitude toward noncontrolling equity participation by foreigners in their markets. Perhaps more significant, to what extent will investments in these markets become substitutes for investments in industrial countries' markets?

All told, cross-border capital flows exploded in the 1990s. Developing nations are more important participants, as borrowers and as lenders. There has been a shift in the mode of financing from official finance to private finance, and a significant shift away from international bank lending to FDI, portfolio equity, and bond finance, although there are sizeable differences in the shares of these types of flows for the countries and groups targeted for analysis in this study.

It is important to distinguish between bank finance and bond and equity finance. The key difference is that the terms of a bank contractual agreement are set, initially and for the life of the agreement, whereas the terms of bond and equity finance vary because they can be traded. For example, once a bank loan is agreed to, the length of the loan (e.g., three months) and the terms of interest payment (e.g.,

10 percent fixed or 2.5 percent variable over an internationally quoted interest rate such as LIBOR) are known for the life of the agreement.[15] The borrower knows how much to pay, and the lender knows how much will be received in interest and principal.

In contrast, the terms on bond and (particularly) equity finance, after being initially set in the contract or issue price, will be changed by market demand. For example, even if the contractual length to maturity and interest rate of a bond are determined at issue (such as a 10-year bond with a 10 percent coupon issued at $100 per bond), the bond is marketable. The price of the bond (along with the value of that bond to the holder and the value of the liability to the issuer) will change as the prospects for the issuing country or company change. This marketability effect is even more obvious in the case of equity instruments, where the return to the investor derives mainly from the capital gains on the instrument and not from a regularly scheduled interest payment.

The distinction in terms of marketability can be important for a developing country. When there is a downturn in economic prospects, the terms of a bank agreement are unchanged; the bond valuation or stock price will fall, however. Thus, with marketable instruments, some of the burden of lowered economic prospects is absorbed or borne by the holder of the financial instrument. On the other hand, this feature of marketability can negatively affect countries by making it easier for the holder to sell the bond or equity (which might imply a withdrawal of funds) when economic prospects look poor. In sum, the marketability of portfolio bond and equity finance is a double-edged sword.

Sources of Private Finance Have Changed as Well, As Has the Marketplace

One reason for the increased participation by developing countries in private portfolio bond and equity finance is the growing value of and desire for international diversification of wealth portfolios by investors in industrial countries. In a sense, developing countries increasingly find foreign investors knocking at their door, whether those countries are looking for foreign investment or not.

A similar dynamic was evident in the period following the first oil shocks in the 1970s as well. The severity of the debt crisis of the 1980s in developing countries (particularly in Latin America) stemmed in large part from the very limited range of financial instruments available to both investors and the countries in need of financing (as discussed above). What is different now is that the investors that are seeking opportunities in developing countries are not predominantly banks, and the financing instruments being chosen by these investors are not predominantly bank loans of relatively short-term and fixed maturity. Yet greater use of financial instruments that are marketable, and the wider diversity of investors, may not prevent another crisis; they may simply change its characteristics.

Industrial country savers increasingly are putting their capital to work through nonbank institutional investors such as pension funds, mutual funds, and insurance companies. These institutional investors increasingly are looking to developing countries' financial instruments to raise returns on their portfolios, as well as to diversify those portfolios. These institutional investors allow an individual saver in an industrial country to take a position in a developing country market without having to do extensive analysis himself or herself—the institutional investor does (or is supposed to do) the requisite analysis. In addition, the institutional investor can create portfolios of assets, which by virtue of their internal diversification should (although there is no certainty) provide lower risk than any individual investment would carry.

Despite the theoretical advantages of a diversified portfolio—which are borne out in both simulated and actual portfolios—it is commonly understood that investors hold a disproportionate share of assets issued by their own country in their wealth portfolios. This situation is known as "home bias." There are a number of reasons for this home bias. First, regulations in some portfolios prevent investors from holding assets issued by foreigners (for example, some government-backed pension funds have a limit on the share of the fund that can be invested in nondomestic assets).

Similarly, some markets (mainly in developing countries) restrict purchases by foreigners. The bulk of wealth portfolios remains overwhelmingly invested in assets of the home country; because industrial country wealth has increased so much in recent years, however, even small increases in the portion allocated to international investments can represent significant flows of capital into developing country markets.

By way of illustration, total pension assets in the OECD countries rose from $4.8 trillion in 1990 to $7.9 trillion by 1995. Over the same period, the share of these assets held in assets issued by OECD countries fell from 92.8 percent to 88.9 percent. While this decrease in the share of OECD assets invested in OECD countries may seem very small, it represents an outflow of $308 billion more than if the "home bias" within the OECD had remained unchanged over the five-year period.[16]

The preference among industrial country investors to hold their wealth in international assets varies by industrial country. In the United States, the increase in the share of international assets in the institutional investor's portfolio has ranged from about 5 percent in 1990 to about 10 percent in 1994. In the United Kingdom, Germany, and the Netherlands, mutual funds hold about 40 percent of their assets in nondomestic assets, although pension funds and insurance assets are much more home-based. Japanese institutional investors held about 10 percent nondomestic assets as of 1994, and the comparable figure for Canadian institutional investors is about 15 percent.[17] These shares probably rose during the 1990s because of deregulation of both funds and markets. Although the breakdown of the nondomestic assets into those from developing countries versus those from other industrial countries is unknown, the trends highlighted in table 4.2 suggest that the shares of developing countries' assets probably have risen at least a bit.

The marketplace of investment changed dramatically during the 1990s. As shown by table 4.5, the increase in the international flows of traded goods and services (which increased about 2-fold during the 1990s) is dwarfed by the increase in the international flows of capital, namely a 20-fold increase in the daily turnover of foreign exchange, a 3-fold increase in the issuance of international bonds, and a 30 percent increase in equity market turnover.

The international capital markets are different from the international trade markets for another reason: speed. Technological change, separation of finance and trade, and several other factors have allowed financial capital to move very quickly across borders in response to changes in wealth-holders' portfolio preferences. By contrast, the exports and imports of goods and services that underpin financing sources and needs still change slowly. Thus, although the trade accounts (the net of exports and imports of goods and services) and the capital accounts (the net of capital inflows and outflows) respond to the same economic forces associated with growth of income and rates of inflation in the trading countries, they do so in very different time frames. These economic forces are reflected nearly immediately in capital flows and in asset prices such as interest rates and exchange rates, but they work to change "real flows" of trade in goods and services much more slowly.

In addition, expectations for a country's profile of risk and return are particularly important in the quick-response market of financial capital.[18] When real or expected economic performance changes, a tension develops between the very rapid response of financial flows and the slower response of trade flows. This tension invariably will be reflected in the flows and prices that can adjust most quickly and freely—namely, capital flows and asset prices.

Indeed, volatility of investor sentiment can lead to very large and rapid changes in available finance as well as in asset prices. During the 1990s, there was one international financial-market crisis after another: the breakdown of European Exchange Rate Mechanism (ERM) in 1992–1993, the Mexican peso crisis of 1994-1995, the Asian financial turbulence that started in 1997, and the Russian financial collapse in 1998. In each case, rapid changes in investor sentiment precipitated the outflow of financial capital, which required a complementary move of the trade account toward or into surplus.

Computer technology has enhanced the role of exchange rates and capital market flows. Flexible exchange rates create incentives for financial transactions that are completely divorced from trade transactions. Computer technology combined with analytical models (such as the so-called Black-Scholes formula for pricing financial options[19]) give financial intermediaries the ability to create new financial instruments to meet new investor demand. Some of these instruments remove the unwanted exchange risk (swaps) or insure against it (options and future-dated contracts). Others meet the business demand to take on more market risk—and with it more potential return on investment—than would be created by any underlying real transaction.

In the context of the oil economy scenarios addressed later in this chapter, speed and volatility mean potentially rapid changes in both the financing available and the financing need for target countries. When international capital flows rapidly and asset prices (exchange rates and interest rates) change radically, developing countries are particularly vulnerable because their financial systems are less well developed. Countries can reduce the potential impact of the volatility of international flows by encouraging flows that have generally lower measured volatility. As shown in table 4.6, the direct investment flows, or FDI, are more stable than overall flows or portfolio flows.

Another essential factor in the more fluid international economy is leverage—the degree to which an investor's exposure is greater than an investor's actual equity stake. Greater leverage through the use of derivative financial instruments is one way that technological change in financial intermediation appears in certain markets. As shown in table 4.7, measures of leverage in international capital markets increased in many markets in the latter half of the 1990s. On the one hand, leverage enables financial intermediaries to make greater commitments to financing using less capital; thus, more financing is available—and at a cheaper price.

Leverage also adds to volatility and speed, however. When investor sentiment changes, not only is the base capital withdrawn, so is all of the financing that is built on (or "derived from") that capital base. Hence, leverage is a double-edged sword. Rapid de-leveraging (a change in investor sentiment that causes the investor's exposure and actual position to become closer to unity) can put both economies and financial intermediaries at risk of severe disruption.

Leverage is one gauge of investor sentiment; another is the degree of differentiation between initial ratings and secondary market yields on traded financial instruments such as U.S. dollar-denominated Eurobonds issued by developing countries.[20] Following the Asian and Russian financial crises in 1997–1998, international lenders reassessed the microeconomic structure and macroeconomic policies of developing countries.[21] In the first half of 1997, about 20 percent of bond issues were not rated, and another 50 percent were not rated "investment-grade"; thus, only about 25 percent of the total bonds issued were investment-grade—indicating a lack of attention to properly assessing risk.

In contrast, in the first half of 1999, nearly all bond issues were rated, with about 40 percent receiving investment-grade ratings and about 55 percent receiving various noninvestment-grade ratings. Similarly, secondary market yield spreads on U.S. dollar-denominated Eurobonds issued by various developing economies diverged substantially from one another during the latter part of the 1990s—a notable change inasmuch as the spreads tended to be both quite small over U.S. government bonds and tightly grouped as recently as 1996.[22]

The different scenarios for oil prices in 2010 outlined in chapter 2 will help some and hurt other key oil-producing and consuming countries in terms of the how the global investor perceives the risk and return of investing in a given country. Consequently, it is increasingly likely that the international financial markets will discriminate among countries through pricing or availability of funds, depending on which oil price condition prevails.

The increased differentiation of, and marketability of, non-bank financial instruments can be a mixed blessing. Although they provide a greater diversity of financial instruments and encourage a wider range of investors to invest in industrial and developing markets, they also make it easy to get out quickly if need be. Consequently, a key manifestation of the extreme high or low oil price scenarios will be increased volatility in international capital markets. How well the developing countries and the international capital markets can absorb this volatility is key to how the oil price scenarios will affect the United States, other key countries specifically targeted for analysis, and the global economy as a whole.

ECONOMIC IMPLICATIONS OF EXTREME OIL PRICE SCENARIOS IN 2010

Historical Observations and the Base Case

Table 4.8, in three sections, provides background information for the oil price scenarios. Section A gives data on the average growth for various countries and regions of the world, first for the 1980s and 1990s and then, in column 2, for two alternative economic scenarios created by the OECD to illustrate future prospects for GDP growth. The "high growth" scenario shows how future growth could benefit from structural adjustment in the world's economies, which would be undertaken to liberalize domestic and global markets for trade and finance and to maintain domestic fiscal stability. The "low growth" scenario assumes that none of these beneficial changes have occurred.

Section B of table 4.8 shows initial conditions for the level of the current account (which for some countries is approximated by net exports)[23] and for GDP, for specific countries and groups of countries targeted for analysis. Section C of table 4.8 pulls together in one place the estimates for production and consumption of oil under all three price scenarios from chapter 2.

Extreme Oil Prices: Impact on Level and Distribution of Global Financing Sources and Needs

Methodology. The methodology for determining how international capital flows might change with a sustained high or a sustained low price for oil is as follows: We start with the base case production minus consumption; this is assumed to be the quantity of net exports of oil in million barrels per day (shown in column 1 in table 4.9a and table 4.9b). This figure multiplied by the base price (shown in column 2), yields the value of net exports in millions of dollars per day in the base case. In a similar manner, we obtain the value of the net exports of oil in the extreme high and low oil price cases, respectively. (Production minus consumption for the high or low price is shown in column 3 in both tables.)

The difference between the value of net exports in the base case and the value of net exports in each alternative case, calculated on the basis of million barrels per day (mmb/day), is shown in column 5 in both tables. To compare this figure to the initial conditions of the annual dollar value of net exports for the country and regions (from table 4.8), the mmb/day figure must be grossed up to an annual dollar basis, shown in column 6 in each section of table 4.9. Thus, column 6 is the change in net exports or, equivalently, the change in international financing needed or available resulting from the change in oil prices, and its feed-back effect on production and consumption.

Interpretation: High Oil Price. The scenarios are relatively straightforward to interpret. Generally, high oil prices have the expected effect on changes in net exports and in financing sources and needs. As the "Summary Observation" column 7 in table 4.9a notes, net exports of the major oil producers and the countries that are net exporters of oil—among which are Canada, Mexico, and the former Soviet Union (FSU)—are increasingly positive because the value of production exceeds consumption by a greater amount as prices rise. Thus, these countries are providing more capital flows to international capital markets when prices are high.

Countries that are net importers of oil generally have increased financing needs because their net exports start out negative (see table 4.8) and become increasingly negative as their production does not expand much and the value of their consumption of oil increases.[24] For example, U.S. net exports start out $155 billion in deficit and become further negative by some $25 billion in the case of the sustained high oil price scenario.

China and Latin America present a different picture under the high oil price scenario than is the case for the key industrial economies that are large net importers of oil. For both China and Latin America, apparently the drop in consumption in the face of high oil prices is large enough that the net export deficit (e.g., financing need) shrinks under the high-price scenario—evidence of highly elastic demand for oil in these regions.[25] For example, in China, net exports (and financing need) under the high-price scenario falls by some $8 billion (while retaining a net export deficit and therefore requiring international capital inflow). For Latin America, the net exports and financing need shrink by some $9 billion. The reduced difference between production and consumption for both China and Latin America is about 55 percent, which is greater than the percentage increase in price from $21.30 to $30.00 per barrel (about 40 percent).

A check of the production and consumption estimates for these two areas (section C of table 4.8) shows that the change is almost entirely on the side of consumption. Production does not increase much in response to higher oil prices, but consumers do respond actively to the higher price by reducing their consumption of oil. Thus, we would conclude that the elasticity of demand for imported oil in these two areas is greater than 1.0.[26] As noted in part 4 of this book, some developing economies, when faced with high oil prices that must be paid in dollars (and at a time when their own currency is likely to be depreciating), actually sell their scarce oil supplies to raise hard currency. This behavior would tend to amplify the price elasticity further.

A similar outcome of an elastic response to the high-oil price obtains for the "unallocated" region. An inspection of the underlying data in section C of table 4.8 suggests that it is the combined change in production (which increases in response to higher prices) and consumption (which decreases in response to higher prices) that yields the elastic result.

Interpretation: Low Oil Price. For the sustained low-price scenario (table 4.9b), there are no real surprises for the specified regions of the world. For the major oil producers, their external positions remain positive but smaller. Similarly, other net exporters of oil (such as Canada, Mexico, and the FSU) remain net sources of financing, but of a smaller amount. Net importers of oil remain net importers, but the financing required to cover the balance is smaller in all cases. The outcome for world totals is somewhat surprising, however, because of the behavior of the "unallocated" region.

The "unallocated" region is a bit of a mystery. Its behavior probably is a result of the fact that it is a residual entry derived from the *World Total* less *OPEC* less *Total non-OPEC* (and it may be further affected by the incompleteness of consumption data available for the major oil exporters, including OPEC). According to the estimates for production and consumption in section C of table 4.8, however, the biggest change is on the production side. In the base case, although the unallocated region is a net importer of oil, it is a fairly substantial producer as well. Under the low oil price scenario, this region becomes a more significant net importer because production drops from 9.8 million barrels per day to 0.2 million barrels per day. (Consumption rises, as one would expect, with lower prices.)

These estimates are consistent with the significant changes in the location of production under the extreme low-price scenario, as discussed in chapter 2. In that scenario, Caspian and other marginal high-cost producing regions (which are included in the "unallocated" region here) lose out in favor of the low-cost oil producers in the Middle East, who pump more oil under the low-price scenario.

The shifts in sign of the world totals from the high-price case to the low-price case reflect the significant shifts in financing sources and needs that result from the extreme oil price scenarios. The world total financing shifts from a net financing "source" under the high-price scenario to a net financing "need" in the low-price scenario.

Judging the Significance of Changes in Financing Source or Need. How important are the changes in net exports (that is, in financing source or need) for the world or for any of the specified countries or regions? Tables 4.10a and 4.10b present some measures. In each table, the first column indicates the importance of the change in the value of net oil exports relative to the dollar value of 1997 net exports of the country or region (taken from section B of table 4.8). The second and third columns give two estimates of the importance of these changes in net exports (or changes in financing available or needed) relative to two alternative estimates of the dollar value of GDP for the country or region.[27] (Two alternative ways to estimate dollar values for GDP are shown because such estimates can differ substantially, particularly for developing countries whose exchange rates are either pegged or traded by only a few international investors.)

The difference in net exports under either extreme price scenario was measured relative to the 2010 base scenario in dollars. How significant an amount this represents as a financing source or need should be examined in several ways. First, how important is the world total compared to the gross flows of international capital? Second, how important is the change in the value of net exports, measured in millions of U.S. dollars per year, for a country or region? For this measure, we need to compare the financing source or need caused by the oil price change to the country or region's initial total resources (GDP) or external resources (net exports).

Thus, tables 4.10a (high-price scenario) and 4.10b (low-price scenario) show the ratio of change in net exports on account of the oil price shock to the initial net export figure for the country or region (column 1) and compared to the two alternative measures of GDP for the country or region (columns 2 and 3). These ratios give a sense of the magnitude of the change in financing need or source compared to the country's initial position in the base case.

The overall observation from these exercises is that some countries and regions will experience changes in financing source or need that are huge—both in terms of their external resources (e.g., net exports) and in terms of their overall resources (e.g., GDP, as measured by either "atlas" or "ppp" (purchasing power parity). Notably, because they are not diversified in their source of production, the oil producers experience very substantial changes in their net exports; thus, the significance of this change in net exports compared to their initial external position in 1997 is large.[28] On the other hand, for the world as a whole, the net financing source or need relative to the initial positions actually is quite modest—well under 0.5 percent of global GDP.

Comparing the figures for financing need or source for broad areas of the world (OPEC and non-OPEC) to the figures for the size of international capital markets (table 4.5), it is apparent that the projected global demands of a 2010 "oil shock" on international capital markets are not nearly as great as in the 1970s and 1980s. The international capital markets were much deeper by 2000 and will be all the more so by 2010. For example, neither the change in net exports of the OPEC countries in the base–high scenario comparison (about $91 billion) nor the change in the net exports of the non-OPEC countries in the base–low scenario comparison (some $93 billion) is so big compared to the issuance of international debt securities of $1,225 billion in 1999.

Turning to selected major industrial regions (e.g., the United States, Japan, Western Europe), capital flows needed in a 2010 oil price crisis are not large. In the high-price case, the United States needs about $26 billion more, Japan needs about $12 billion more, and Western Europe needs about $13 billion more. These amounts are about 50 percent of the additional financing seen to be available in the OPEC countries. If OPEC countries allocated their portfolios 50-50 to industrial and developing countries, the financing would be relatively straightforward to achieve.

In fact, an allocation of 50 percent of the available financing to assets of the developing countries probably is high (and an allocation of only 50 percent to assets of industrial countries too low). The industrial countries probably would receive a greater share of available financing from OPEC. In this situation, interest rates in industrial countries would fall and economic activity there would rebound a bit, as the higher oil prices traded off against the lower interest rates to affect overall economic growth as well as growth within different sectors. In the developing world, growth would be relatively more slowed in response to the double whammy of the higher oil prices and higher interest rates, although these countries might get some spillover benefit through trade with industrial countries.

Notwithstanding the modest overall impact of high prices relative to the base case, for some countries and regions the changes in both net export (NX) and NX against GDP are dramatic. For example, for the OPEC countries and the FSU, the change in the financing source would represent a huge change in their external balances: the net increase in financing from the high oil price would be about $90.7 billion (for OPEC) against a net export surplus of about $21.8 billion in 1997. Thus, as in 1970s and 1980s, the OPEC countries would be looking to invest substantial additional funds. Compared with the collective GDP for OPEC, the additional funds from the high oil price would represent either 7.5 percent or 15 percent of

GDP, depending on the measure of GDP. This analysis provides an idea of how important the oil sector is for these economies.

For some of the smaller OPEC countries, such as Venezuela and Nigeria, the infusion of funds relative to the starting net export is even greater, indicating the relatively more precarious position of their initial net export positions. The FSU experiences similar gains—and for these countries, the importance of the oil sector for the net export position is even greater.

Using the same line of reasoning, it is clear why the 2010 low oil price scenario would be disastrous for these countries (table 4.10b). The net impact of the lower oil price on OPEC countries is a huge 15 percent or 30 percent of GDP (depending on the measure). It is interesting that the FSU does not experience quite such large-scale adverse effects: the change in net export relative to GDP is only about 8 percent (4.7 percent by the alternative measure).

In the case of net oil producers with more broad-based economies, such as Canada and Mexico, the dramatic changes in oil prices would have more muted effects on their net export positions as well as on their GDP. In the high-price scenario, these countries' net exports would improve substantially, nearly closing any negative position as measured in 1997 dollars. In terms of GDP, the increase in net exports under the high-price scenario represents a major improvement for Mexico (increase by 2.3 percent of GDP); the change in NX compared to GDP is less dramatic for Canada. The same basic outcome shows up, with the plus-minus signs reversed, in the low-price scenario.

For the developing countries, the effects of extended low oil prices on their net export accounts are large in 2010, though generally not so large compared to what happened in the 1970s. The NX/GDP ratio represents a not insignificant change. A change of approximately 1 percent in the NX/GDP ratio would be the outcome of these scenarios for most developing countries. The biggest change under the low oil price scenario is for India and South Korea, as each would benefit substantially (i.e., about 2 percent of GDP) from the lower oil prices. The Latin American region is relatively unaffected by the changes in oil prices when measured as a share of the region's current account or GDP. This outcome contrasts with the 2 percent worsening of their position relative to GDP experienced in the 1970–1980 period (compare column 2 for 1970 with column 2 for 1980 in table 4.1).

In sum, although the undiversified producers of oil would experience dramatic changes under either extreme oil price scenario, the moderately diversified developing countries would be less affected by oil market developments from now to 2010 than they were in the 1970s. These extreme price scenarios have only muted economic impacts on industrial countries. Moreover, the financing available or needed is fairly small in comparison to the gross flows in international capital markets anticipated for 2010, or even present-day levels of activity and depth in the international capital markets.

One important concern, however, could be that in the high-price scenario, only a portion—in some cases, perhaps a very small portion—of the financial windfall for the leading oil producers would be recycled out of their own countries into the international financial markets. Global interest rates would then have to play a very important role, as discussed next.

Impact of Scenarios on the United States

The direct impact of the sustained high or low oil price conditions on the United States in 2010, through their impact on U.S. net exports, is remarkably small. In the high-price case, the net export position does worsen relatively more, but only by about 0.3 percent of GDP. As a point of comparison, the U.S. net export deficit widened only about 0.1 percent of GDP as a direct consequence of the Asian financial crises of 1997–1998. And then over the course of 1999, the robust U.S. economy pulled in additional imports of all kinds of goods, so that the net export deficit grew by about 1 percent of GDP.

Thus, the extreme high oil price scenario in 2010 is not so dramatic, in macroeconomic terms, even compared to events that the U.S. economy experienced from 1997 to 1999. Nevertheless, the political reaction in Europe and the United States to the disproportionate effect of high oil prices on certain sectors and regions, as seen throughout 2000, shows the limitation of considering only macroeconomic aggregates.

The direct improvement on net exports and the NX/GDP ratio in the case of the sustained low oil price case is more significant: NX/GDP would narrow by some 0.6 percent. Given that the net-export-deficit-to-GDP ratio was about 3.6 percent as of mid-2000, a narrowing on the order of 0.6 percent of GDP is significant.

The United States also will be affected indirectly by the ways in which extreme oil prices—high and low—affect its trading partners. As noted in table 4.11, the United States trades substantially with Mexico, Japan, Canada, and the European Union (EU).

The low oil price scenario would affect the United States mostly through the channel of trade. With lower oil prices, many regions have increased purchasing power to buy U.S. exports instead of spending as much of their income on oil. The opposite effect would hold true for the high-price scenario. However, some of the regions most negatively affected by high oil prices (India, for example) are not major buyers of U.S. products. Even though China ends up being positively affected by both scenarios, it is not a large buyer of U.S. products either. On the other hand, South Korea is a significant purchaser of U.S. exports, so the high-price scenario would hurt the U.S. indirectly through this channel.

Looking forward, as they participate more fully in international markets, China and India are likely to become more significant trading partners of the United States. Consequently, in the 2010 time period, the impact on their domestic economic activity of extreme oil price movements probably would affect the United States more than current trade figures might suggest.

EXTENDED SCENARIOS

There are several ways in which the markets might change in this decade that are important to the relationship between financial flows and oil flows. First, the way in which economic value is created by combining natural resources, human resources, financial capital, and knowledge has changed dramatically over the past 20 years. Technology is a much more important source of value-creation in the economy of the United States and some other countries, displacing to some degree the role of the more energy-intensive manufacturing base. Second, deregulation of some financial markets (and possibly reregulation of others) is likely to be an important driver of change in the characteristics and geographical distribution of international capital flows in the future. A third factor is the energy intensity of production within the economies of key large trading partners, such as India and China, which could affect international financing requirements.

High-Tech America Is Less Energy Dependent

Table 4.12 shows that from 1980 to 1996, the United States became less energy-dependent in generating GDP. The information technology revolution could accelerate this trend. Thus, with the passage of time, the United States becomes less directly affected by changes in international oil prices. What this means is that the relatively small effects of these oil prices directly on the U.S. economy will become even smaller in the present decade and beyond.

The United States will continue to be affected indirectly through trade flows as noted above (and discussed further below). In addition, to the extent that production by U.S. multinational corporations occurs abroad, there will be linkages back to the United States through higher or lower profits for those corporations as they absorb higher or lower oil prices into their overseas production costs.

Stay-at-Home Capital or Re-Regulation of Capital Markets

A key question for the future is whether the major oil-producing countries will invest their funds on international markets in the case of the high oil price, as they did in the 1970s. Some of these countries were running small current account balances as of the late 1990s. But many have large fiscal budget deficits that need financing, or great domestic needs. Consequently, if there were an inflow of funds associated with higher oil prices, these countries could find plenty of expenditure outlets at home, including investment activities, in contrast to the "petrodollar recycling" situation in the 1970s.

In the case of the extended high oil prices, however, there still be will be the same financing need in the non–oil-producing countries. If oil money "stays home," fewer funds will be lent into the international capital markets. In such circumstances, global interest rates would tend to rise relatively more, slowing economic activity more. Through this mechanism, demand and supply for oil would be brought back into balance.

Compare the foregoing situation to one of extreme low oil prices. In this case, the financing needs of the oil producers would be dramatically large, yet the incentives to invest there by multinational oil companies or other financial investors would be limited. These countries probably would experience deterioration in their internal activity and fiscal balances. Additional funds available on international markets because of the low oil prices would tend to reduce global interest rates, boost economic activity (including oil consumption) outside the oil-producing regions, and gradually bring supply and demand for oil back into balance. This is what happened—albeit very gradually and overlaid by other economic events—during the 1990s, when oil prices were quite low.

A second issue is whether the dangers highlighted by the Asian financial debacle of 1997–1998 will result in re-regulation of some types of capital—in particular, portfolio flows of capital. As noted in the first section of this chapter, gross flows to emerging markets of this type of capital have risen more than 50-fold in the past 15 years. One consequence of re-regulation to restrict the inflow of such portfolio capital would be that developing countries might be less likely to receive inflows of such capital to finance growing net export deficits in a high oil price scenario. A return to reliance on bank flows is possible, although there are limits on how much banks might be willing to lend to developing countries in times of high oil prices and reduced prospects for growth—as indeed has been observed in 2001.

Moreover, if oil-producing countries do invest windfall proceeds abroad in 2010, they are not likely to do it via bank intermediation. Over the 30 years since the last major oil crisis, Saudi Arabia at least has become a much more "mature" investor that will use a range of financial instruments to recycle (e.g., invest) its oil proceeds abroad, if it decides to do so. Similarly, Canada, Mexico, and Venezuela are not strangers to international financial markets today. Only some oil-rich areas such as Iran, Iraq, and the Caspian Basin countries are relatively new to the markets; they have great internal needs, how-ever, and therefore are less likely to generate large external capital flows.

Alternative Scenarios for Energy Intensity

What if development processes in China and India cause them to become much more intensive users of energy in this decade? Com-pare their kilograms of energy equivalent per capita against other developing countries (table 4.12). In the case of China, if the energy-intensity of production rose, it is less likely that the elasticity of de-mand for oil would be above 1.0, as has been suggested by the scenarios presented in this book. With a less elastic demand for oil, China would have a net increase in financing need in extended high oil price conditions, not the reduced financing need as suggested by the high-price scenario. Moreover, India would have an even greater increase in its financing need if the energy-intensity of its production increased.

Compared with the values in the tables in this chapter, the global demand for financing almost certainly would be greater. Because India and China are large countries, even greater financing needs in the 2010 high oil price scenario imply greater stress on international capital markets to recycle funds to these countries. Yet these coun-tries are not very open to international capital today, and they re-main quite dependent on official capital flows (recall table 4.3). Consequently, absent a significant degree of economic maturation in these countries in the near future, it may be difficult for the inter-national private markets to service their financial needs in 2010.

Similarly, if Latin America became more intensive in its use of en-ergy, its consumption would not fall as much as we have posited un-der the high-price scenario. This region would require additional financing, and the demand on world oil markets also would be greater. Therefore, the posited character of the high-price sce-nario—that total world production will exceed total world con-sumption so that the high price cannot be sustained—is not as clear. If many countries increase their use of energy in the first decade of the twenty-first century, oil prices would be more likely to remain high for a longer period. Therefore, energy intensity is an important factor in determining the economic effects of extreme oil price trends.

On the other hand, developing countries could take advantage of innovations in technology and use energy more efficiently, even as they grow. That is, China and India could become much more efficient in their use of energy to produce GDP. Compare the GDP per unit of energy for these countries against the other developing countries in table 4.12; if energy efficiency rises in China and India, then their need for financing could remain at about the same value as in the scenarios discussed in the third section of this chapter. In this situation, the financial aspects of an individual country could remain stable in the face of higher oil prices, even if the global financial markets were not.

IMPLICATIONS OF BIGGER, MORE EVOLVED GLOBAL CAPITAL MARKETS

This chapter has focused on the links between international capital markets and international oil markets. It addressed how the characteristics of international capital markets have changed from the 1970s through the 1990s and discussed the possible outcomes for international financing sources and needs of sustained extreme high and low oil prices in the 2010 timeframe.

What we have seen is that international capital markets have become much richer and deeper. Compared with the 1970s, the international markets by 2010 will offer a much greater range of financial instruments, which will enable many different kinds of countries and institutions to borrow and lend. In addition, financial institutions now operate with much higher leverage ratios, which tends to further increase the flow of international capital. Thus, we conclude that even in the face of large, sustained oil price changes, the international capital markets have the *capability* to intermediate these financing sources and needs (although see the caveat below).

Regarding the financial situation in individual countries and regions, oil price effects will be more of a concern. For the less-diversified economies of many of the oil producers, sustained high or low oil prices can have dramatic effects through changes in their net exports. For many OPEC countries, these price trends could have huge impacts on the sources of financing for their GDP; the impact on the FSU also is significant. Extreme oil price scenarios have a much less dramatic impact, however, on many other countries and regions highlighted for examination in this study because their economies have a much more diversified production base and source of value-creation. Yet even for most developing countries, the changes in their net external balances relative to the overall size of their economies (NX/GDP) are smaller in 2010 than was the case in the 1970s and 1980s.

For the United States, these possible sustained high or low oil prices result in smaller impacts on U.S. net exports and NX/GDP ratio in 2010 than those experienced from 1997 to 1999, as the U.S. economy grew robustly and Asian demand collapsed following the financial crisis there. The U.S. economy and the international financial markets generally have been able to absorb these changes in international financing sources and needs.

Looking forward, an important issue is whether the oil-producing countries will want to recycle the funds generated in a high-price scenario. Many of them have significant internal obligations to work off before looking to investments abroad. If this is the case, the "supply" of international funds will be lower than projected in our scenarios, with upward pressure on global interest rates more likely. When global interest rates rise, investors tend to shift their portfolios to investments in the advanced industrial economies. Thus, the developing countries probably will feel more of a pinch by 2010 from rising interest rates than from insufficient flows of finance.

The collapse of oil prices in the low-price scenario suggests lower global interest rates, with relatively more funds allocated toward the non–oil-producing developing world. Growth rates of these countries, on the margin, would tend to be more robust.

All of this analysis suggests that the international capital markets a decade from now will be able to provide the financial liquidity, smoothly, from the part of the world where capital is generated to the part of the world that needs it. The increased range of financial instruments and diversity of countries and investors participating in financial markets even today would tend to support this notion of smooth adjustment.

The increase in financial leverage is a double-edged sword, however. When financial markets work well, financial leverage can help intermediate the oil monies from the countries earning them to the countries that need additional financing. When market sentiment about the prospects for growth in one country's economy changes, however, the leverage in the international capital markets tends to exacerbate the withdrawal of funds from those markets and send greater inflows into others.

Clearly, for example, the international capital markets did not smoothly adjust international capital flows to changes in market sentiment regarding the Asian countries' macroeconomic situation in 1997–1998, in part because the financial markets were surprised day after day with new revelations about the true situation in these countries. In the end, although the change in the level of financing was large, the more important features of the Asian financial crisis were the speed and volatility of the financial flows; these factors are what caused the greatest economic chaos for the affected countries.

By analogy, a sustained high or low oil price shock probably will not yield great drama in the international financial markets in 2010. What will matter more for the ability of the markets to smoothly provide financing to oil importers and recycle oil earnings from producers is whether the oil price change occurs as a complete surprise and—as likely as not—in conjunction with some other unanticipated crisis circumstances. Such surprises lead to rapid and widespread shifts in market sentiment that will magnify the simple equilibrium flows of financial needs and sources suggested by the oil price scenarios analyzed here.

Ultimately, the oil price change per se would not cause the greatest economic difficulty; the key factor is the speed and volatility of financial movements in response to a surprise shock. These are the hazards of the twenty-first-century global financial system, and they will only grow as the world's economy gains in size and sophistication.

How should policymakers prepare now for potential financial chaos in the future? The best offense is a good defense: ensure that each country's financial systems are appropriately monitored and have sufficient reserves against dramatic changes in market sentiment. Be prepared to engage in coordinated action to calm international financial markets. Acknowledge a role for an international "lender of last resort."[29] The next oil "crisis" can be ameliorated by international capital markets—or these markets can make it worse. Policymakers can and ultimately will play a large role in determining which of these outcomes is more likely.

Notes

[1] In this chapter as well, the direct impact of the oil price scenarios on country, regional, and global macroeconomic activity has been incorporated into the consumption and production figures used in the quantitative analysis that follows.

[2] Official aid includes grants and loans from sovereign governments and international financial institutions such as the World Bank. This type of aid also is also known as official finance. It is distinguished from "private" finance (e.g., the sources of funds from the private financial markets).

[3] Flows of private finance are classified, broadly, into "direct" and "portfolio." Financial investment from a single private source that accounts for more than 10 percent ownership of the purchased asset is called "direct" investment. In "portfolio" investment, the flow of capital represents less than a 10 percent share of the purchase price of the asset.

[4] This description oversimplifies history a bit to make the point.

[5] Derivative financial instruments are a type of financial instrument that has no intrinsic value but whose value is based on—that is, "derived" from"—assets that do have intrinsic value. For example, an option to buy stock in a corporation at a particular price on a particular date in the future is a derivative financial instrument.

[6] Direct investment and portfolio investment represent the two largest categories of private finance. Gross flows are an indicator of the rising importance of financial markets; looking only at net flows (which is the difference between flows of capital into and abroad from a country or region) can mask the rising importance of finance.

[7] South Korea was a large net recipient in 1997 because of the financial crisis.

[8] World Bank, *Private Capital Flows to Developing Countries* (Washington, D.C.: World Bank, 1997), pie charts, p. 11.

[9] OECD, *World in 2020* (Paris: OECD, 1997), chart, p. 41.

[10] World Bank, *Private Capital Flows to Developing Countries,* pie charts, p. 11.

[11] Bank of International Settlements, *69th Annual Report* (Basel, Switzerland: BIS, 1999), graph 7.2, p. 123, on nationality structure of international bank lending; graph 7.3, p. 124, on banks' external claims on countries outside the reporting area; graph 7.4, p. 126, on main features of international bank claims by region.

[12] International Monetary Fund, *International Capital Markets 1998* (Washington, D.C.: IMF, 1998), table 2.3, p. 26.

[13] "Turnover" is defined as total value traded (buy and sell) divided by average market capitalization.

[14] See IMF, *International Capital Markets 1998,* table 2.5, p. 33.

[15] LIBOR is the London Inter-Bank Offer Rate, which is the rate at which banks lend to each other in the overnight interbank market.

[16] Calculated from OECD, *World in 2020,* table 1.9, p. 52.

[17] World Bank, *Private Capital Flows to Developing Countries,* figure 2.7, p. 100. See also IMF, *International Capital Markets 1998.*

[18] "Return" in this context is just another way of describing prospects for growth in income and the rate of inflation.

[19] The Black-Scholes formula is named for economists Stanley Black and Myron Scholes, who derived it. The formula allows investors to price derivative instruments from the underlying value of the asset as well as the behavior of the asset price over time.

[20] Many developing countries issue U.S. dollar-denominated bonds in the international capital markets—the so-called Eurobond market. These instruments are issued at a particular price with a particular coupon, based in part on the riskiness of the country as measured by the "rating." The secondary market yield of these instruments is a measure that combines the market price of the instrument and the coupon. The "spread" compares the yield on these instruments to a common denominator, such as the yield on U.S. government bonds.

[21] Such reassessments are frequent and can be observed in data following other financial crises, such as the Mexican devaluation in 1994.

[22] See IMF, *International Capital Markets 1999,* box 3.7, p. 57, and figure 3.2, p. 40.

[23] The current account for a country is the sum of net exports, net interest on outstanding international obligations, and various transfers, such as official grants, worker remittances, and the like. Differences in terminology should not affect the analysis here.

[24] Although the higher oil price does cause consumption of oil to fall, the rise in price is great enough to cause the value of consumption (change in price multiplied by change in quantity) to be higher than in the base case. In other words, elasticity of demand for oil is less than 1.0 (see following discussion).

[25] Elasticity of demand is a very important concept. It measures the extent to which demand responds to a change in price. In this case, the demand for oil has fallen more than the price has risen, so that net exports (in dollar terms) are smaller for high prices than for the base-case prices.

[26] An elasticity of demand greater than 1.0 has this characteristic of greater percentage response of demand given any percentage change in price.

[27] We need to convert the local currency-denominated value of GDP into the value of GDP in dollar terms because the value of net exports and the changes in net exports are measured in dollars. The first measure of GDP is the value of GDP in 1998 dollars, as estimated by the World Bank "atlas method," which uses a three-year average exchange rate to convert the value of GDP in local currency to the value of GDP in dollars. The second estimate of GDP is the "ppp basis," or purchasing power parity, which converts GDP from local currency into dollars using an estimate of what the exchange rate would be that roughly equilibrates the value of a consumption basket in the United States and in the country in question.

[28] For Saudi Arabia, not only is the estimated change in net exports large, but the value of net exports in 1997 (table 4.8, section B) is rather small (particularly in comparison to the figures for other OPEC countries); thus, the large percentage figure for Saudi Arabia in column 1 of table 4.10.

[29] These recommendations are discussed in much greater depth in *Safeguarding Prosperity in a Global Financial System The Future International Financial Architecture*, a report of an independent task force sponsored by the Council on Foreign Relations, Carla A. Hills and Peter G. Peterson, cochairs, and Morris Goldstein, project director (Washington, D.C.: Institute for International Economics, 1999), which was written in response to the turmoil of the Asian financial crisis.

Table 4.1
International Capital Markets of the 1970s and 1980s

Country/Region	1970				1980			
	Col. 1 Current account ($ billions)	Col. 2 CA/GDP (% GDP)	Col. 3 Net resource flows[a]	Col. 4 % intermediation by banks	Col. 1 Current account ($ billions)	Col. 2 CA/GDP (% GDP)	Col. 3 Net resource flows[a]	Col. 4 % intermediation by banks
United States	2.33	0.2	n/a	n/aa	-10.75	0.04	n/a	n/a
Japan	1.99	1,0	n/a	n/a	1.2	-1.0	n/a	n/a
Germany	0.9	0.5	n/a	n/a	-14.25	-1.2	n/a	n/a
All developing countries	-6.1	-5.4	11.3	61.1	17.6	6.1	82.8	78.7
East Asia/Pacific	-2.3	-1.1	2.2	54.5	-11.8	-2.6	13.1	80.9
Latin America/Caribbean	-3.6	-2.1	4.2	69.0	-29.9	-4.0	29.9	77.6
South Asia	-0.7	-0.9	1.4	71.4	-4.0	-2.1	6.5	53.8
Middle East/North Africa	0.7	1.6	1.2	33.3	59.1	13.0	8.5	83.5

Sources: International Monetary Fund, *Balance of Payments Statistics,* for industrial countries; World Bank, *Global Development Finance Analysis and Summary Tables,* for all developing countries (LDCs) and regions.

[a]Net resource flows ($ billions) are inflows for nations running current account deficits and outflows for those running current account surpluses.

Table 4.2
Changing Geography, Type, and Magnitude of Gross Flows of International Capital
(in U.S.$ millions)

	1986	1989	1991	1995	1997
Total Capital Flow					
Industrial countries					
Direct inv. abroad	-89,735	-207,164	-185,654	-308,334	-389,336
Direct inv. inward	66,382	166,557	113,688	207,370	235,909
Portfolio inv. abroad (assets)	-186,319	-274,989	-321,879	-345,345	-634,061
Portfolio inv. inward (liabilities)	176,963	304,258	418,303	538,394	847,865
Other investment assets	n/a	n/a	-4.4	-567.3	-1,166.2
Other investment liabilities	n/a	n/a	36.7	586.0	1,154.1
Developing countries					
Direct inv. abroad	-1,861	-10,420	-7,068	-18,555	-29,335
Direct inv. inward	12,444	25,804	40,717	21,788	182,162
Portfolio inv. abroad (assets)	2,084	-4,536	-11,705	-17,359	-40,527
Portfolio inv. inward (liabilities)	977	5,027	31,015	47,188	127,606
Other investment assets	n/a	n/a	48,102	-62,363	-145,061
Other investment liabilities	n/a	n/a	64,075	165,291	91,018
Selected countries					
Net direct investment (abroad–inward)					
United States	18,520	38,870	-9,368	-39,001	-28,396
Japan	-14,250	-45,220	-30,334	-22,469	-22,859
Europe[a]	24,979	28,230	37,123	50,194	90,166
Net portfolio investment (assets–liabilities)					
United States	71,590	43,500	96,424	137,401	295,533
Japan	-102,040	-32,530	44,401	-36,575	28,736
Europe[a]	-2,625	-14,296	25,381	-15,125	52,651

Source: International Monetary Fund, *Balance of Payments Statistics.* Data for 1991, 1995, and 1997 come from Parts 2 and 3 (1998): Table B24 for direct investment, Table B27 for portfolio investment, and Table B31 for other assets and liabilities. Data for 1985 and 1989 come from Part 2 (1993): Table C17 for direct investment and Table C18 for portfolio investment; data for other assets and liabilities are not available.

[a]Europe consists of Belgium, France, Germany, Italy, Luxembourg, the Netherlands, and the United Kingdom.

Table 4.3
Characteristics of International Capital Flows to Developing Countries
(in U.S.$ millions)

Destination	1970		1980		1990		1997	
	Official	Private	Official	Private	Official	Private	Official	Private
Total net flow	3,400	4,000	21,700	43,400	27,700	15,700	13,300	105,300
Mexico	142	216	791	6,026	4,171	5,057	-4,563	6,003
Brazil	184	1,144	825	3,745	-639	-427	-1,820	19,890
China	n/a	n/a	195	1,731	1,727	4,620	4,315	8,134
India	606	-12	906	789	2,334	1,606	-312	2,839
Indonesia	354	162	806	807	2,382	1,830	535	5,889
South Korea	147	124	650	1,776	308	-250	4,396	8,968
Russia	n/a	n/a	n/a	n/a	3,474	5,562	2,418	5,006
Caspian[a]	n/a	n/a	n/a	n/a	n/a	n/a	488	1,556

Source: World Bank, *Global Development Finance 1999* (formerly *World Debt Tables*).

Note: n/a = not applicable/available. Official is "official creditors"; private is the sum of "public and publicly guaranteed, private creditors" and "private nonguaranteed." A negative figure implies a net outflow of that type of capital.

[a]Caspian consists of Azerbaijan, Kazakhstan, and Turkmenistan.

Table 4.4
Characteristics of International Private Capital Flows to Developing Countries
(in U.S.$ millions)

Destination	1970			1980			1990			1997		
	LTD*	FDI*	Portfolio*	LTD	FDI	Portfolio	LTD	FDI	Portfolio	LTD	FDI	Portfolio
Total private capital flows	6.9	2.2	0.0	65.2	4.4	0.0	43.4	24.5	3.7	118.7	163.4	30.2
Country												
Mexico	358	323	0.0	6,817	2,156	0.0	9,228	2,634	563	1,440	12,477	2,052
Brazil	327	421	0.0	4,570	1,911	0.0	-1,066	989	0.0	18,070	19,652	3,835
China	n/a	n/a	n/a	1,927	0.0	0.0	6,346	3,487	0.0	12,449	44,236	8,457
India	594	46	0.0	1,695	79	0.0	3,940	162	105	2,528	3,351	2,116
East Asia/Pacific (standard group)^a	389	284	0.0	4,666	1,132	0.0	n/a	n/a	n/a	8,814	37,111	3,803
Indonesia	517	83	0.0	1,613	180	0.0	4,213	1,093	312	6,423	4,677	298
South Korea	271	66	0.0	2,426	6.0	0.0	58	788	518	13,363	2,844	1,257
Russia	n/a	n/a	n/a	n/a	n/a	n/a	9,037	0.0	0.0	7,424	6,241	1,206
Caspian^b	n/a	n/a	n/a	n/a	n/a	n/a	n/a	0.0	n/a	2,045	2,056	50

Source: World Bank, Global Development Finance 1999 (formerly World Debt Tables).

*LTD is "net flow of long-term debt (ex. IMF)"; FDI is "foreign direct investment (net)"; portfolio is "portfolio equity flows."

^a East Asia and Pacific Standard Group excludes China, Indonesia, and South Korea, which are portrayed individually.

^b Caspian consists of Azerbaijan, Kazakhstan, and Turkmenistan.

Table 4.5
Dimensions of International Trade and Financial Markets in the 1990s
(U.S.$ billions)

	1989	1997
Gross trade value (exports + imports)	6,800	13,650
Foreign exchange market (daily turnover)	718	19,719
International bond net new issuance	172	596
Equity market turnover ratio (%)	63.8	82.8

Sources: International Monetary Fund, *International Financial Statistics Yearbook*; Bank for International Settlements, *Central Bank Survey of Foreign Exchange and Derivatives Market Activity in April 1998*, Table 2 (total reported turnover net of local double-counting; data for 1989 and 1998); International Finance Corporation, *Emerging Stock Market Factbook*, 1998 (annual trading value/market capitalization); International Monetary Fund, *International Capital Markets*, September 1998, Table 4.4.

Table 4.6
Volatility of International Capital Flows, 1980s and 1990s
(coefficient of variation of quarterly flows)

	Overall net flows		FDI		Portfolio	
	1980s	1990s	1980s	1990s	1980s	1990s
Developing countries	0.2	0.3	0.3	0.4	0.7	0.6
Indonesia	0.9	0.7	0.8	0.4	3.4	1.6
Korea	334.2	0.9	1.2	0.6	4.6	0.8
Mexico	3.9	0.7	0.5	0.6	3.3	1.3
Latin America	0.9	0.3	0.3	0.5	5.3	0.6
ASEAN4+Korea[a]	0.8	1.1	0.5	0.2	1.0	0.9

Sources: World Bank, *Private Capital Flows to Developing Countries*, 1997, Table 1.3, p. 31; International Monetary Fund, *World Economic Outlook*, 1998, Table B2.2.1, p. 64.

Note: The coefficient of variation is standard deviation divided by the mean.

[a] The ASEAN4 are Philippines, Thailand, Malaysia, and Indonesia.

Table 4.7
Measures of Leverage

Top 25 U.S. Commercial Banks	Gross Off-Balance Sheet Leverage Ratio		
	Q4 1995	Q4 1996	Q4 1998
	77	70	91

OTC Derivatives Markets	Approximate Gross Leverage Ratio		
	March 1995	June 1998	Percentage change
Foreign exchange contracts	12	22	80
Interest rate contracts	41	35	-14
Equity-linked contracts	12	7	-42
Commodities contracts	11	13	14
Total contracts	22	28	29

Sources: Internationational Monetary Fund, *International Capital Markets 1999*, Table 4.1, p. 86, and Table 4.2, p. 87.

Notes: Gross off-balance sheet leverage ratio is the ratio of notional amount of derivatives outstanding divided by equity capital. *Gross leverage ratio* adds absolute amount of short (negative) asset equivalents to that of long (positive) positions; it is an approximate measure because the activity of institutions in the derivative markets is not fully known.

Table 4.8
Background Information for the Scenarios

Section A: GDP Growth: Historical Perspective and Prospects (in percentages)

	Column 1		Column 2	
	Real GDP growth (average)		Real GDP growth (projected) 2000–2010 (avg) OECD	
	1980–1990	1990–1998	High growth	Low growth
World			5.0	3.1
High income	**3.1**	**2.1**		
United States	3.0	2.9	2.7	2.1
Japan	4.0	1.3	2.9	2.0
Canada	3.3	2.2	n/a	n/a
Europe[a]	n/a	n/a	2.7	2.0
Low and middle income	**3.5**	**3.3**	**n/a**	**n/a**
Mexico	0.7	2.5	n/a	n/a
Brazil	2.7	3.3	6.1	3.0
China	10.2	11.1	8.2	5.3
India	5.8	6.1	7.2	4.3
Indonesia	6.1	5.8	7.0	4.1
South Korea	9.4	6.2	n/a	n/a
Russia	n/a	-7.0	5.9	3.6

Sources: Column 1—*World Development Report 1999*, Table 11, p. 250; Column 2—OECD, *The World in 2020 Towards a New Global Age*, Table, p. 92; for Russia, Figure 2.4, p. 68, covering the period 1996–2020.

[a]Europe is Austria, Belgium, Denmark, Finland, France, Germany, Greece, Ireland, Italy, Luxembourg, Netherlands, Norway, Portugal, Spain, Sweden, Switzerland, and the United Kingdom.

(continued)

Table 4.8 (continued)

Section B: Initial Conditions for Countries and Regions

	Net Exports ($million) 1997	GDP, atlas method ($billion) 1998	GDP, ppp basis ($billion) 1998
OPEC			
Saudi Arabia	257.00	128.88	n/a
Iran	5,232.00	109.60	n/a
Iraq	n/a	n/a	n/a
UAE	6,700.00 (1991)	48.70	52.70
Kuwait	7,935.00	n/a	n/a
Venezuela	4,684.00	81.30	190.40
Nigeria	552.00	36.40	99.70
Middle East	21,874.00	585.60	1,203.30
United States	-155,375.00	7,921.30	7,922.60
Canada	-9,261.00	612.20	735.60
Mexico	-7,454.00	380.90	785.80
China	29,718.00	928.90	3,983.60
Russia	2,569.00	337.90	579.80
Japan	94,354.00	4,089.90	2,928.40
South Korea	-8,167.00	369.90	569.30
India	-5,811.00	421.30	1,600.90
Latin America (including Brazil)	-40,373.00	1,977.90	3,401.50
Western Europe	160,500.00	8,483.00	7,663.00
World totals	**122,815.00**	**28,862.00**	**36,556.00**

Source: World Bank, *World Development Report.*

Notes: "Atlas" method and "ppp" basis are alternative ways to calculate the dollar value of local currency-denominated GDP. (For full description of these methods, see *World Development Report.*)

Except where noted below, net exports are measured using current account data. The differences between the current account and net exports include (1) net investment earnings or payments on outstanding international obligations and (2) various transfers, including military, official, and private worker remittances. For the purpose of this exercise, the difference between net exports and current account is not relevant.

For Middle East, net exports (GDP) is net exports (GDP) of Middle East and North Africa. For Latin America (including Brazil), net exports (GDP) is net exports (GDP) of Latin America and Caribbean countries. For Western Europe, net exports (GDP) is calculated as the sum of the current accounts (GDP) of Germany, France, the United Kingdom, Italy, the Netherlands, Spain, Belgium, Norway, Finland, Greece, Ireland, Sweden, Switzerland, Denmark, and Portugal. For the world, net exports (GDP) is net exports of the world. For Russia, net exports (GDP) are those of the Russian Federation.

(continued)

Table 4.8 (continued)

Section C: Elements of the Base and High/Low Cases: Oil Production, Consumption, and Production minus Consumption (Prod. less -cons.)

	Base case: $21.30/barrel (1997 $)			High case: $30/barrel for 3 years			Low case: $10/barrel for 3 years		
	Prod. (mmb/d)	Cons. (mmb/d)	Prod. less Cons.	Prod. (mmb/d)	Cons. (mmb/d)	Prod. less Cons.	Prod. (mmb/d)	Cons. (mmb/d)	Prod. Cons.
OPEC									
Saudi Arabia	14.10			12.90			17.30		
Iran	4.50			4.20			5.30		
Iraq	3.80			3.20			6.00		
UAE	3.40			3.10			4.00		
Kuwait	3.20			3.10			3.70		
Venezuela	5.10			4.90			6.30		
Nigeria	3.20			2.80			3.50		
Subtotal	*37.30*						*46.10*		
Middle East		7.50			6.20			9.00	
Total OPEC	**43.30**		**35.80**	**39.90**		**33.70**	**52.60**		**43.60**
United States	9.00	22.70	-13.70	9.50	21.60	-12.10	8.10	23.70	-15.60
Canada	3.20	2.10	1.10	3.30	2.00	1.30	3.20	2.30	0.90
Mexico	4.00	2.60	1.40	4.10	2.30	1.80	3.90	2.80	1.10
China	3.50	6.40	-2.90	3.60	4.90	-1.30	3.40	7.30	-3.90

(continued)

Table 4.8 (continued)

Section C: Elements of the Base and High/Low Cases: Oil Production, Consumption, and Production minus Consumption (Prod. less -cons.) (continued)

	Base case: $21.30/barrel (1997 $)			High case: $30/barrel for 3 years			Low case: $10/barrel for 3 years		
	Prod. (mmb/d)	Cons. (mmb/d)	Prod. less Cons.	Prod. (mmb/d)	Cons. (mmb/d)	Prod. less Cons.	Prod. (mmb/d)	Cons. (mmb/d)	Prod. Cons.
FSU[a]	10.10	4.70	5.40	10.30	4.30	6.00	9.80	5.70	4.10
Japan	0.00	6.00	-6.00	0.00	5.40	-5.40	0.00	6.70	-6.70
South Korea	0.00	3.40	-3.40	0.00	2.80	-2.80	0.00	4.00	-4.00
India	0.00	3.10	-3.10	0.00	2.60	-2.60	0.00	3.60	-3.60
Latin America (incl Brazil)	4.40	7.40	-3.00	4.50	5.80	-1.30	4.30	9.40	-5.10
Western Europe	7.70	15.30	-7.60	7.80	14.40	-6.60	7.50	16.20	-8.70
Total non-OPEC	41.90	73.70	-31.80	43.10	66.10	-23.00	40.20	81.70	-41.50
Total unallocated[b]	9.80	12.30	-2.50	10.00	10.80	-0.80	0.20	8.70	-8.50
World totals	95.00	93.50	1.50	93.00	83.10	9.90	93.00	99.40	-6.40

Sources: Production—OPEC, Western Europe, and country details from Chapter 2; consumption—Western Europe, Middle East, and country details from USDOE/EIA, Tables A4, B4, C4. Figures for production and consumption under high (low) case include feedback effects of high (low) price on economic activity and back to production and consumption of oil.

[a] This and subsequent references to FSU in this chapter are derived from data under that heading (denoting countries of the former Soviet Union) from chapter 2.

[b] Unallocated is residual from World totals minus Total OPEC (or Middle East for consumption) minus Total non-OPEC.

Table 4.9a
High Oil Price: Production Minus Consumption and Change in Net Exports

	Col 1 Base Prod-Cons (mmb/d)	Col 2 Base Price	Col 3 High Prod-Cons (mmb/d)	Col 4 High Price	Col 5 $ millions Change per Day	Col 6 $ millions Change per Year	Column 7 Summary Observation: Direction of change in net exports and financing sources (positive) or needs (negative)
OPEC							
Saudi Arabia	14.10	$21.30	12.90	$30	86.67	31,634.55	Larger positive
Iran	4.50	$21.30	4.20	$30	30.15	11,004.75	Larger positive
Iraq	3.80	$21.30	3.20	$30	15.06	5,496.90	Larger positive
UAE	3.40	$21.30	3.10	$30	20.58	7,511.70	Larger positive
Kuwait	3.20	$21.30	3.10	$30	24.84	9,066.60	Larger positive
Venezuela	5.10	$21.30	4.90	$30	38.37	14,005.05	Larger positive
Nigeria	3.20	$21.30	2.80	$30	15.84	5,781.60	Larger positive
OPEC/Middle East	**35.80**	**$21.30**	**33.70**	**$30**	**248.46**	**90,687.90**	Larger positive
United States	-13.70	$21.30	-12.10	$30	-71.19	-25,984.35	Larger negative
Canada	1.10	$21.30	1.30	$30	15.57	5,683.05	Larger positive
Mexico	1.40	$21.30	1.80	$30	24.18	8,825.70	Larger positive
China	-2.90	$21.30	-1.30	$30	22.77	8,311.05	Smaller negative; very elastic consumption
FSU	5.40	$21.30	6.00	$30	64.98	23,717.70	Larger positive
Japan	-6.00	$21.30	-5.40	$30	-34.20	-12,483.00	Larger negative
South Korea	-3.40	$21.30	-2.80	$30	-11.58	-4,226.70	Larger negative

(continued)

Table 4.9a (continued)

	Col 1 Base Prod-Cons (mmb/d)	Col 2 Base Price	Col 3 High Prod-Cons (mmb/d)	Col 4 High Price	Col 5 $ millions Change per Day	Col 6 $ millions Change per Year	Column 7 Summary Observation: Direction of change in net exports and financing sources (positive) or needs (negative)
India	-3.10	$21.30	-2.60	$30	-11.97	-4,369.05	Larger negative
Latin America (including Brazil)	-3.00	$21.30	-1.30	$30	24.90	9,088.50	Smaller negative; very elastic consumption
Western Europe	-7.60	$21.30	-6.60	$30	-36.12	-13,183.80	Larger negative
Total non-OPEC	**-31.80**	**$21.30**	**-23.00**	**$30**	**-12.66**	**-4,620.90**	Larger negative
Total unallocated	**-2.50**	**$21.30**	**-0.80**	**$30**	**29.25**	**10,676.25**	Smaller negative; elastic production and consumption
World total	**1.50**	**$21.30**	**9.90**	**$30**	**265.05**	**96,743.25**	Larger positive, because of response of unallocated region

Sources: See table 4.8.

(continued)

Table 4.9b
Low Oil Price: Production Minus Consumption and Change in Net Exports

	Col 1 Base Prod-Cons (mmb/d)	Col 2 Base Price	Col 3 High Prod-Cons (mmb/d)	Col 4 High Price	Col 5 $ millions Change per Day	Col 6 $ millions Change per Year	Column 7 Summary Observation: Direction of change in net exports and financing sources (positive) or needs (negative)
OPEC							
Saudi Arabia	14.10	$21.30	17.30	$10	-127.33	-46,475.45	Still positive, but smaller positive
Iran	4.50	$21.30	5.30	$10	-42.85	-15,640.25	Still positive , but smaller positive
Iraq	3.80	$21.30	6.00	$10	-20.94	-7,643.10	Still positive, but smaller positive
UAE	3.40	$21.30	4.00	$10	-32.42	-11,833.30	Still positive, but smaller positive
Kuwait	3.20	$21.30	3.70	$10	-31.16	-11,373.40	Still positive, but smaller positive
Venezuela	5.10	$21.30	6.30	$10	-45.63	-16,654.95	Still positive, but smaller positive
Nigeria	3.20	$21.30	3.50	$10	-33.16	-12,103.40	Still positive, but smaller positive
OPEC/Middle East	**43.30**	**$21.30**	**43.60**	**$10**	**-486.29**	**-177,495.85**	**Still positive, but smaller positive**
United States	-13.70	$21.30	-15.60	$10	135.81	49,570.65	Still negative, but less negative
Canada	1.10	$21.30	0.90	$10	-14.43	-5,266.95	Smaller positive
Mexico	1.40	$21.30	1.10	$10	-18.82	-6,869.30	Smaller positive
China	-2.90	$21.30	-3.90	$10	22.77	8,311.05	Still negative, but less negative
FSU	5.40	$21.30	4.10	$10	-74.02	-27,017.30	Smaller positive
Japan	-6.00	$21.30	-6.70	$10	60.80	22,192.00	Still negative, but relatively less need for financing

(continued)

Table 4.9b (continued)

	Col 1 Base Prod- Cons (mmb/d)	Col 2 Base Price	Col 3 High Prod- Cons (mmb/d)	Col 4 High Price	Col 5 $ millions Change per Day	Col 6 $ millions Change per Year	Column 7 Summary Observation: Direction of change in net exports and financing sources (positive) or needs (negative)
South Korea	-3.40	$21.30	-4.00	$10	32.42	11,833.30	Still negative, but relatively less need for financing
India	-3.10	$21.30	-3.60	$10	30.03	10,960.95	Still negative, but relatively less need for financing
Latin America (including Brazil)	-3.00	$21.30	-5.10	$10	12.90	4,708.50	Still negative, but relatively less need for financing
Western Europe	-7.60	$21.30	-8.70	$10	74.88	27,331.20	Still negative, but relatively less need for financing
Total non-OPEC	-31.50	$21.30	-41.50	$10	255.95	93,421.75	Still negative, but relatively less need for financing
Total unallocated	-2.50	$21.30	-8.50	$10	31.75	-11,588.75	Larger negative; elastic consumption
World total	1.50	$21.30	-6.40	$10	-32.36	-11,811.40	Flips from positive in high price to negative because of unallocated

Sources: See table 4.8.

Table 4.10
Significance of Change in Net Exports (NX)
(expressed as % of denominator)

Section A: High Oil Price

	Column 1 Change NX NX in 1997	Column 2 Change NX GDP atlas method	Column 3 Change NX GDP ppp basis
OPEC			
Saudi Arabia	123.1	24.5	n/a
Iran	2.1	10.0	n/a
Iraq	n/a	n/a	n/a
UAE[a]	1.1	15.4	14.3
Kuwait	1.1	n/a	n/a
Venezuela	3.0	17.2	7.4
Nigeria	10.5	15.9	5.8
OPEC/Middle East	**4.2**	**15.5**	**7.5**
United States	0.2	-0.3	-0.3
Canada	-0.6	0.9	0.8
Mexico	-1.2	2.3	1.1
China	0.3	0.9	0.2
FSU	9.2	7.0	4.1
Japan	-0.1	-0.3	-0.4
South Korea	0.5	-1.1	-0.7
India	0.8	-1.0	-0.3
Latin America (incl Brazil)	-0.2	0.5	0.3
Western Europe	-0.1	-0.2	-0.2
World totals	**0.8**	**0.3**	**0.3**

Sources: See table 4.8.
[a]UAE uses current account data for 1991 in column 1.

(continued)

Table 4.10 (continued)

Section B: Low Oil Price

	Column 1 Change NX NX in 1997	Column 2 Change NX GDP atlas method	Column 3 Change NX GDP ppp basis
OPEC			
Saudi Arabia	-180.8	-36.1	n/a
Iran	-3.0	-14.3	n/a
Iraq	n/a	n/a	n/a
UAE[a]	-1.8	-24.3	-22.5
Kuwait	-1.4	n/a	n/a
Venezuela	-3.6	-20.5	-8.8
Nigeria	-21.9	-33.3	-12.1
OPEC/Middle East	**-8.1**	**-30.3**	**-14.8**
United States	-0.3	0.6	0.6
Canada	0.6	-0.9	-0.7
Mexico	0.9	-1.8	-0.9
China	0.3	0.9	0.2
FSU	-10.5	-8.0	-4.7
Japan	0.2	0.5	0.8
South Korea	-1.5	3.2	2.1
India	-1.9	2.6	0.7
Latin America (incl Brazil)	-0.1	0.2	0.1
Western Europe	0.2	0.3	0.4
World totals	**-0.3**	**-0.1**	**-0.03**

Sources: See table 4.8.
[a]UAE uses current account data for 1991 in column 1.

Table 4.11
Trade Links between the United States and Selected Countries and Regions
(in U.S.$ millions)

Partner	1989		2000	
	Export	Import	Export	Import
U.S. total merchandise trade with world	383,812	473,211	753,636	1,222,772
All industrial countries	234,669	290,020	549,491	759,167
Japan	44,494	93,553	65,254	146,577
Canada	78,809	87,953	178,786	229,209
EU-11	86,424	85,292	164,825	220,366
All developing countries	149,143	183,209	223,813	463,605
Mexico	24,982	27,162	111,721	135,911
Brazil	4,804	8,410	15,360	13,855
China	5,755	11,990	16,253	100,063
Indonesia	1,247	3,529	2,547	10,385
Korea	13,459	19,737	27,902	40,300
India	2,458	3,314	8,726[a]	4,033[a]
Russia	4,284	709	2,318	7,796

Sources: U.S. Department of Commerce, *Survey of Current Business* and *U.S. Foreign Trade Highlights 1991.*
[a]Year-end data for 1999.

Table 4.12
Energy Intensity of Selected Countries and Regions, 1980–1996

	Per capita Kg of oil equivalent		Per capita average annual growth in commercial energy use	GDP per unit of energy used		Net energy imports % commercial energy use	
	1980	1996	1980-1996	1980	1996	1980	1996
World	**1,622**	**1684**	**2.9**	**3.1**	**3.2**	n/a	n/a
High-income	**4,792**	**5,346**	**1.6**	**4.1**	**5.0**		
Japan	2,967	4,058	2.4	9.3	10.5	88	80
Canada	7,848	7,880	0.3	2.1	2.5	-7	-51
United States	7,973	8,051	0.4	2.7	3.4	14	21
Low and middle Income	**910**	**998**	**4.5**	**1.4**	**1.3**	**-32**	**-28**
Mexico	1,464	1,525	0.2	2.3	2.1	-51	-51
Brazil	896	1,012	1.0	4.7	4.4	43	31
China	604	902	2.6	0.3	0.7	-3	0
India	352	476	1.9	0.6	0.8	8	13
Indonesia	402	672	3.5	1.3	1.6	-116	-66
Korea	1,148	3,576	8.1	3.1	3.0	72	86
Russia	5,499	4,169	-3.6	0.5	0.5	2	-54

(continued)

Table 4.12 (continued)

	Per capita Kg of oil equivalent		Per capita average annual growth in commercial energy use	GDP per unit of energy used		Net energy imports % commercial energy use	
	1980	1996	1980–1996	1980	1996	1980	1996
Lower middle income	2,040	1,763	7.4	1.7	1.0	-13	-20
Upper middle income	1,557	1,861	2.8	2.8	2.6	-98	-65
East Asia and Pacific	588	925	4.6				
Europe and Central Asia	3,349	2,739	7.6				
Latin America and Caribbean	1,062	1,163	2.4	3.5	3.2	-24	-35
Middle East and North Africa	842	1,244	5.1	2.2	1.6	-577	-225
South Asia	334	441	3.9	0.7	0.9	10	15

Source: *World Development Report 1999*, Table 10, p. 248.

CHAPTER FIVE

JAPAN'S DOLLAR TRAP AND THE IMPACT OF A FUTURE DOLLAR CRISIS ON THE OIL ECONOMY

R. Taggart Murphy

CATHERINE MANN'S ANALYSIS IN CHAPTER 4 OF THIS BOOK demonstrated the intertwining of oil price movements with the many changes that have occurred over the past quarter century in the magnitude, composition, and complexity of international capital flows. The "separation of finance and trade" she discusses in her study has been driven by the demands of institutional investors for higher returns than those available from traditional trade financing. The highest returns—as well as the highest risks—stem from speculative plays, and in the international financial arena, no more lucrative returns or quicker profits exist than those available from astute bets placed on currency movements. That is why daily foreign exchange trading on global markets now dwarfs by many orders of magnitude the foreign currency needs of exporters and importers.

This fact ought to draw our attention because the birth of speculative trading in foreign exchange coincided with the birth of the international oil regime we know today. Indeed, one can argue that turbulent currency markets and turbulent oil markets are twin offspring of the same parent—the collapse of the Bretton Woods system of fixed exchange rates. Although geopolitical considerations played a role, what ultimately drove OPEC's wresting of control over oil prices from the majors in 1973–1974 was a determination to restore real oil export earnings that had dropped dramatically in the wake of the dollar's plunge after Bretton Woods collapsed in 1971.

At this writing, with the dollar strong against the Euro and strengthening against the yen, the possibility of another dollar crisis may seem distant. Yet given the dollar crises that have occurred since 1971—in 1978, 1987, and 1995—it would be foolhardy to count on no recurrence between now and 2010, particularly inasmuch as the causes of the earlier crises have by no means all disappeared. Indeed, one of those causes—ballooning U.S. current account deficits that now stand at historical highs as a percentage of gross national product (GNP)—is even more pronounced than it was in 1971.[1]

It behooves us, therefore, to incorporate into our analysis two evaluations: the likelihood of a dollar crisis and the effect that any such crisis would have on oil markets.

THE "DEFICIT WITHOUT TEARS"

The strains that led to the collapse of Bretton Woods included the gathering inflation in the American economy brought on by the refusal of the U.S. government to finance the Vietnam War with tax increases; the growing restiveness of European countries—particularly France—over the inflation that the Bretton Woods system allowed the United States to export; the twin emergence of American trade deficits and Japanese trade surpluses; and the refusal of Japan's policy elite to consider any resetting of the yen/dollar peg to reflect changing economic realities.[2] (West Germany, the other major emerging surplus country, had agreed to a revaluation of the mark in 1969).

Today, inflation in the United States is largely an historical memory. Moreover, the floating rate system that emerged in the wake of Bretton Woods theoretically makes it impossible for the United States to export inflation.[3] But the American trade and current account deficits now stand, as noted, at historic highs. With employment and capacity utilization rates likewise at historic highs, under no conceivable economic scenario save that of a severe recession are these deficits likely to fall substantially. Meanwhile, Japan has continued to pile up current account surpluses to the extent that the country is now far and away the world's largest net creditor nation—with some $1.3 trillion in net claims on the rest of the world.

Theoretically, the foreign exchange markets ought long ago to have brought these imbalances down by reducing the value of the dollar and boosting that of the yen, thus eroding the price competitiveness of Japanese exports while making imports into the United States so expensive that Americans would be unable to afford so many of them. Indeed, this happened to some extent in 1973 and again in 1978, and OPEC succeeded in restoring its eroded earnings by hiking the dollar price of oil. I consider briefly at the conclusion of this essay the question of OPEC's reaction to another severe drop in the dollar's value—a matter on which, in any case, others are more qualified to comment than I. For the time being, however, let us consider why the twin external imbalances of the United States and Japan have persisted for so long and why the dollar continues to be relatively strong despite the imbalances.

One can, of course, explain continued dollar strength by noting that investors and traders worldwide believe that the U.S. economy will continue to be buoyant and thus keep buying American equities, bonds, and other dollar instruments. This dynamic, however, really begs the question. A sharp fall-off in the dollar's value would inevitably be part and parcel of a sudden deterioration in U.S. economic prospects. A serious drop in the dollar's value would signal the end of the world's willingness to finance U.S. current account deficits. In a full-employment U.S. economy with high capacity utilization rates, the inevitable adjustment would have to come through reduced spending—in other words, a weaker economy.

For the time being, however, bullish sentiment on the U.S. economy translates into bullish sentiment on the dollar, and that bullishness flows from the belief that somehow the United States has escaped the normal constraints that prevent countries from running excessive and endless current account deficits. Because the ability to run a "deficit without tears" permits the United States to enjoy a full-employment, high-growth economy without inflation, betting that the United States can continue to run these deficits amounts to a bet on the continuation of the U.S. economic expansion. In a self-reinforcing virtuous circle, that bet translates into market demand for dollar instruments, which helps soothe concerns over mounting current account deficits, which in turn boosts confidence in the U.S. economy and so forth ad infinitum—or at least until foreign exchange markets suddenly, for whatever reason, begin to fret over the deficits.

The term "deficit without tears" was originally used by the French economist Jacques Rueff in complaining about advantages enjoyed by the United States in the Bretton Woods system. It serves equally well today, however, and understanding it begins with a look at the largest foreign holders of dollars and their motives for holding those dollars rather than switching them into other currencies—or, rather, whether those motives extend beyond simply betting that the U.S. economic expansion will continue for the foreseeable future.

FROM OPEC REVENUES TO JAPANESE CURRENT ACCOUNT SURPLUSES

In the years immediately after the collapse of Bretton Woods, the largest pools of dollars outside the United States were those held by the OPEC nations. They were mostly placed on deposit in the London branches of the major international banks—predominantly American—and on-lent, as noted in chapter 3, to oil-importing countries. OPEC nations may have considered billing their customers in currencies other than the dollar and/or hedging their dollar earnings by denominating a substantial portion in other "hard" currencies. A large-scale move out of the dollar by OPEC, however, would have been regarded as a hostile act by a United States that provided a security umbrella for the leading OPEC powers (including the Shah's Iran).

Meanwhile, despite grave concerns worldwide in the late 1970s about American inflation and the competence of American macroeconomic management, no alternative global currency existed. The Euro had yet to be conceived, and the relative sizes of the West German and Japanese economies were far too small to foster any notion of the mark or the yen as serious alternatives to the dollar's role as the world's preferred currency.[4] Any large-scale move by OPEC nations to overthrow the dollar would simply have destroyed the global financial infrastructure that financed their customers' oil purchases. In any case, OPEC's ability to engineer price hikes seemingly at will amply compensated them during the 1970s for the dollar's weakness.

As Peter Fusaro documents in his chapter, however, the 1980s saw control over oil prices begin to slip out of OPEC's hands. As the decade proceeded, OPEC's dollar holdings were replaced by the Japanese current account surpluses as the world's largest pool of dollars outside American control.

SOURCES AND DEPLOYMENT OF JAPANESE SURPLUSES

The financing of the so-called Japanese economic miracle came, as a matter of deliberate policy, out of domestic savings rather than foreign investment. A panoply of instruments, from tax regimes though compensation practices and the stunting of consumer credit, assured a household savings rate in Japan that has remained well in excess of 15 percent for the past half-century. After the 1974 recession, however, Japan never returned to the double-digit growth rates that had prevailed between 1955 and 1973. Household savings nonetheless remained extraordinarily high.

As Japan emerged from the temporary slowdown brought on by the Iranian revolution and the 1979 OPEC price hikes, Japanese industry simply could not use all of the savings available to it. The inevitable result was a ballooning current account surplus that has continued to accumulate for 20 years and is now running at an annual clip of well in excess of $100 billion.

The macroeconomic regime that prevailed in the United States in the early 1980s steered the initial surge of the Japanese surplus into U.S. dollar instruments—primarily Treasury instruments. The combination of the strong fiscal stimulus provided by the 1981 U.S. tax cuts and the tight-money/high-interest-rate regime of Paul Volcker's Federal Reserve sent the U.S. Treasury on a marketing spree to finance the resulting exploding federal deficits. The notes, bills, and bonds on offer carried very high interest rates—six to seven full percentage points more than those available on comparable Japanese securities—and they were snapped up by Japanese banks, insurers, and brokers looking for a place to deploy the dollars pouring into their coffers.

I have argued elsewhere that the surge of Japanese money into the Treasuries market permitted the so-called Reagan Revolution to succeed without a financial reckoning—or at least postponed that reckoning until 1987.[5] For our purposes here, however, I note that the surge of money set a policy trap that has hobbled the Japanese economy ever since. The question of whether the Japanese policy elite finally shakes Japan free of that trap or succumbs to it also is, to a very large extent, the question of the sustainability of the American "deficit without tears."

THE 1987 STOCK MARKET CRASH AND JAPAN'S BUBBLE ECONOMY

The nature of the trap first became obvious with the stock market crash of October 1987. Japan had agreed to a politically engineered effort by the world's major economies to reduce the value of the dollar—the so-called Plaza Accord of September 1985—thereby heading off the growing protectionist clamor in the U.S. Congress and, so it was hoped, reducing politically troublesome American trade deficits.

Despite a fall in the dollar's value that was far greater than anticipated, the August 1987 trade numbers announced a week before the crash demonstrated that the near-halving of the dollar's value over the preceding 18 months had had virtually no effect on the U.S. trade deficit. Japanese institutional investors, convinced that yet more dollar weakening was in the offing, dumped large quantities of Treasuries into the market. Seeing cheaper bonds (another way of saying higher interest rates), American investors piled out of the stock market and into the bond market, bringing on the worst stock market crash since 1929.

The threat of a global meltdown followed by recession was averted in part by deliberate moves to prop up the Tokyo stock market and flood the Japanese economy with credit that spilled over into the international financial arena. The events of October 1987 demonstrated to the Japanese policy elite, however, that the country's financial institutions had accumulated such an immense position in dollar markets that any attempt to reduce Japan's dollar holdings would simply trigger crashes in those markets that would rebound negatively onto Japan itself.

At the time, the Japanese policy elite was in the midst of efforts to spark a domestic investment boom, thereby weaning the country from its heavy reliance on export-led growth. With the full knowledge and consent of the authorities, year-on-year growth in Japanese bank lending had grown to more than twice nominal GNP growth. Scared by the implications of the 1987 crash, the authorities redoubled their efforts, cutting interest rates to historical lows while opening the monetary spigots all the way. The resulting flood of credit into Japan's asset markets brought on the largest financial bubble in history: the net worth of the land on which greater Tokyo sits grew to exceed that of the entire United States plus the net worth of every company listed on the New York Stock Exchange.

POST-BUBBLE JAPAN AND THE DOLLAR TRAP

The collapse of the bubble in the early 1990s did not free Japan from the policy trap, however; indeed, the jaws closed ever tighter as Japan's current account surpluses continued to mount. The bubble's collapse represented the failure of attempts to put domestic investment in the driver's seat of the Japanese economy, leaving exports again as the sole engine of growth. Yet any moves to replace exports with domestic demand were fraught with peril. Freeing up consumer spending involved dismantling the entire economic infrastructure that had suppressed spending and generated high savings for a half-century. Moreover, the excess savings of the Japanese economy have become increasingly vital to supporting the vast pool of dollars that Japan holds.

Japan's net creditor position—the sum of its claims on the outside world less outside claims on Japan—stands today, as noted, at some

$1.3 trillion. Most of these claims are denominated in U.S. dollars. That these claims have become an economic millstone for Japan may not seem obvious at all; theoretically, they should permit the country to enjoy income streams from the rest of the world and buy whatever it wishes.

Any move to spend these dollars on any considerable scale, however, threatens their value—not to mention flooding the country with imports that would destroy whole sectors of an already fragile economy, with widespread job losses further depressing consumer spending. Exchanging the dollars for yen is not an option either. So little yen circulates outside Japan that the result today of any attempt to redenominate Japan's claims in yen would be a catastrophic decline in the dollar/yen exchange rate, devastating Japan's export industries.

That leaves Japan holding the claims. But if foreign currency holdings are not converted either into domestic currency or imports, they must be financed. As long as the dollars remain unredeemed as an asset on the books of the Japanese financial system, they must be funded either by monetary creation or by a deflationary shrinkage of the national balance sheet, as it were, to bring assets and liabilities into line.[6]

Akio Mikuni and I argue in a book commissioned by the Brookings Institution[7] that efforts to cope with Japan's huge pile of dollar assets hold the key to understanding the deflationary stagnation of the Japanese economy over the past decade. Many economists worldwide have, to be sure, advised Japan's policy elite to counteract this deflation with the deliberate creation of inflationary expectations by gunning the money supply. We argue, however, that given the monetary regime that has prevailed in Japan since the 1950s—a regime that creates money primarily through bank lending at the behest of the financial authorities—this strategy is much easier said than done, particularly in an environment in which banks no longer trust the ability of Japan's bureaucracy to guarantee the viability of loans.

Instead, the Japanese policy elite has attempted to use fiscal stimulus both as a means of pump-priming the economy back into life and for offsetting the deflationary effects of the dollar assets. Neither goal has been reached, despite periodic massive injections of public works spending that have now saddled the Japanese government with the largest debt burden as a percentage of GNP among the OECD countries. Signs are everywhere that these tactics cannot continue much longer without a ruinous rise in Japanese government bond yields, as the government is forced to turn to genuine investors responding to price signals to sell its securities rather than unloading them on public-sector institutions led by the postal savings system.

A DOLLAR CRISIS AND OIL MARKETS

The very real possibility exists, then, that sometime in this decade, Japan's ability to support and fund its ever-expanding pool of dollars will end. The result almost certainly would be a dollar/yen crisis that pushes the yen's value against the dollar far below anything imaginable today. It is difficult to see how such a crisis would not affect dollar/Euro rates as well. Frightened investors worldwide would likely dump dollar instruments, bringing an end to the American "deficit without tears" as a steep decline in American consumer spending—another way of saying a recession—became the only way to bring U.S. external accounts back into balance in a world no longer willing or able to finance U.S. deficits. Indeed, it is precisely to forestall such an eventuality that U.S. Treasury officials have cooperated with their Japanese counterparts in helping to head off surges in the yen's value—most dramatically in the summer of 1995 in the wake of a postwar record low for the dollar of 79 yen—and repeatedly urged pump-priming on an already heavily indebted Japanese government.

It is, of course, impossible to predict precisely how a dollar crisis would play out in oil markets. But we can say with certainty that the effects would be profound. OPEC surely would wish to recapture real earnings eroded by any plunge in the dollar's value; Peter Fusaro suggests in chapter 2 that OPEC's power over energy markets, if not oil markets per se, has waned since the halcyon days of the 1970s. Particularly because any dollar crisis would likely be accompanied by recessions in the world's two greatest oil importers—the United States and Japan—OPEC's ability to sustain price hikes is of course, not at all clear.

Attempts by OPEC nations to diversify out of dollar holdings could, however, complicate matters further. The existence of the euro provides OPEC—and everyone else, for that matter—with a credible alternative to the dollar as both a settlement and an investment currency, an alternative that did not exist in the 1970s.

Even if the combined efforts of Tokyo and Washington succeed in averting a dollar crisis, efforts by Japanese policymakers to extricate Japan from the deflationary trap in which the country finds itself will have very wide implications for oil markets—and not simply because Japan is such a large importer of oil. Paradoxically, high oil prices actually could benefit the Japanese economy by reducing Japan's current account surplus in a way that neither creates political problems nor damages the competitiveness of Japan's leading export industries because their foreign competitors would suffer the same price increases. But, of course, oil prices must not rise to the point that they bring on recessions in Japan's principal export markets—the United States and the rest of Asia.

Notes

[1] For a notable analysis, see Catherine L. Mann, *Is the U.S. Trade Deficit Sustainable?* (Washington, D.C.: Institute for International Economics, 1999).

[2] A superb in-depth study of the Japanese policy elite's handling of the collapse of Bretton Woods is Robert C. Angel, *Explaining Economic Policy Failure: Japan in the 1969–1971 International Monetary Crisis* (New York: Columbia University Press, 1991). Angel's description of the policy paralysis in the face of unprecedented economic challenge could serve equally well to depict the situation of recent years in Tokyo.

[3] In practice, the dollar's central role as a universal settlement and reserve currency could permit the United States to export a certain degree of inflation. A return of 1970s-style inflation probably would destroy this role, however, and in any case, the Federal Reserve has given no indication whatsoever that it would countenance any such return.

[4] Indeed, conventional wisdom regarded the OPEC price hikes as fatal to the Japanese economy—evidenced by a run on the yen and the first emergence of

the "Japan premium" that Japanese banks had to pay for funds in the international money markets. (Japanese officials were so fearful of a cut-off in access to international credit that they arranged a secret $1 billion loan from Saudi Arabia.) In fact, Japan emerged from the 1974 OPEC-induced recession more quickly and more thoroughly than any other industrialized power—but that was not evident until 1977.

[5] R. Taggart Murphy, *The Weight of the Yen* (New York: W. W. Norton, 1996), particularly chapter 5.

[6] These issues did not arise for thinly populated OPEC nations such as Saudi Arabia and Kuwait in the 1970s and thereafter because oil revenues far exceeded production costs and practically every good other than energy in those countries had to be imported. In effect, they were dollar economies; thus, there was no real need to convert dollars into domestic currency to compensate producers.

[7] R. Taggart Murphy and Akio Mikuni, *Japan's Policy Trap* (Washington, D.C.: Brookings Institution, 2002).

PART FOUR

NATIONAL INTERESTS IN
THE 2010 GLOBAL ECONOMY

The research and commentaries on the evolution of U.S. national interests and the future oil and capital markets in parts 1, 2, and 3 of this volume provided the basis for a policy conference held at the Center for Strategic and International Studies in Washington, D.C., on March 1, 2000. The panelists for this event were five distinguished foreign policy experts from the United States and Japan: Robert Zoellick, Yukio Okamoto, Janne Nolan, Robert Manning, and Paul Wolfowitz.

The panelists received summary briefing presentations from contributing authors Peter Fusaro and Catherine Mann, followed by commentators Adam Sieminski and Kevin Nealer, respectively. These energy and global economics presentations were accompanied by questions and comments from conference attendees. Following these briefings, the foreign policy expert panel presented its views and participated in open discussion with attendees.

James A. Kelly presided over this conference event; the panels were moderated by Ambassador Richard L. Armitage.

Part 4 of this book is organized in two chapters. Chapter 6 contains the briefings and commentaries on oil and the international economy, including comments by conference attendees. Chapter 7 contains the presentations by the foreign policy panelists, followed by selected comments from the open discussion with attendees.

CHAPTER SIX

EXECUTIVE BRIEFINGS AND COMMENTARIES ON ENERGY AND FINANCE

COMMENTARY ON ENERGY TRENDS

Peter C. Fusaro

I WOULD LIKE TO TALK A LITTLE BIT ON THE "MEGATRENDS" of the energy industry. The energy industry is very different from the one that existed during the oil shocks of the 1970s and 1990. It is driven by markets. Oil price discovery is now global; it is on computer screens. In the past year we have seen oil prices increase more than 100 percent—from a $12 low up to $30—so we really have both of our price scenarios to some extent already bracketed.

This is a time of technological change in the production, refining, distribution, and end use of energy. But we also are seeing a real swing into the "e-commerce" space. This is going to be a very different industry: much more information-intensive and less people-intensive. It is going through tremendous consolidation, and that consolidation will extend into the electric utility space . Why? Because we have global deregulation—which means competition and new market entrants.

We also are going to see a rising importance for natural gas. Gas can be looked at over the next 20 years as a transitional fuel, but gas consumption globally will double, particularly in the power generation segment, because of environmental imperatives, using new technology such as combined-cycle turbines. There also are new technological implications on the lower end of the market; in recent months, micro-turbines and fuel cell companies have shot up like a skyrocket on the stock markets. Why? Because we are going to see a fundamental shift into self-generation and distributive generation.[1] This dynamic of energy is extremely information-intensive, but it also is starting to coalesce around new technologies.

Finally, global environmental awareness is now a given. This is not the fuel reformulation of 1975 (when I worked on unleaded gasoline lead phase-down). In the early 1990s, we saw fuel reformulation globally in the oxygenation of fuel. We are now seeing growing movement on greenhouse gas emissions, regardless of what happens with Kyoto,[2] and we will see how this trend affects project finance and the use of energy. Thus, the message is very simple: we are looking at an industry in which change is constant and dynamic and ideas are disseminated much more quickly. We are seeing flattened organizations in the petroleum sector, as well as within the other energy industries that are restructuring—that is, natural gas and electric utilities.

The 2010 oil price scenarios are not meant as modeling exercises; they are not meant as forecasts. They are meant to drive ideas. We are using Department of Energy data for the base case, and we have two extreme scenarios—which, frankly, are not that extreme now when we see $30 oil. The "extremes" were $10 oil as a low-price scenario and $30 oil as a high-price scenario.

This analysis has dramatic implications for the Asia-Pacific region, which has been the growth engine for energy over the past 10 years. Even though the Asian economic surge has stalled, there will be tremendous growth in oil imports to the region given the future needs of countries such as China, India, Indonesia (when it becomes a net importer), Japan, and South Korea. Moreover, there will be rising supply dependency on Middle Eastern sources. Therefore, there are some obvious energy security issues to consider.

The idea of the two extreme scenarios is to drive home clearly what is changing in this industry. Oil is still a political weapon, but it is becoming less of an economic weapon. The low-price scenario (see table 2.6) will delay Caspian production, shift to lower-cost suppliers in the GCC, and sustain OPEC's market power. It also will decelerate technology transfer and alternative fuel development, and it obviously will lessen inflation.

The converse is true for the high-price scenario (see table 2.7). It will accelerate technology transfer and lead to fuel switching. It will maximize conservation opportunities. It will create unconventional supply such as heavy oil and tar-sands and diversify supply choices. It also will boost renewables as well as fuel cells and some of the smaller technologies that are starting to be capitalized will come into play.

The key factor in both scenarios is that the share of OPEC supply will increase in this decade. The second factor is that we are moving into a gas-driven world in which we no longer flare natural gas. We create value in LNG and in piped gas. We are seeing new technologies that will use gas much more efficiently, with increases from 30 percent base-load coal-fired capacity to 50–70 percent gas-fired capacity. Across the board, it bears reemphasizing, energy will be used much more efficiently in the future. The technologies are emerging; they are commercializing, and they are going to be there.

Basically, the emerging new energy world has access, across the board, to supply and value. It is not a business-as-usual, stagnant industry. Rather, it is a consolidating, competitive, technology-driven industry in which concern for the environment is a major market driver. Never underestimate e-commerce; we are just getting started on the Internet, and markets bring price discovery. Therefore, this is the right time to review foreign policy in this arena.

COMMENTARY ON ENERGY ISSUES

Adam Sieminski

I have found, in 20-some years following the oil market from a global perspective, that the most important thing is to know what questions to ask. The answers are easy, so I have some easy answers to some really good questions from Ambassador Armitage (see chapter 1).

Will oil be as important to the economy in the future as it was in the past? Some of the best work on that question has been done by Larry

Goldstein.[3] He said that oil accounted for about 9 percent of GDP in 1980; it is now down to 3 percent. Consider some quick numbers that anybody can do on the back of an envelope: take the price of oil, multiply by demand here in the United States, and divide that by GDP. It was 6 or 7 percent in 1980, and it is less than 2 percent now. In strict economic terms, oil is not as important now as it was, which is why Alan Greenspan has not been saying as much about the price of oil now as the Fed would have—and did—back in the 1980s.

Is security of oil supply still a central concern of international security planning? In effect, Peter Fusaro just said that. *What are the circumstances in the oil sector that policy planners should most fear?* I think the answer is quite simple. Virtually all of the excess capacity to produce oil in the world is now in three or four countries in the Gulf—notably Saudi Arabia, Kuwait, and the United Arab Emirates. There probably is not a lot in Iran; there could be some in Iraq; there is not a lot in Venezuela, and not a lot in Nigeria. There is no excess capacity in the free world. The United States does not hold anything back, and producers in the North Sea do not hold anything back.

Industry is not investing a great deal in upstream exploration activity. Exploration spending declined substantially in 1998 and did not rebound in 1999. In 2000, we have not seen a lot of major announcements from Exxon, Mobil, BP Amoco, and Total Fina Elf about upstream investments. Why? Because they are too busy cutting costs after their mergers. The lion's share of the world's excess production capacity is in Saudi Arabia.

So here is an interesting question that Ambassador Armitage did not ask: *What have the Saudis been up to recently?* I used to think it was the Saudis who would protect us from the dangers of $30–$40 oil, but I am not so sure anymore. Yet the Persian-Arabian Gulf is where the bulk of the new production is going to be coming from.

The security of oil supplies from the Gulf will be significantly more important to other major actors besides the United States, especially to Asia, as we move into the future. Think about where the consumption is coming from over there: in Japan, roughly 6 million barrels a day of consumption will be imports in 2003; in South Korea, imports will be 2.5 million barrels (and growing very rapidly);

in China, imports will total 2 million barrels; in India, imports will be 2 million barrels. China's oil imports probably will grow faster than India's. For the rest of Asia, add another 7 million barrels. So in the immediate future we will have well in excess of 20 million barrels a day of consumption in the region, and most of that is imports because—with the exception of Indonesia—there are not a lot of major oil producers in the Asia-Pacific area.

Are there other aspects of the emerging 2010 international economy that raise national interest considerations for the United States? If you look at the past five years of energy and oil growth relative to economic growth, it turns out that the Asian countries, with the exception of Japan—a developed country—have higher ratios of oil consumption to GDP than developed Western economies. In the United States, by rough calculations, the ratio of oil consumption to GDP is 0.6 or 0.7. In many of these emerging economies in Asia, the ratio is more than 1—perhaps 1.2 or 1.3, maybe even higher. These countries are in the early stages of their economic growth. So as they move up their economic growth chain, the energy consumption levels are going to grow very rapidly, and a lot of that consumption is going to be oil.

What new global dynamics that might be visible over the next 10 years should we be thinking about? Let me bring up a supply issue. For the past 20 years, the North Sea has provided two-thirds of the growth in non-OPEC production (from the UK, Norway, and a little bit in Denmark). A group associated with Deutsche Bank called Wood Mackenzie Consultants says that 2000 represents the peak production year for the UK. Peaks in North Sea production have been predicted incorrectly in the past, so many analysts are complacent on this issue. Why? Recovery techniques such as 3-D seismic technology, horizontal drilling, sub-sea completions, and even existing platforms have been used to produce more oil, and miraculously the forecast decline disappeared.

Now the technology card has been played, however, and there does not seem to be any new technology breakthrough on the horizon—not that there couldn't possibly be one. Over the course of the next three to five years, however, it is hard to see how production is going to grow in the UK sector. Continuing growth in Norway is possible, and the Norwegian government could make some tax changes that might help things along, but not at the same level: production went from zero in the North Sea to 7 million barrels a day; that is not going to happen again. So, the question is: Where is this non-OPEC oil production going to come from if not the North Sea?

We could say the Caspian. There are a lot of political problems there, and a pipeline will need to be built. A group at CSIS has been looking at this issue recently, and it would be interesting to have their views on how quickly the Caspian can really grow.[4] West Africa clearly is going to be a big growth area, but there are political problems in key oil countries such as Nigeria and Angola that might slow things down. Nigeria's production probably could be higher than it is, and why isn't it? Because of political issues that might not get solved. Adding deepwater Gulf of Mexico and deepwater Brazil, I can still count all of those on one hand, and I am beginning to run out of other big options.

So now we are back to OPEC again, maybe with Iraq stepping up production. Think about that. The future of the world's oil markets, and whether we are going to have stable prices, if it is not to be accomplished through production increases by Saudi Arabia, for whatever political reasons, instead might require Iraq to fill the need. The stability of oil flows from Iraq, controlled by the regime in Baghdad, might become increasingly important over the next 5–10 years. That probably is a subject deserving of a separate study.

What about Russia? There certainly is the possibility of growth there. Again, however, not unlike Mexico, the Russians seem to be incapable of moving forward strongly to allow foreign investment, which clearly is the way to move quickly and steadily on oil production growth. The likelihood that the governments in Russia or Mexico are going to foster huge increases in production on the back of foreign investment seems to be low.

So that brings us right back to the foreign policy panel. *Is oil and the security of oil supply going to be a central concern for security planners looking out over the next 10 years?* Absolutely—and I hope you can do something about this issue because I am concerned about it.

OPEN DISCUSSION ON ENERGY ISSUES

(Question from U.S. Department of Defense policy official about industry's objectives—specifically, what kinds of things industry wants from government.)

Peter Fusaro: It obviously is looking for tax incentives in many countries, but if you look at the pending BP Amoco-Arco merger, I do not think the Federal Trade Commission is really against larger energy companies per se. Yes, they will divest some because of excessive market power concerns, but the reality is that the industry is changing in many respects. For example, end-use energy service providers will be providing financing, new technology implementation, and so forth. We have advanced metering. The key insight is that we are going to use energy more efficiently because of new technologies, and we are going to do so because of environmental imperatives—because it is the right thing to do. Companies want to be perceived as "green." So the thesis here is that it is not just one factor. It is many factors that cannot readily be quantified. There are no models, there are no templates, there are no data; we are in new space.

Adam Sieminski: Let me offer a slightly different response. I would say that what industry ultimately is looking for is growth in earnings and return on capital employed. Historically, one of the best ways to achieve that has been in the upstream—that is, oil and gas exploration and development—rather than in refining and marketing and chemicals or some of the other businesses in which the industry engages. So how do you get upstream profitability? The answer is that you have to produce oil, mainly. How do you do that? You need access to land and offshore leases. So, from a strategic standpoint, the key priority for industry is access to developable reserves.

In fact, we have seen a remarkable change over the past decade, starting around 1990, when several nations—some OPEC and some non-OPEC—began to realize that the concept they had been working under since the 1970s really was no longer operable. That concept was to develop everything internally, via national oil companies. The worldwide move to allow the industry back into places in Latin America—notably Venezuela—and into the Caspian,

Russia, and even some of the countries in the Gulf has been critically important. What the industry really wants, therefore, from a strategic standpoint, is access to land and long-term stability in the deals they make with those countries.

Larry Goldstein, president, Petroleum Industry Research Foundation: The market will take care of a lot of things Adam is talking about. The industry is not homogeneous, but where they are of one mind is on the issue of sanctions. In all our conversations, public and private, the industry does not quarrel with the U.S. government's perspective on what certain foreign governments are all about. At the same time, however, most of us come to the conclusion that unilateral sanctions are counterproductive. They do not serve the U.S. national interest. Iran is a case in point. The sanctions policy has not only complicated the development of productive capacity, it has precluded American companies from being involved in countries where other companies are going to be involved anyway, and it is now complicating our policy on developing the Caspian.

Going beyond the issue of sanctions, the issue that seems to trouble the industry most is the growing realization that oil risks are moving away from producer country disruptions and control of supply as a political tool and more to transit risks. A lot of new oil is being developed in very insecure, politically unstable parts of the world where that resource has to transit many other borders that are just as unstable as the place where the original resource is being produced. The issue of transit risk is the growing issue that will concern the industry over the next 10–20 years.

Amy Myers Jaffe, senior energy adviser to the Baker Center, Rice University: The Baker Center's first study on the Persian Gulf was more or less in line with some of the things that have been said here about the lack of spare capacity in the world, which is partly how we get the $30 oil price today. We had a chart that showed what OPEC was planning to do in their investment policies in the late 1980s and what would have happened if the sanctions policy had not erupted—not to suggest that the sanctions policy wasn't necessary at the time, just examining the cost. We showed how OPEC today would have a capacity of something like 33–34 million barrels a day instead of the

27–28 million barrels a day that we believe they really have, even allowing for the inflated production capacity of Saudi Arabia; I don't really think they have what they say they have.

If OPEC were at 33.5 million barrels a day capacity today, we would not all be sitting here in a $30 world. We would be talking about an $8 scenario. Because the sanctions policy has been so pervasive, because it has been such a knee-jerk, "I-can-solve-my-public-relations-problem-by-slapping-a-sanction-on-this-country" approach, we haven't given a lot of consideration of how many oil producers we can sanction at a time without raising the price of oil.

I also would note—with regard to where the industry sees its security problems coming from—that as the presentations have made clear, markets are global, and we have transparency and all these things that make them work. Our economy is much more protected against oil disruptions because of the rise in natural gas and other factors that have been discussed, but military security and economic security are really two different compartments. The Navy is not going to be able to put a futures contract in its aircraft carriers. The invasion of Kuwait taught us a lesson when we realized that we were buying 90 percent of our jet fuel from Kuwait, and the military suddenly had to go out and buy jet fuel on the spot market, raising the price to a $10 spread, when the historical level of the spread had always been as low as $2.

So there is a physicality to fueling, and the risk here is not just transit risk (because we have piracy on the Asian sea-lanes and other things which are complex) but also an internal stability risk, which is a much more complex matter. I think the U.S. military has proven that they can go in and handle somebody rolling a gun across somebody else's border. I have not seen very effective policymaking, however, showing us what we can do inside a society that has imploded. I would submit that Yugoslavia has been a very useful lesson in just how incredibly difficult that is. Imagine an implosion like that in a major oil-producing country. That's a much more serious risk.

Lincoln P. Bloomfield Jr.: Listening to the two presentations this morning, one could get the feeling that "the old strategic thinking remains valid: The focus of energy security still resides with the Gulf, and the Straits of Hormuz remain a critical choke point." Peter's presentation about the commoditization of oil suggests, however, that perhaps we ought to consider whether future U.S. policy planners should be thinking about tools not only to address the internal stability of producing countries and transit risk—including the security of sea lanes into the Gulf—but also the vulnerability of the global economy, in the advanced and developing economies alike, to potentially serious harm from extreme oil price volatility. While we are revalidating and updating the Cold War era security concepts, is there something else the policy planning community needs to think about relating to price volatility and the potential turbulence and fragility of the global economy?

Larry Goldstein: In terms of public policy, my answer is: I hope not. That's not government's business. My sense is that politically, there would not be symmetry. Consumer countries—the United States in particular—would be more concerned with high prices than when prices are low. Yet both are damaging. One is more visibly and politically damaging and much more pointed to end-use consumers, and government has the tools to tinker—hopefully not tamper—with those concerns. The president and the Secretary of Energy, quite responsibly, understood this in standing up to the northeast senators during the winter of 1999–2000 and declining to release the Strategic Petroleum Reserve as a price-dampening mechanism—a tool it was not designed to be.[5] Instead, the administration released low-income home energy assistance for that segment of the population pained by high prices at a point in time.

Government policy is not going to be as responsive, however, in a low-price environment. Yet the costs are still very real. We lost 500,000 barrels a day of productive capacity in 1999 in the United States. We probably lost the same amount in Venezuela, and we have a real problem in Venezuela because of that. I am not sure the Venezuelans—who have had both feet in the U.S. camp historically—know where to plant their feet today because if they cannot benefit from increased production, they may have to be price hawks in the short term, given their economic troubles. Thus, as long as you do not have confidence that the government is going to be responsive on both sides of price volatility, my sense is to keep the government out of it.

Robert E. Ebel, director, Energy and National Security Program, CSIS: Adam mentioned the project that we have underway, which is a strategic energy initiative looking at the geopolitics of energy to the year 2020. He asked where the non-OPEC oil will come from in the years ahead. Will it come from the Caspian? If drilling programs are successful and if pipelines are available, you might see something on the order of less than 3 percent of world supply coming out of the Caspian by the year 2010.

How about Russia? In 1988, the Soviet Union was the largest producer of oil in the world, at 11.4 million barrels of oil a day. In 1999, Russia produced 6.1 million barrels. I think it has bottomed out. You might see some small increments coming up in the years ahead— maybe to 6.5 or 6.6 million in five years and maybe even to 7 million by the year 2010. But much of that oil is going to stay at home as the economy begins to rebuild.

So that leaves us (as our study found) with the so-called "rogue states"—although I understand that term is not in favor any more, so perhaps we should say "sanctioned states." If we do not get this additional oil out of sanctioned states such as Iran, Iraq, Libya, and Sudan, and if our forward estimates of rising global demand are correct, we are going to have some difficulties.

Robert McNally, Tudor Investment Corporation: In hindsight, it seems that one of the main reasons we find world prices above the high scenario and rising is that people were late to realize the importance of the Saudi and Iranian political rapprochement and how that restored trust within OPEC—that plus the change in the Venezuelan government. So two questions flow from that. The first is: Does this logic mean that OPEC is less likely to increase production by as much as is needed and necessary to keep prices contained in the short run and to project a downward path in prices after that? Secondly, over the longer term, as we look to 2005 and 2010, does this Saudi-Iranian rapprochement threaten to destabilize and realign political relationships in the Gulf—particularly the perception that the United States is the dominant actor in that important region?

Adam Sieminksi: On the first question—Is it possible that OPEC will not be adding enough production in the near term?—I would say that the evidence is very clearly accumulating that the answer to that is Yes. Just this morning, there was an announcement that Saudi Arabia, Mexico, and Venezuela, who have been huddling about what to do with production, have said that they will add about 1.2 million barrels a day. Another number that I heard whispered yesterday was 1.5 million barrels a day. My own calculations say you need 2 million barrels to balance the market. I have heard other people say that we need as many as 3 million barrels a day in increased output to make supply and demand balance this year.

So the OPEC members seem to be running into a political issue wherein Iran and Venezuela, for example, do not have the proportionate capacity to make an equal contribution to the total increase that is necessary. Iran opposes increasing production because that will bring prices down and they cannot push their volumes up, so they become a net loser. Venezuela could be a net loser, as could others, making the political decision very difficult. That is why I think OPEC will end up adding some production into the market, but probably not enough—with the result that oil prices stay much closer to $25 a barrel, maybe even a little higher. Because the number that is in most of Wall Street's official forecasts for prices is closer to $21 a barrel, this makes a big difference to the cash flow of the companies and ultimately could make a difference in the growth in demand.

BRIEFING: OIL PRICES AND THE FUTURE GLOBAL ECONOMY

Catherine L. Mann

We have talked here mostly about the economics of oil and the politics of oil. I would like to differentiate between the real economic effects of oil on economic activity in an equilibrium sense and how the market reacts to the effects of oil. So the question that I am asking is: Would an oil shock today be channeled through international capital markets and affect economies and financial markets in the same way as in the 1970s and the 1980s debt crisis that followed, or are we looking at a very different environment?

The answer is, very simply, no. Oil price changes today, under either of these extreme price scenarios, would have a relatively smaller impact on financing requirements of countries generally, although I make some distinctions about that in a minute. The market—the financial markets, the international capital markets—can easily finance these requirements and intermediate the funds.

The problem that I see instead is one of volatility. There is a tremendous amount of capital in the financial markets. It has a tendency to move in large denominations; it "sloshes," as we have observed lately with the Asian financial crisis and the Russian default and so forth. So the problem really will be volatility. Because of the new market structure of the past 25 years, market sentiment will tend to magnify the underlying real effects of oil price changes; and this volatility has far greater potential to cause disturbances—perhaps even leading to political issues—than the oil price effect by itself.

In reaching this answer, I used the production and consumption numbers that came out of Peter Fusaro's exercise to generate scenarios of how much various countries and regions in the world would need in terms of net financing requirements, either drawn from the financial markets or offered to the international financial markets, in the high-price and low-price scenarios. I calculated those numbers, but then we need to ask: Are those large numbers? Are those little numbers? How do we know?

To answer these questions, I looked at data for regions of the world and individual countries of interest to this group and examined the numbers relative to common denominators. These denominators included GDP, how much financing these countries had been using from the international markets in the past, and total demand for financing from the high and low oil prices relative to the overall amount of capital that is normally in the financial markets by themselves. So if my answer is, "No, we really don't have to worry about the real effects of the oil price, but we do have to worry about the potential disturbance coming from this magnification effect through the conduct of the capital markets," then I have to tell you what has changed in international capital markets.

There are good and bad sides to this story. Both are part of the reason that, on one hand, in an equilibrium sense we don't have to worry about the financing but on the other hand, we may have to worry about the magnification effect. The good news is that capital markets are much deeper and richer in terms of the financial instruments that are available, and the contracts are more market-oriented. There are secondary markets and derivative markets for virtually every type of financial arrangement. In the 1970s, when we had to recycle petrodollars, banks accounted for about 80 percent of the financial intermediation. A single type of financial intermediation process accounted for 80 percent of the financial intermediation that had to be done—and those bank contracts basically had no secondary market.

In contrast, we now have about 15 percent of financial intermediation done by banks and the rest about equally divided between foreign direct investment (FDI) and bond and equity portfolio investment. This latter category comprises many more market-oriented instruments for which there are secondary markets. Although we can question liquidity at times, there are secondary markets. The second positive aspect about changes in the capital markets over the past 25 years is that there is much broader participation in capital markets. Developing countries are not just recipients of international capital flows; they also are participants in outward flows, including outward FDI and outward portfolio investment.

Thus, the international capital market today is much closer to being a fabric as opposed to a pipeline. In the 1970s, capital more or less went from OPEC to industrial countries and then to developing countries in a triangular flow, intermediated though banks. Now, by contrast, there is much more of a web-work or fabric of international capital sources and uses. This fabric is very thick because of these very different kinds of financial instruments.

In addition, I think an important ingredient in this broader participation is that institutional investors in industrial countries increasingly are looking to investments outside their own markets. Most people in any market tend to hold in their wealth portfolio assets that are denominated in their own country. This feature is called "home bias." That tendency has changed some over the past 25 years (actually rather a lot); what these institutional investors in developed countries have created is a much greater flow of financial capital into the capital markets of developing countries.

The third characteristic of capital markets that has changed—and this is the part that is potentially more worrisome—is that international capital markets are much more leveraged than before. Leverage is a double-edged sword. On the positive side, leverage is a way in which financial intermediaries essentially can create additional financial capacity. So there is more capacity in the financial markets now to lend to areas that need it in the case of, say, a high oil price.

On the other hand, the sharp side of leverage is that when market sentiment changes, the tendency is for leverage to move capital in a large flow, away from areas that are now deemed to be more risky. We observed this dynamic in a very big way in the Asian financial crisis. To provide some numbers on leverage: New derivative instruments on interest rate and currency swaps were about $18 trillion in 1999—much larger than the underlying trade flows associated with that activity. In combination with the technology of computers and electrons, leverage also means that we can get much faster movements of financial capital, which will be reflected in very large changes in asset prices, interest rates, and exchange rates.

So how does all this play out in terms of extreme oil price trends? The high and low oil price scenarios both have very dramatic effects on OPEC countries. Changes in their current accounts and GDPs are major—on the order of 15 percent of GDP on the high-price side and a reduction in current account as a share of GDP of about 30 percent on the low-price side. These changes represent potentially huge demands on international financial markets, but only from OPEC countries. These numbers for 2010 are much larger than the relative impact of oil price shocks on the OPEC countries in the 1970s. This difference reflects how much more dependent those key producing countries are on the oil sector now than they were back then. For the OPEC countries, then, the extreme oil price scenarios are very, very severe in terms of what they need from the financial markets or what they are offering to the financial markets.

For the rest of the world, on the other hand, the effects in 2010 are very small. Some countries will receive more of a shock in terms of oil price change. India and South Korea would benefit substantially from low oil prices, with a change of about 3 percent in their net external balance relative to GDP. These countries would not be as well off with a high price. Net financing requirements for China or Latin America might be 0.5 percent of GDP—the same number as for the United States.

These numbers are very small in relation to what the figures were in the 1970s, for two reasons. The first is that in the United States, we are much less energy dependent than we were in the 1970s, so the economic impact of energy prices essentially is not a major issue for the United States. Developing countries also have a much more diversified base of GDP value creation than they did in the 1970s. Thus, even though they are becoming more intensive in their energy use, they also are producing a lot of other things (much more so than in the 1970s), so their economic base was much more diversified by 2000—and will be even more so in 2010.

With regard to the numbers that come out of these price scenarios, in terms of what the net financing requirements might be or net financial offerings to international capital markets, we are talking about maybe $100 billion or $150 billion, on either the upside or the downside. Compare these figures to the international capital markets, which today are trillions of dollars. The international capital markets very easily have the capacity to intermediate these flows. The key point, however, is that they have the capacity to intermediate these flows if they happen smoothly, over a year, and if there is no shock or market sentiment that changes the attitude of institutional investors and the general investing public.

I think what we have observed in the past two years in the case of Asia, however, is that international capital markets do not intermediate and price different kinds of risk very well. They do not smoothly adjust flows to changes in market realities involving which countries are perceived to be moving faster versus slower. Financial markets tend to move in a herd, and leverage only tends to magnify those changes in market sentiment.

The years 1999 and 1998 were very difficult for Asia, but not so much because of the impact of changes in the overall financial environment. The impact was magnified by the very rapid change in asset prices and very rapid overshooting of their exchange rates. The magnification effect was far more important for Asia. So if we look forward to the next oil shock, the question is: Will the markets recycle these funds smoothly? The answer is, "Probably not," because a true oil price shock would be a surprise.

What we are looking at right now—this $30 per barrel oil—is no real surprise. We could see it coming, so we are not seeing a huge change in market sentiment. If there were a true surprise, market sentiment about the potential impact on certain areas of the world would tend to magnify financial attitudes toward those countries. Flows of financial capital would either dry up or zoom in, creating huge changes in asset prices; that disturbance causes crashes of banking systems within domestic economies and even crashes of national economies.

In conclusion, I return to Lincoln Bloomfield's question about whether governments should be concerned about this issue and whether they should try to do something about it. There certainly has been a concern in the past year about the impact of this volatility. That has been the focus of all the hotly debated policy prescriptions in the five or so books written over the past year about rebuilding the international financial architecture so that it can manage better in the face of very large flows of financial capital and rapid changes in asset prices.

Interest in that type of restructuring of international financial markets truly has been tempered in the past year because all of the financial capital has streamed right back into most of the markets from which it had exited only months earlier. Thus, in considering what governments should do, the policy community should not put those books about international financial architecture on the shelf to gather dust so quickly. They are going to want to bring them off the shelf the next time there really is a surprise oil shock, either up or down.

COMMENTARY ON INTERNATIONAL ECONOMIC ISSUES

Kevin G. Nealer

For those of you who think you're in on the joke, go back and read Catherine Mann's study [chapter 4] again because for most people—with the exception of those in the investment community—it has been 25 years since you have had a model in your head about how international financial flows work. She has given you the crib sheet. You need to read her study again because it will give you not only the vocabulary but also the reality that is animating the $800 billion worth of global capital movement that happens every night.

You spend a lot of time in the policy community chewing over the $4–5 trillion annual trade in goods and services and its impact on the financial markets. You had better go back and look at how the real world works, invisibly, every evening. If you are not running a hedge fund, Catherine Mann has written the primer for you.

Among the most important changes she documents are a more than 50-fold increase in the level of portfolio investment in developing markets. That volume of capital now exceeds direct investment flows—real money going in and buying factories. We all knew that changes had occurred, but as a data point, that one is staggering. It also is important to look at the emergence of this new class of tradeable instruments, with profound effects on the market: equity and commercial paper, as well as the reliance on what Dr. Mann describes as noncontractual, or market-driven, rates of return. It also will be important for the oil markets and how we think about them.

At the risk of seeming needlessly contrarian, I would like to pull out one thread in her study and add my speculation that these two factors—the proliferation of instruments and the volumes and size of these portfolios—require that we think about the emergence of a new and potentially different kind of investor in the oil-producing countries and perhaps in the emerging markets as well. Dr. Mann speculates—I think very reasonably—that the high oil price scenario could lead producing countries to invest more in their home markets, in contrast to the petrodollar recycling that inflated the U.S. economy and other economies in the 1970s.

Maybe so. I believe, however, that it is at least as likely that under these changed conditions, whoever is managing the inflow of dollars in the oil-producing countries may turn them right around and seek returns wherever they are most attractive. This could mean a flight to value in the United States, Japan, Europe, and the OECD that replicates the problem of the 1970s, or it could be very different. In the decade ahead, it also may mean that money floods into emerging markets in the form of infrastructure spending through bonds or equity portfolios. Thus, emerging market financing needs might be met with less difficulty, and producers—in particular the former Soviet Union—may not see as much of the domestic investment potential, as much of that home market bias, as the model may lead us to believe.

If telecommunications privatization in Sri Lanka and Laos looks like a better bet than a long, slow payout for a sewer system or a new ring road in Moscow, it is not hard to figure out where the money is going to go. Certainly I have my doubts that there will be a strong need, and the market will feel a strong need, for yet another U.S.-built airbase in Saudi Arabia. I do not know where petrodollars might end up, but I think the emergence of these new instruments, and what Dr. Mann has documented in the volumes of capital, could inspire a very different kind of investment pattern in the decade ahead, in the hands of people who are not as constrained by the national good or a home market bias in the oil-producing countries that otherwise would have captured the rents from these higher prices. Obviously, this dynamic would ease the upward pressure on global interest rates if my contrarian model is true, but it also would have a lot of other follow-on, or "knock-on," effects that need to be considered.

I also would like to conjure, as Dr. Mann did, with the idea that China and Latin America operate with very different demand elasticities for oil than other consumers. I caution against feeling too confident as we model the behavior of consumers in those very different markets. For example, my own firm has done a lot of work in China in the automotive and energy sectors, and what I have seen there are widely varying pricing models, developed to portray a range of options for Chinese fuel use. We see much greater consumption for transportation than was true five or even two or three years ago. The state may own about 90 percent of all automobiles, but don't take that number to the bank. At the top of a Chinese consumer's wish list is a car. Chinese people don't want a color TV, they want a car—and increasingly, they are getting it.

By the way, if you want an example from real life, the recent corruption scandal in China's Fujian Province offers some real insights into how porous China's borders are becoming. What was going on there? It was fuel smuggling. By whom? Some of the highest-level officials in the local government. All of this goes to say that I am not really confident—and I do not know how confident we can be—about the government controls or past consumer disciplines that Peter Fusaro had to use to develop the model.

The prices of cooking oil, rice, and other staples have long been the stuff of retail politics in China. I simply want to suggest that fuel might soon rise to that same level of expectation. If I am right in worrying about China's growing dependence on imported oil, we could imagine a significant dent in the $150 billion in foreign exchange reserves that China's government is so confident about. Bob Manning has done a lot of significant work on the changing architecture of the Chinese energy industry, and I invite his thoughts on the exquisite policy problem that Jiang Zemin's successor is going to be faced with in this regard.

I think Dr. Mann is importantly correct in drawing our attention, for the purpose of this analysis, to what happened to the role of capital markets in the recent Asian crisis. There really is a lot to be learned. In a matter of months we watched $400 billion in value destroyed, and we saw governments collapse in Indonesia, South Korea, Thailand, and Japan. Investors adjusted quickly—some observers say too quickly—to these breathtaking events, and the reallocation of capital left the international financial institutions as well as local consumers and businesses to pick up the pieces. Today, unless you are a Bangkok-based exporter in the manufactured goods sector, or maybe an Indonesian colonel, you can almost be forgiven for imagining that the whole thing really never happened.

Dr. Mann raised the question about volatility and whether as a result of the Asian crisis we can expect to see a form of re-regulation of financial markets. Perhaps we should not say "re-regulation"; I am not sure we can look back over our shoulder or see authentic regulation in the rear-view mirror. We can safely say, however, that the little bit of increased visibility that we have seen since 1997 on financial movement is about the extent of regulatory discipline. Those of you in the market who disagree with this statement, I would like to hear about it. Looking at what the central bankers are trying to do (I may regret saying this), however, is like watching dogs chase cars. You wonder: If they caught it, what would they do with it? They are chasing the $800 billion that rushes around the world every night, but the tools simply are not there.

There comes a moment within the international financial community when there is a consensus about some feature of the market or, in this case, a need for regulation. I do not think we have nearly reached the point of consensus yet in the international financial institutions—the "IFIs"—or in the real markets themselves. Hence, I do not foresee constraints on capital movement that would affect the adjustment if it happened under the high oil price scenario.

I urge that we take to heart the warning implicit in Dr. Mann's final comments. It is a cautionary note that informed my reading of Peter Fusaro's and Herman Franssen's essays. We look at several factors—such as technological improvements in exploration and production and in the oil market, the increased depth and sophistication of financial markets, and the relative decline in the importance of oil to increasingly high-technology economies—and I think we risk some complacency here. If the oil shock comes as a result of a new war in the Middle East, a long-term disruption in markets such as Mexico or Venezuela, or a regime-threatening crisis in Russia, the whole idea of managing the risks to our security interests, for Japan and the United States, is not going to end with improved financial intermediation or increased flexibility in commercial paper markets; we all know that.

The truth is that in extremis, things do get simpler; they don't get more complicated. Here, mature capital markets are necessary, but they are certainly insufficient for crisis management if we face these kinds of systemic risks to our security.

Those risks require clear understandings about our respective interests and what the two largest economies in the world are prepared to do to underwrite successful crisis management initiatives through the U.S.-Japan alliance. Despite recent improvements wrought by the U.S.-Japan Defense Guidelines, I have my doubts about the quality of the bilateral dialogue in an attempt to manage some of these scenarios.[6]

I close by departing from the writ that I have here and offering a final thought on R. Taggart Murphy's provocative thesis [chapter 5]. Subject to your correction, especially those of you in the markets, I do not believe that a dollar crisis is either inevitable or—absent the benefit of better thinking here—even likely. In March 1999, Japan was exporting about $9 billion per month as capital sought better returns, and we are likely to see continued liberalization of the Japanese capital markets. That exodus has slowed, but the real problem in bilateral relations is not as interesting, precise, or well-defined as a currency crisis.

I see U.S.-Japan cooperation, on an entire range of interests, fraying around the edges, with little back-channel dialogue or genuine consensus about policies. This fraying is conspicuously true with regard to the dialogue, or lack thereof right now, between Japan's Ministry of Finance and the U.S. Department of the Treasury. That drift is dangerous, and I am afraid it is likely to accelerate in the more than a year that it is going to take a new U.S. administration to get settled and get serious about having a conversation with Japan about shared interests.

OPEN DISCUSSION ON INTERNATIONAL ECONOMICS ISSUES

Larry Goldstein: I am less sanguine. I believe that the capital markets are efficient enough that things will work out over time. It is that intermediary period where the capital markets need the time to work themselves out. What concerns me most in an oil price shock caused by a supply disruption is that the Asian economies are at a substantial relative competitive disadvantage. Volatility is created not on averages but at the margin; what we saw happen in late 1997, and why we became very bearish on our markets in early 1998, was our view of what was happening to Asian currencies.

Oil is bought internationally. The medium of exchange is dollars. A major oil price shock upward creates a tremendous sudden demand for dollars. That has very negative effects on the Asian economies because if those currencies collapse, the real price of imported oil to them skyrockets. Inasmuch as we all recognize that oil is more important to their economies than it is to Europe and the United States, we can see that the currency impact creates the greatest damage to those economies. At this point I am simply unsure what oil price shocks do to the relative value of those currencies.

In addition, hedge funds played an important role in the destabilization of markets for a moment in time in 1998. Lack of transparency is a major issue. I do not think governments can or should do much, if anything, about it, there is a risk out there, and one has to distinguish between short-term and long-term capital, as well as between hard capital and investor capital. It is a real concern. We know the Federal Reserve Board got involved in international problems in 1998 by lowering interest rates three times, in part because of the default in Russia but also in part, I argue, because of Long-Term Capital Management.[7] It became very complicated, and I think all of that was triggered by overnight relative changes in currency values. Currency is a missing part of the equation with which I remain very uncomfortable.

Catherine Mann: You are singing the same song I am; we are just using slightly different terminology. You are talking about currency value, whereas I talk about asset prices. To me, currencies are assets, so that is an asset price. You are absolutely correct to say that with a higher oil price scenario, the Asian countries do bear more of a financing requirement because the value of their currencies tends to be depreciated relative to the dollar, so their import costs go up. Taking an example in the scenarios, South Korea has to spend about 2 percent of GDP more to finance higher oil expenditures. On the other hand, 2 percent of GDP is not a huge number for a country like South Korea. It is relevant, and it does have an effect on the economy, but that is not the biggest problem.

You are right that it is an equilibrium number, whereas to get to 2 percent you probably first have a significant change in the *won* (the South Korean currency), which has an impact on the financial system. Indeed, we observed bank closures in South Korea and further "knock-on" effects through the economy from that weakening of the currency. So you are absolutely right that the transition, not the end point, is the problem and that currency valuation changes are a very important ingredient to the transition.

Larry Goldstein: There are two significant points here because the transition could be particularly severe. What we saw in Asia was a lot of dollar-denominated loans, and companies simply could not afford to operate. When you know where the currency equilibrium is going to be, it is very easy. Because the *won* was devaluing and the (Thai) *baht* was devaluing, however, and they had not reached an equilibrium level yet, companies faced the prospect of having to take local currency and convert it into dollars to buy oil to put into refineries to get local currency back. Guess what? No one would do that.

Indeed, what you had was not only the normal negative effects; in addition we actually saw rationing going on. In fact, many of the governments encouraged rationing. People were exporting oil in those countries to get the hard currency dollars. They were actually shortchanging their economy, just as the Russians were doing during their August 1998 devaluation; they were leaving their local economy short of oil by exporting large volumes to accumulate dollars.

Kevin Nealer: We should not talk about currency movement as if it is incidental—something that happens on the margins or that you watch through the side mirror. Let me add one thought about the Asia crisis and the hedge funds. We all love to beat them up, but in fact, about 80 percent of the capital movement was done by the banks. It was not done for the hedge funds accounts. It was done by the banks because that is what the banks do: They are big speculators.

Who hit the door first? Who made the currency movements first? Who put the initial pressure on? It was local investors, who know best; they were gone first. That is what happened to currency. The speculative community did step in, but the energy did not come from outside; it came from inside. That is one of the authentic lessons from the Asian crisis. It is not to say that volatility and what you have said about volatility is not a real problem. I wish I could tell you about how somebody is going to step in and fix it, but I have not seen a consensus to do that yet.

Question for Dr. Mann from Amy Jaffe: In conducting your study and using Peter Fusaro's scenarios, did you just look at one scenario versus another or did you take into consideration a very realistic possibility that you would have constant volatility? In the past year we have seen the price go from $8 to $30, and it went up and down in a zigzag manner. In a lot of years you can go from $8 to $20 and $20 to $8 and $8 to $20 and $20 to $8 four times in a year. Did you look at the impact of those kinds of changes on a regular basis for a lengthy period of time? Or did you look only at sudden moves that last for a period of time?

Catherine Mann: I stayed within the parameters of the study, which examined sustained extreme conditions. What I was given was a base case, a high case, and a low case, and those were equilibriums. I can respond to your question, however, by saying that the financial markets deal with tremendous volatility every minute of every day, so they do not have a problem. Financial people make money which-ever way the money goes; up and down is good for the financial markets.

How well do economies respond in real terms? That is one of the essential questions to be addressed in several recent books on the is-sue of international financial architecture. My view is that volatility is a state of the world right now, and it will increasingly be that way. It is as though we lived in a world with a lot of germs; you cannot put yourself in a bubble and say, "I'm not going to live in that world." All you can do is exercise, eat right, and wear proper clothing if you're going out in the rain.

Hence, the prescription for a country's economic planners is to build yourself up internally to withstand the volatility that is around you all the time. This is one of the ingredients of the changes in the international financial architecture as well as domestic financial architecture that will make the international financial system more of a boon to a country than a bane. There are other questions having to do with whether exchange rates move too much and whether we should put sand in the wheels, but those are different questions.

Professor John D. Langlois, Jr., Princeton University, and president and executive director, Center for International Political Economy: If you think about types of volatility, you could say there are two types. One is the type you see in the market, which is day-to-day through capital markets. The other one is the kind you might see in the bank markets, which is hidden. Banks do not mark to market their books, typically, and they refuse to pass on information; they bottle it up.[8] Then, as we saw in the Asian crisis, not only Asian banks but banks all over the world suddenly overreacted and withdrew liquidity. People call that volatility; it is a kind of "bumpy" volatility, and it is a product of nontransparency. It is very destructive.

If you look in Asia, the places where we had the real crises were the places where the markets were less developed, except for China, where there were other reasons why they escaped it. So in terms of going forward, I am considering the notion that the greater market development we have, the better off we probably will be. Moreover, the less bank intermediation of risk we have, the better off we will be.

Dr. Mann pointed out that in 1972, banks intermediated about 80 percent of risk. Even in Japan today, banks are still intermediating 70 percent of finance, and in China the figure probably is 90 percent, so I would say that these places are ripe for trouble. Japan has started to introduce mark-to-market accounting. China has not hit the speed bumps yet, but they are going to, and people's heads are going to hit the top of the car and pop through. I think we are going to see trouble in China when people start to realize the hidden volatility that they thought did not exist. Pent-up volatility, in the form of unrealized write-offs, is going to come to the fore. What should we be doing about this? Rather than worrying about the United States, we should be worrying about China and other places like it.

Catherine Mann: There is volatility on a daily basis that can be relatively well contained within the markets; then there is volatility in individual countries and the question of how they respond to it. It is true that banks in the Asian countries that were in crisis were the first to get out after they had gotten the signal from the domestic investors. By and large, however, the banks that left these Asian crisis countries were not American banks; they were German and Japanese banks.

Why did those banks have to get out so quickly? Because they did not learn the lessons of the savings and loan crisis that we had. They did not learn from the debt crisis in the less-developed countries (LDCs) that our banks bore relatively more, which is that you have to price your risk better, and you have to have reserves against potential losses. You may not mark to market for accounting purposes, but you better have really good internal risk management guidelines so that you are effectively marking to market three or four times a day. In the international financial system meetings at the Bank for International Settlements (BIS), the International Organization of Securities Commissions (IOSCO), the Joint Forum, and elsewhere[9]—and increasingly within the financial task force being set up at the BIS—the focus is on how we can get financial intermediaries within countries and global intermediaries to better prepare themselves to avoid overreacting in a volatile episode. How do we get them to avoid acting like a herd, to avoid responding by sloshing all of their capital out of South Korea in one six-month period and bringing it all back in the next six-month period?

Some of the answer is reserves, some of it is internal risk management techniques, and some of it is increasing the number and menu of financial instruments. For example, we could look at credit risk derivatives,[10] which could alter the dynamics of a crisis situation. It is like insurance: "Credit risk derivatives" equals "insurance" from the standpoint of vocabulary. It is an insurance mechanism that kicks in when the market crashes. People who have bought insurance do not have to exit, and they do not become part of this herd that takes capital out. So you are absolutely right in saying that further market development is an essential ingredient to managing the impact of volatility and diffusing the impact of market volatility, which is around us all the time and will continue to be there.

Paul Wolfowitz: I have wondered whether some of that volatility, particularly the actions of German and Japanese banks—although in the case of Indonesia it also was French and Dutch—had anything to do with the fact that a lot of that lending initially was not conceived on fundamentally commercial banking terms but was a form of export subsidy. Certainly I saw in Indonesia an awful lot of "crony" banking to support Japanese and European exports. Perhaps that was a factor elsewhere in Asia.

Francis A. Finelli, The Carlyle Group: I would like to raise a question from the perspective of the equity market and the financial health of the oil industry. We are seeing megamergers here and in other industries such as defense, and they are having a profound impact. Some people could argue that the large oil companies confront a lot of the same problems that the defense industry does; they certainly are hostage to government policy and aspects of international security, and they are operating in markets that do not really demonstrate key growth characteristics going forward.

Merging is one way to try to generate earnings growth. We have seen disappointments in the defense sector as synergies do not accrue and the companies find that they cannot generate the economies of scale that they originally projected. I would appreciate any assessments on the prospects for these megamergers in the oil industry, or the broader energy industry, and the implications if they follow a similar path to what we are seeing in the defense sector.

Adam Sieminski: These mergers have been very defensively oriented for the reasons that you have stated. The oil companies were finding that their rates of return on capital were very low. They needed to find ways to cut costs, having already gone through an internal calculus of cutting costs. Once you have done everything you can on the inside, you have to find somebody else's costs to cut. There are some very serious structural problems that this industry is facing. One of those problems is that, in spite of the new technology and the reality that there is a lot of oil and resources out there, industry's ability to develop reserves profitably has been somewhat limited over the past few years. Growth in production has not been as strong as the companies themselves thought they could do just two or three years ago. That does imply that prices might have to go up.

What are all these mergers about? The companies need to find ways to cut costs because they are desperate to provide rates of return that will attract capital into the industry. Volatility is increasing, if you think about what Peter Fusaro was saying and some of the comments I and others in this discussion have made. Oil demand is coming increasingly from volatile economies; supply is coming increasingly from volatile producers. Because industry is so keen to control its costs, it does not want to hold inventories. It is setting up a really unique situation compared to the prior history of the oil industry, where there is really nobody available to be the supplier of last resort other than Saudi Arabia and the strategic petroleum reserves [of the United States, Europe, and Japan].

I can see that we are going to go through another cycle. Prices actually are going to go higher than where they are already, which will establish a wave of investment by the industry in places where there is oil. The major U.S. and European oil companies will go out and start finding oil in several of these non-OPEC places, and demand is going to come down because of what Catherine Mann was saying in terms of weakening currencies in a high-price environment. The result will be that OPEC will lose market share, and they are going to be right back where they were in 1998, with prices having to collapse to some new low level to discipline producers all over again.

One thing I have seen change very dramatically in 25 years is the speed with which all of this happens. The roller coaster has much shorter hills, it seems, and they may be higher and coming faster. My concern is that although the first time around the financial community concluded that it seemed to have dealt with it, I wonder how well we are going to deal with it the second time.

Amy Jaffe: Adam has absolutely hit the nail on the head. Let me share an anecdotal story to dramatize his point. Adam is saying that in the 1970s we were in a pattern in which it took until the mid-1980s for the new oil to come on line. We had a giant price collapse, and then we thought the collapse would be forever. I recall that in the 1970s and 1980s we were running out of oil in the United States. There was no oil to find, and the prospect of drilling in 7,000 feet of water was something for the distant future—perhaps 2010.

I remember going to the offshore technology conference in 1991 and interviewing people from Shell and Petrobras, who were the industry leaders in deepwater technology. While I was thinking that deepwater looked like it would turn out to be a big play, they pulled me aside and said, "Amy, you don't understand. The technology isn't there yet. People have lost billions of dollars. You have to be the largest oil company in the world to do this. It's going to take us 10 years to get the technology."

The company with the first successful deepwater field was Shell, and although I do not have the details of their first field, I will give you the details of the second field, which was Augur.[11] They figured out how to do it; it took them about 8–10 years. They had to hedge a derivative[12] with Bankers Trust to lock in a $14 per barrel price because they determined that to make a sufficient rate of return on investment they needed at least the $14 or $15 price of oil to cover their costs. The project was successful. As I recall, the depth of Augur was approximately 2,000 or 3,000 feet of water. When Shell found that field, they told me that there was a lot of oil at 7,000 feet, but I would not see them out there in my lifetime.

This year, BP Amoco announced a 1 billion barrel field in 7,000 feet of water. I was at a conference in Dallas recently, and a representative from BP Amoco was talking about the development of that field. He said it was going to take them two years and cost them $3 a barrel to develop.

That story can give you an idea of how timelines and costs are shrinking. Mobil went into West Africa, to Equatorial Guinea, and developed an oil field in 18 months. So what used to take 10 to 12 years, 8 years on the fast track, can be done today in 2 years, and with computer technology it is compressing further. Soon we will be talking about oilfields that we can turn around in a year because of processing capabilities.

Notes

[1] Self-generation refers to a situation in which the electricity end user produces its own power through means such as cogeneration, microturbines, fuel cells and batteries; distributive generation is a term that describes an electricity system in which self-generation is practiced.

[2] The reference is to the international environmental summit held in Kyoto, Japan, in December 1997, and the multilateral agreements agreed there—the Kyoto Protocol—that set performance goals and timetables to reduce greenhouse gas emissions.

[3] Mr. Larry Goldstein, who attended and participated in this discussion, is president of the Petroleum Industry Research Foundation.

[4] The CSIS Strategic Energy Initiative, led by Project Director Robert E. Ebel, director of the Energy and National Security Program at CSIS, has been examining the geopolitics of energy into the twenty-first century.

[5] When comparable conditions arose in the fall of 2000, however, President Clinton reversed course and released 30 million barrels from the SPR—*Ed.*

[6] Revised Guidelines for U.S.-Japan Defense Cooperation, September 23, 1997.

[7] Long-Term Capital Management (LTCM), a very large private investment firm operating a highly leveraged global hedge fund with many important institutional subscribers, was "rescued" from collapse by a bailout that involved many of those client institutions, organized by the Federal Reserve in September 1998. The Federal Reserve acted out of concern that the failure of LTCM's fund could create widespread major financial losses. According to the President's Working Group on Financial Markets (April 1999), at the time of the near-collapse, the LTCM Fund "reportedly had over 60,000 trades on its books.... [T]he gross notional amounts of the Fund's contracts on futures exchanges exceeded $500 billion, swaps contracts more than $750 billion, and options and other Over the Counter derivatives over $150 billion." The Fund itself held equity capital of only $4.8 billion as of January 1, 1998; its balance sheet leverage ratio apparently exceeded 25 to 1. Its losses, the Working Group reported, "greatly exceeded what conventional risk models...suggested were probable."

[8] The practice known as "marking to market" refers to the discipline of periodically valuing positions at current market prices.

[9] The BIS—often termed the "central bankers' bank"—is a forum where the central bank heads meet to discuss the state of the world economy, where bank supervisors discuss and promulgate bank supervisory standards, and where

international coordination can be effected at times of financial crisis. IOSCO is a body of securities regulators with a similar mission. The Joint Forum is where the two bodies—bankers and securities regulators—meet to discuss cross-cutting issues in international financial markets.

[10] A "credit risk derivative" is a derivative financial instrument that pays off when the riskiness of the underlying country or company changes. For example, if the rating on a country's sovereign bond falls from BAA to BBB, the likelihood that the country will have difficulty paying off the bond contract is said to have risen. This raises the level of risk of holding that bond in an investment portfolio, and the portfolio investor might want to sell the bond. If the investor has purchased a credit risk derivative that—like an insurance policy— pays off when the bond rating falls, however, this payment will compensate the investor for this higher risk on the underlying asset.

[11] Augur is an oilfield owned by Royal Dutch Shell, located in the U.S. Gulf of Mexico.

[12] This phrase refers to the practice of trading in equity or fixed income securities with the promise to buy or sell these instruments at a pre-agreed price at a fixed point in the future. The two parties involved in such a transaction in effect are "betting" against each other with regard to the actual market price or value of the commodity represented by the securities—in this case, crude oil.

CHAPTER SEVEN

FOREIGN POLICY PRESENTATIONS AND DISCUSSIONS

Robert B. Zoellick

I DISCUSS INTERCONNECTIONS AMONG FOUR TOPICS. FIRST IS information on changes occurring in the energy markets. The second is to relate what I have seen occur in financial markets, in government and the private sector, to draw some connections to the changing energy markets. Third, I offer some hypotheses on how information as an asset, a key driver of value creation, is going to affect both of these markets. The fourth relates to changes in our concepts of geopolitics and security.

In the spirit of Woodrow Wilson—or perhaps because of my poor organization—I briefly note 14 points. First, I want to underscore Peter Fusaro's point about information as an asset because I think that development is going to be one of the critical drivers in looking at energy markets and security differently. In particular, I would stress the importance of more, better, and more accessible information about where to find oil and natural gas, how to tap it efficiently, the trade-off among different energy sources, how to finance the assets, how to manage producers' risks, and, ultimately, how to reduce customers' costs and risks in this information exchange.

Second, I want to highlight the increased integration of energy and financial assets. This integration is inherent in risk management, but as Peter Fusaro notes in his chapter 2, it also involves monetizing the value of the assets, in part through the securitization process.[1]

One consequence is that, in my view, this development increases the risks that market failure in energy markets will carry over to financial markets. To give you a flavor of this dynamic, remember that in the 1980s, the failure of PennSquare Bank—an energy-related bank connected to Continental Bank—in turn led to the biggest bank failure in the United States. That occurred in an entirely different financial market from today's, but you can get a sense of the scope we could be talking about in the future.

Third, it was interesting to note the scaling back in the development of hard, physical energy assets. As others have noted, the name of the game now is to acquire existing assets and maximize value with information and financial efficiencies. That is what these companies are trying to do now—the principal way they are trying to add value.

Fourth, even with less development of new oil production, the world probably will have ample supply, if the world remains relatively open to intermediation and development of these existing productive assets.

Fifth, I think it is very interesting that even though the energy sector may be less important economically for the United States and other countries given the reduction in the energy component of production, the Persian Gulf is relatively more important because of its role as the low cost producer.

Sixth—moving to what I think is a key theme, is increased volatility—Catherine Mann's study [chapter 4] triggers a host of recollections about the effects of greater volatility in integrated capital markets. Just think about what happens in integrated capital markets when you can process information faster and transmit decisions much more quickly through the networks. You have had some anecdotal examples. The good news is that individual users will have tools to manage the risks and dampen them, but the system as a whole is going to face larger and more frequent movements.

Coming back to Lincoln Bloomfield's point, this increased volatility will cause problems for people who do not manage risk well, just as has happened in national financial systems. Over time, the markets will get better and better at risk management. Just think, however, of the fallout from the Asian financial crisis, all the discussion about how the IMF was involved and how its support creates a moral hazard.[2] In a sense, you could see that whole debate and set of problems show up in this broader energy-financial market.

The seventh point is a key reminder that integrated markets and risk management are based on two key assumptions that people sometimes forget when they talk about theory as opposed to institutional reality. The first assumption is that these calculations are based on certain parameters and certain assumptions about these parameters. As we have seen in financial markets, some of these parameters are based on historic assumptions about how different things interrelate. Some of them are based on historic assumptions about ranges of movement.

Long-Term Capital Management was a classic case of people making certain assumptions about how certain financial instruments related to each other—and yet they didn't. Now the markets have learned. For some of you who watch closely what happens in the long-term Treasury market when prices go up sharply, the developments in early 2000 would have led some people to assume that there would have been another problem in the market because the historical relationships between long-term Treasuries and other financial instruments were thrown awry. Yet instead we find that the market had adjusted. I would say, in this case, that as we learn how the energy and financial markets interrelate, there will be lessons. Indeed, there will be failures, just as there was in the case of LTCM.

The second key assumption about integrated markets is that they have to have an ability to clear. Keep in mind that with financial markets, this is partly the role of capital: Capital allows institutions to bear losses and still perform contractual responsibilities. In the energy case, I think there is going to be another distinction, however: At some point in the process one has to deliver hard commodities to points on the map. People still have to use energy commodities; it is not just a question of electronic notations and an income statement or balance sheet.

Financial markets have problems when they cannot clear. I was at the Treasury Department in 1987, and the big worry at the time of the stock market crash was not whether the markets would equilibrate; of course they would. The question was whether you would have a host of firms go down in the meantime, having lost their capital, and then they would not be able to perform on their contracts. If this had happened, the markets would have had difficulty clearing quickly, exchanges would have frozen, and confidence could have been hit—reinforcing a downward spiral. So this assumption on clearing leads to the question of the duration of the swings and the ability of capital to cushion volatility. One company on whose advisory board I serve has a strategy in this market that is quite advanced. It assumes that there is a need for a market maker to have physical resources, which is different than intermediaries in most financial markets.

Eighth, given these changes, I would ask: What actors or actions would disrupt the availability of the system?—and, as subquestions about such disruptions: How much, how long, and how frequently?—because the nature of these disruptions could lead to perceptions of insecurity of access among players.

The ninth point starts to move to the geopolitical: I think emerging powers and those less used to markets may be particularly sensitive to the complexities of this dependence and the uncertainty factor. To link this topic to a subject that Paul Wolfowitz and I have written about, some of the changing shifts in power relationships in the world today are eerily similar, and you can draw analogies to what happened about 100 years ago. So you have to factor in how countries view themselves and their relationships with other powers, in addition to changes in this marketplace.

My hypothesis is that the first impulse, particularly for emerging powers and those less likely to know markets, is to try to assure their own access. They will not recognize that the global commodity market leads to extraordinary interconnections. To be fair to them, people in the United States don't either. They still assume that we can have independent energy security, and people even talk about being "separate" from the world. That is a trick when you have a market for a fungible commodity with a world price and, moreover, when your growth depends on everyone else's growth.

So we shouldn't be too hard on what I suspect will be Chinese or Indian efforts to secure their own access to resources. I would look at how China is going to view its national interest relationships with Central Asia, Russia—or, to be more accurate, parts of Russia that are sources of energy—and the Gulf. I suspect the same thing is going to happen with India as its market reform process moves forward.

Tenth: My sense is that a producer strategy of keeping supplies off the market is of very limited political use unless an actor can dominate a key supply region over time. Why? Because given the markets we have described, others will offset short-term supply disruptions. Strategic reserves remain very important. There is a reference in Dr. Franssen's commentary (chapter 3) about policies to promote strategic reserves for other countries. Oil exporters will need to keep in mind that they do not gain if their high prices create recessions—or worse, lead to substitute resource development or more exploration and development.

The ringer here, however, given what we have said about the marketplace, is that a player who dominates the Persian Gulf could play for larger stakes. The Gulf is the one region with that potential. That brings us right back to the questions of what is Iraq's real strategy? Is it continuing to develop weapons of mass destruction? Is it developing missiles? How do these possibilities relate to Iraq's long-term strategy in the region and perceptions of whether it is on the rise or falling as a power? I would add, tangentially, that I do not think the United States has been doing so well on that front.

Eleventh: Other than the aforementioned problem, the greater concern from the security side is the short- or medium-term disruption, which leads to a focus on choke points that could trigger volatility relationships that fall outside prevailing assumptions. People have mentioned transit risks, including disruptions in sea-lanes. I would broaden transit risks to include the whole scale of distribution, transportation, and grid infrastructure; that also includes, in my view, the whole information technology system on which this is based. Information technology attacks, terrorist attacks that could disrupt choke points, and missiles that target transit points could move the price range outside expectations. All of these possibilities are security issues that affect this new marketplace.

Twelfth: Japan has assumed for 40 or 50 years that the U.S. Navy's Seventh Fleet provides its energy security. The Navy provides the assurance of the old-fashioned transit system. If that confidence ever erodes, what does Japan do? What becomes Japan's security response?

The thirteenth point, which is related to the twelfth, is a question I asked my midshipmen at the Naval Academy: If you were a policy official in China, would you accept the Seventh Fleet as your guarantor of security? Japan does; will China? If not, and if China decides that it needs to build its own maritime force, what will be the second-order effects on Japan and other countries if China develops a major blue-water navy? This issue takes you into the whole question of what type of security and alliance structure we should be developing to deal with the possibility of these changed circumstances.

The fourteenth and final point—and perhaps my greatest concern—is that all of these changes, with private markets integrating on the product, financial, and information sides, are taking place in an international economic system that reveals a lot of tension among key players today. I would just cite the breakdown of the December 1999 World Trade Organization (WTO) meeting in Seattle, at which I think many people thought, "Well, there are differences, but at least they can get this trade round launched." It ought to be a wake-up call that the key parties all approached this round in such a defensive fashion they could not even get a negotiation launched.

On top of that you have public anxiety, driven in part by deeper global integration. This anxiety is not just a matter of radical reactions from activists such as Ralph Nader. When Europeans do not trust their own food, health, and safety systems because of their own history with food problems and blood supplies, it is not surprising that in a world of deeper integration they are going to question their food from other countries.

So I am concerned that the trading negotiations and system are not moving ahead. The handling of disputes is eroding confidence in the dispute-resolution mechanism, not because of a fault in the mechanism but because of resistance to rulings in these cases and lack of political ability to resolve them. Political ability to resolve these issues is weakening at exactly the time that volatility is likely to lead to more public demands and public insistence on government action. When we deal with volatility, the key question is, what are the parameters and assumptions of the marketplace in which it is going to operate? That question leads us to a series of financial questions related to capital and how one manages the institution and exchanges of the system.

Recognize also, however, that we are dealing with real people here, and real people are going to object to extreme volatility, as we have seen even in this country in extraordinary economic times. Over time, the market can partly get better at handling volatility. For example, a company can go to a risk management business and say, "We need certainty of supply, within certain prescribed parameters and assumptions, for energy at a certain price for 10 years." How are average individuals going to cope with these things, however?

I think the solution is not what the United States did in the 1970s, which was to control prices and restrict and regulate. That makes the problem much worse. You need to think of strategies that help people adjust or in some way expedite the adjustment process. These strategies relate to a free trading system but also to everything from education to worker retraining and, in the energy field, to things such as short-term income support for affected people in certain categories.

We have to come back, however, to the questions of how to offer this adjustment support without creating a vested interest structure that perpetuates the subsidy and how to avoid the moral hazard issue. Underlying these specific concerns is the whole question about how our political and social systems can adapt to this increased volatility. Those are the conclusions that I have drawn at this point.

Yukio Okamoto

I am only going to speak about three points. Because I am the only Asian on the panel, my comments center on the situation as it is viewed from Japan. Clearly in that part of the world, the most important unknown factor is China. Adam Sieminski and Kevin

Nealer touched on it, but I want to ask the audience a question: How many of you think that sometime in the twenty-first century, Chinese per capita GDP will reach one-half of the per capita GDP of Japan today, in the year 2000? I think it will. It is not an unrealistic situation to perceive, but how it translates into reality may be very important.

Chinese per capita GDP is one-seventieth of Japan's today, so to assume that China's per capita GDP will come to one-half of Japan's means that China's per capita GDP will increase 35-fold. Do you think this is unrealistic? No, it is not. Japanese per capita GDP grew 35-fold over the past 40 years. China today is growing at a faster pace than Japan did in those years. Although we must welcome Chinese economic development, maybe 40 years from now China will be consuming 35 times as many resources as today. Of course, they are not going to eat 35 times more food, but the country's potential to consume resources, including oil, will be enormous.

In the short term, China's quest for oil will be a nightmare for U.S. security policy officials. They will have to go out to Iran, Iraq, Sudan, and other countries with which the United States does not have friendly relations, as well as Southeast Asian coastal areas. A 35-fold increase in Chinese per capita GDP also means that we have to multiply that against their impressive population of 1.3 billion. So we are talking about a new economic equivalent population of almost 40 billion people coming to earth anew. If you add India to that projection, it is almost unimaginable how the earth can sustain such an explosion of economic resource consumption unless something is done very quickly on the supply side.

My second point concerns the Japanese role. Japan has to be commended on what it has done with its own economy. Conservation of energy has really changed the economic and industrial structure of Japan. We are consuming much less oil for economic growth than during the time of the oil crisis in the 1970s, but the Japanese effort has not been exported elsewhere in Asia. Moreover, Japanese diplomacy for securing resources and diversifying its energy sources has not been very successful, in my view.

Japanese dependence on Middle Eastern oil was less than 80 percent during the time of the initial oil crisis. It has gone up, not down, by 10 percent since then. You may be aware that Saudi Arabia, at the end of February 2000, rejected the renewal of the expiring concession agreement sought by Japan's Arabian Oil Company. We in Japan have not been able to establish a credible and coherent policy toward the Middle East. During the 1970s oil crisis, we had been very passionate in cultivating a new relationship with the Middle Eastern countries. Once that crisis was over, however, we went back to where we were. It is doubtful that we have established very trustworthy channels with oil producers in the Gulf.

What should the Japanese role be? I think we ought to be leading Asian efforts to go forward with alternative sources of energy supply. I sit on the Working Group of the Japan Atomic Energy Commission, and we are working on the long-term energy policy of Japan, especially with regard to nuclear energy. Japanese nuclear electricity production has gone up substantially. At the time of the oil crisis, it constituted only 0.3 percent of the total Japanese energy supply. Now it is up to 14 percent. Looking to the year 2010, the Japanese government projects this figure to increase to 17 percent.

Considering only electricity, 37 percent of total electricity used in Japan comes from atomic energy, whereas the figure for China is a mere 0.2 percent. China is going to build many nuclear reactors. My view is that Japan really should be in the forefront of transferring nuclear technology for peaceful uses, as well as the monitoring regime, to the new nuclear builders in Asia: China, India, Vietnam, and others. Japan has been very shy about doing that, however, because it is still shackled with its political past.

The third point concerns the Japan-U.S. relationship. The two preceding points come back to this important theme of the Japan-U.S. alliance. Kevin Nealer told us that there is a lack of back-channel dialogue between the two countries. I agree. The past decade has been a lost cause. We were good at solving problems, but once the problems were gone, Japan was off the radar screen in Washington. This may sound harsh, but there does not seem to be a great deal of substance, good or bad, in policy consultations between the U.S. and Japanese governments at this point in early 2000.

There are many things we have to sit down and talk about with each other. If you term the Sino-U.S. relationship a strategic partnership, then the U.S. and Japan have to talk anew—something more than just the beautifully dubbed themes of a "common agenda." Scientific cooperation is fine; drug and medical cooperation are fine. There is something fundamentally important for the United States and Japan to talk about in frank terms, however.

Japan must go for nuclear power generation, yet the United States does not want Japan to use spent fuel. Although it does not explicitly say so, it does not support Japan transporting processed spent fuel. The United States does not seem to like Japan going for a fast breeder reactor, much less going for nuclear fusion. Well, let's sit down and talk about it. If you really are opposed to such Japanese policies, we have to talk about alternatives.

We have to talk about Saudi Arabia. Obviously if we take a 10- to 20-year view, Saudi Arabia is the most important factor in the oil situation. The internal political stability of that kingdom is a mutual concern, a mutual interest for the United States and Japan. There must be many ways we can complement each other's efforts to promote the stability of that kingdom. Japan cannot do that alone. The Saudis do not really listen to a country without international security power, but we have means to help them economically and technologically. A Japan-U.S. alliance of efforts in Saudi Arabia would be beneficial to the entire global energy situation.

We have to talk about China. With more decentralization than centralization, more centrifugal forces at play than centripetal forces, China inevitably will strengthen its nationalism because communism is no longer effective in uniting the people. Rising nationalism in China, by definition, tends to be anti-foreign, anti-Japan, and anti-United States. We cannot say, "Hey, China, you mind your own internal situation; if you don't want to have a relationship with us, that's fine." No, we cannot say that because of their importance and their potential energy requirements. So, how are we going to talk with China? Japan cannot do that alone. There has to be a U.S.-Japan alliance.

It is almost pathetic that Japan, under the two rounds of the Miyazawa plan,[3] gave $80 billion to Asian countries and got no recognition for what it did. I recently visited all of those recipient countries, which gave a whole-hearted welcome to the initiative, whereas it was greeted with a sneer and sarcasm in the United States. This is really not the way to conduct the Japan-U.S. alliance.

I think we need to talk about credible crisis management policies. What are we going to do about a Chinese thrust into the Indian Ocean through Myanmar? What are we going to do about the security of the sea lines of communication? The challenges I have tried to highlight really come down to the U.S.-Japan relationship that, in frank terms, seems to have eroded over the past 10 years or so.

We must sit down together and start a dialogue directed at the core issues for our two countries.

Janne E. Nolan

I would like to address three themes. One is the discussion of the oil industry as a metaphor for the broader phenomenon of globalization—not just globalization of financial and industrial interests but globalization of governmental interests as well. Second are the implications for our security instruments, focusing on the United States, and third, what I think are the key flash points as we consider this issue.

I was really struck by Peter Fusaro's analysis of the commoditization of the energy industry, the parallels to the defense industry, and some of the similar implications that emerge from analysis of the two sectors. With regard to some of the observations he makes about the progressive ascendance in importance of market forces and technology's influence, these trends have largely rendered obsolete many of the supply management techniques, as he put it, that were used by producers in the past.

This observation would be applicable to the defense industry as well. It has clear implications for some of the ways we think about managing the diffusion of technology—specifically military technology. In the defense sector, we increasingly see an eroding demarcation between defense technology and commercial technology, with a clear shift toward emphasis on the latter—to a point that it is difficult to make distinctions between the two.

The declining role of government in both cases—that is, declining not in its importance but in its ability to observe and monitor, and certainly to control, the activities of industry and the disposition of resources—is critical. The U.S. government used to be the main agent of technological innovation, whether it was satellites, computers, or other breakthrough technologies. In terms of investment, it is now a small fraction of the overall engine of innovation. The defense industry also has become multinationalized, from the standpoint of the United States as a consumer of goods for technical defense innovations and for U.S. industry as an exporter and active producer of goods.

The point of all this is that, in drawing these similarities, it is important to look at how structural these trends are across industries. Moreover, it is important to understand the degree to which protectionist instruments have become ineffectual, if not counterproductive, in large areas. The idea of sovereign-based production and sovereign-based goods, on which the whole protectionist export control apparatus control rests, has really disappeared. The premises have disappeared, for the most part, for all but a fraction of highly specialized military components, such as missile guidance, but not much more than that. So what we are finding instead is the challenge of governments managing large-scale economic activities over which they have very little authority and about which they have very little knowledge.

It is interesting to participate in a group such as this, which has expertise beyond traditional security experts. At the risk of insulting my colleagues here, security experts are notoriously ignorant about financial markets, economics, and economic trends. Most of them do not make a lot of money, so they are not that concerned about many things that really are directly vital. Bob Zoellick also was at the meeting at the Aspen Strategy Group the year that the Russian ruble collapsed. We had a very different mixture of people than is usually in attendance at the Aspen Strategy Group, especially individuals from international finance and banking. All of the visitors had cell phones and were working them hard—as much to find out the impact on their respective personal interests and portfolios as to obtain the most current news about what was going on. There really is a culture clash here in terms of government and industry, which I think is very pronounced.

What does this mean in terms of policy? One of the weakest links in the defense world with regard to issues such as management of technology diffusion—"proliferation," as we call it—is the absence of any kind of strong linkage between industry and government to help develop regimes for technology diffusion that are not based on outmoded concepts of sovereignty and might actually work. We need to create a situation in which government and industry are not in competition with one another, fighting over policy instruments that serve neither business interests nor, ultimately, security interests.

The second theme relates to implications for key elements of American military strategy. First, on the energy security front, it is not clear that we have ever had an energy security policy, at least at the national level, and that has been a matter of deliberate avoidance. In the 1984 presidential election campaign there was a struggle over this issue in the Democratic Party platform; a minority plank of the platform said that the United States should seek to diversify its oil dependency away from the Persian Gulf. That plank was rejected by the Mondale camp as far too radical. It was therefore adopted as a minority plank and left to languish. The argument at the time was, "Can you imagine Americans accepting a dollar a gallon for gasoline? There would be insurrection."

Second, aside from an energy security policy, it is not clear that a military strategy that would be very important in securing supplies of oil now and in the future really is all that well aligned with these interests. Someone mentioned collapsing states. Many of the regions that we are talking about where there might be new sources of oil supply teeter on the edge of stability or instability, as well as on the edge of abortive efforts at democratization and economic improvements. We still are not very good at promoting these kinds of things or understanding shared interests in difficult regions, not least because of our relationship with Russia; I will not go into that issue, but it is obvious.

In addition, the risks addressed earlier offer excellent examples of how much preparation remains to be done. As Bob Zoellick said, we are talking not just about conventional transit risks but cyber-attacks, space, and other areas that are central to our interests in the globalized, information-driven economy.

My third theme addresses how we deal with regions and their complexities, as well as with specific countries. As Yukio Okamoto mentioned, many of the countries in the particularly vital region of the Persian Gulf are facing difficult political transitions, with Saudi Arabia the most important for immediate U.S. interests. We are not paying as much attention as is warranted to the potential for disintegration of a legitimate government in a state that continues to try to retain a government apparatus that is not really in sync with the modern currencies of power.

I conclude by listing four of what I believe to be our weakest areas with respect to the concept of energy security and global security. First is the United States' relationship with Russia. We are still dependent on what is essentially a relationship based on deterrence by force; we have not really moved beyond the force calculus very effectively.

Second is the concept of "rogue" states, which I do not think is very useful. I tell my students not to use this concept, which I find reminiscent of much of the rhetoric that was used about OPEC in the 1970s—"a band of anarchists, renegades, bent on global disruption, with no stakes in the international system." Such rhetoric is not helpful.

Third is our relationship with China, which we have discussed a bit already. As we continue to hold relations with this country, in particular, hostage—perhaps unavoidably—to domestic politics, we are extremely hamstrung in being able to do anything innovative.

Fourth is the way in which we deal with the looming trends of vast economic disparities across the globe, coinciding with the rise of populations in the poorest regions of the world—demographic trends of people (mostly young) who are going to make huge demands on social infrastructure. We are not really thinking seriously about the implications of that trend for future stability.

To end on a high note: In the United States, groups such as this make clear that we have the ability to recognize these issues and to move forcefully. As long as we have Rich Armitage behind this kind of initiative, we probably can feel a little better than the foregoing comments suggest.

Robert A. Manning

One of the biggest problems we have is bridging the gap between the reality of energy security and the perception of it by many of the key actors. By this I mean the kind of scarcity mentality that animates a lot of policy, versus what I see as essentially an energy glut—an oversupply problem—certainly over the next 10 years and, I would argue, possibly over most of the next quarter-century. Why do I say that?

Let me touch briefly on Peter Fusaro's study on oil and the revolution in the oil industry, in terms of turning it into a commodity very much like financial markets and in terms of the technology of finding and producing it. We are getting twice as much out of wells as we did 20 years ago, for example. As Amy Jaffe points out, it is much cheaper now to get oil at 7,000 feet under water—less than $5 a barrel.

Second, I think one of the interesting things in the whole field of energy is new technology. We are seeing advertisements for Toyota's new Prius gas-electric hybrid car, which gets something like 60–70 miles per gallon. The entire auto industry is moving in this direction, and many people consider these hybrid cars a transition technology, heading toward fuel cells. What is going to happen to the demand for oil when cars are getting 70–80 miles per gallon instead of getting 15, or maybe even running on hydrogen and fuel cells? By the period 2005–2010, when I anticipate that some of these technologies will begin to be mass-marketed in a big way, the world is going to look very different if the emerging Chinese middle class is driving fuel cell cars than if it is driving traditional internal combustion engine cars.

So you add all that up, and you consider countries that have run afoul of U.S. policies. (I don't use the term "rogue states.") We have sanctioned a lot of the major oil producers. Recent elections in Iran suggest the possibility of change in the Gulf region. It is conceivable that five years from now Iran may be, if not a friendly actor, certainly a neutral actor from Washington's perspective. There is a lot of oil to develop in Iraq, Iran, Libya, and places like that; when you add all that up, it seems to me that we have plenty of oil. OPEC is shutting in almost 5 million barrels a day to keep the prices high. Therefore, scarcity should not be the prime consideration in fashioning energy policy.

Having said that, I want to focus on the geopolitics of these oil markets—the revolution in the oil markets. What I see as a structural trend is a kind of bifurcated market. One of the best-kept secrets in Washington may be that we get very little of our oil from the Middle East; it is probably 10 percent or less of our total oil consumption. In this bifurcated market, we are getting oil either from the North Atlantic basin (the North Sea, offshore West Africa) or Latin America; these sources make up the bulk of our oil supply. That is the good news for American energy security. The potentially bad news is that most—60 percent or more already, and by 2010 about probably two-thirds—OPEC production in the Middle East will be going to East Asia. So we are beginning to see a kind of Asia-Middle East energy nexus forming. The big question Bob Zoellick touched on is, What does this mean?

That nexus is a key strategic issue, and it relates to this gap between perception and reality. Scarcity is one myth; I want to mention several other myths. Some people have suggested that the Caspian is going to be a new panacea, but it is not—certainly not any time soon. Given the layers of problems, from drilling to geopolitics to the political risk in that region, it is going to be a long time coming. Even then, it may be, at best, another North Sea—which is not anywhere near the oil reserves and production potential of the Persian Gulf.

Now we see this Asia-Middle East energy nexus forming. Perhaps I was one of the very few who noticed, while we were having our Thanksgiving turkey in November 1999, that Jiang Zemin showed up in Saudi Arabia. It was the first time a Chinese president has ever visited Saudi Arabia; using some very interesting language, he declared a strategic oil partnership. This gives you a flavor of where these relationships are going.

Looking at demand for most Asian countries, notably Japan and China, future projections start from their present import levels of about 12 million barrels of oil per day, roughly 75 percent of it from the Middle East. My assessment is that they are going to be importing somewhere between 17 and 19 million barrels by 2010; by 2020 they probably will import 24–30 million barrels a day. To repeat, I think there is plenty of oil out there. The question is one of price, and there is obviously going to be a lot of commercial competition.

Most of this oil is going to be coming from the Middle East. The capital flow issue has been touched on already. By rough calculation, if you have 20–25 million barrels a day coming out of the Gulf at $20 per barrel, you are looking at $150 billion dollars in annual revenues. Where is that revenue going to go?

I think we have huge problems in the Gulf. Demographic problems—as we see in Saudi Arabia and Iran, for example—are big issues. Political change in Iran, it seems to me, is playing out in our direction. Saudi Arabia is a wild card; I would not want to speculate on its future. What I see happening broadly, however, in the patterns of this nexus, is mostly a commercial relationship. That is, what I see is Asians trying to go upstream and invest in Middle East production, and Arabs and Gulf states trying to invest in downstream Asian refining, marketing, and so on. I do not see any real problem here. They are both covering their markets—one covering supply and the other covering demand—and that is positive.

People are nervous about China: What are the Chinese going to do? I have tried to examine this question carefully in a book that analyzes Chinese military sales in the Middle East.[4] Interestingly, the actual correlation between energy codependence and military cooperation is the opposite of what people fear. If anything, these arms sales are diminishing. The question, then, is, How is China perceiving this whole thing? Are they—as American officials having been telling them for a while now—accumulating more shared interest with us? Perhaps they learned that giving Iran the capability to disrupt tanker traffic in the Gulf is going to disrupt their oil; that is one interpretation.

The larger question Bob Zoellick raised is, For how long and how comfortable is China going to be with the U.S. Navy guaranteeing its sea lines of communication, which are critical to its energy security?

I think this is a very big question. My view, however, is that the whole sea lane issue is misunderstood. Some of the studies that the Center for Naval Analysis has done about the cost of going around Australia and other routes in that region document that alternatives are available and manageable.

When we talk about these sea-lanes, however, we are talking about $2 trillion in annual trade; it seems to me that disrupting the sea-lanes is the economic equivalent of using nuclear weapons. We need to be thinking in terms of Chapter 7 of the UN Charter, and what would need to be done on a regional basis.[5] We need to think about giving the Chinese security assurances about the sea-lanes. It is difficult to foresee a circumstance in which the United States would cut off China's oil other than a protracted World War II-type conflict—which itself is difficult to envision given the nature of modern warfare. If such a security assurance slows down their quest for a blue-water navy, that is something we ought to be thinking about.

The real danger here is this perception problem. Consider if China continues toward a blue-water navy. If you read the literature in India, the Indians also are talking about a blue-water navy; and Japan is not going to be far behind. A naval arms race in Asia will not enhance security in Tokyo, New Delhi, or Beijing; it will increase the likelihood of conflict. The problem of energy security, and the threats I see, are all in the nature of short-term disruption. If there is a revolution in Saudi Arabia, you can have 100 aircraft carriers, but you are still going to have an oil problem. So there is a disjuncture between the kind of thinking on energy security that has real practical consequences in my mind. If you do have this naval arms race, I am not sure anybody ends up being more secure in any way.

The other big question this nexus raises is one of burden sharing. I do not see any alternative to the United States remaining the guardian of the Gulf for the foreseeable future; yet we already have Japan talking about lowering its host nation support for U.S. forces in Japan. Who benefits most from our guarding the Gulf? It is Asia first, and Europe to a lesser degree. I think this has the potential to be a political issue in the United States over time. We can all make sophisticated arguments about how oil is fungible and, therefore, we are protecting our own interests, but we are still left with a disproportionate share of the burden being borne by the American taxpayer. When we are talking about the purchasing power of the EU and Japan, we are not exactly talking about Bangladesh. This issue is looming out there, and we need to think about it.

Yukio Okamoto mentioned Japan's nuclear energy, and again we find a perception gap; indeed, Japan offers a classic example. Let me just cite two of their biggest failed industrial policies. By my calculation, the Japan National Oil Corporation (JNOC) has spent $41 billion since its inception. With the loss of the Arabian Oil Company's concession in Saudi Arabia, they now have a grand total of perhaps 400,000 barrels a day in global production to show for it. Subsidizing companies to make bad investments does not seem to have gained Japan much in energy security.

Similarly, in pursuing the back end of the nuclear fuel cycle—which makes absolutely no economic sense whatsoever—Japan has spent at least $31 billion over the past three decades.[6] If Japan had invested these funds in gas trunklines and infrastructure to expand home and office utilization of natural gas rather than spending it on JNOC and the nuclear fuel cycle, it would have done far more to ensure its energy security.

I also think Japan would get more energy security if it accelerated deregulation because Japan pays the highest cost of any country in the world for energy. Again, do you go with markets or allow notions of scarcity to shape your policy? We also are seeing this kind of scarcity thinking to some extent in China, although the good news is that China does not have nearly as much money to make bad decisions as does Japan.

You may recall that in 1997 the Chinese state oil company, CNPC, made several big purchases around Central Asia, particularly in Kazakstan. I was doing research, and I was poking around China. Because of shifts in domestic pricing, CNPC had accumulated a lot of cash and had to spend it. This imperative dovetailed with People's Liberation Army thinking along the lines that, "We need oil, so let's go get some."

CNPC went out and pursued investments in Venezuela, Sudan, Iraq, and Iran in addition to Kazakstan, with the idea of securing production in those countries for China's own future needs. Chinese refineries, however, are incapable of processing most of the kind of oil that comes out of the Gulf; it is sour crude. They are going to have to spend a fortune to be able to do that. The rumor mill in Beijing was that the officials who had made these expenditures were last seen in a reeducation camp, courtesy of Jiang Zemin, for having wasted all this money. So the West does not hold a patent on flawed thinking with regard to energy planning.

Paul D. Wolfowitz

Although I am in the cleanup position, I am going to talk about the past and about history, which I still think is relevant to the future. I have one point, and it takes the form of a sermon on a text. The text has an anonymous author; I am not sure who originally came up with this line. I thought it was Don Keegan or Fred Ikle, but they both disowned it. It may have been my own teacher, Albert Wohlstetter.

At any rate, the text is as follows: "History has more imagination than all the scenario writers in the Pentagon." We have had a very useful set of papers built around scenarios, and I think it is terrific. It is particularly terrific if you use scenarios the way they ought to be used—which is not to say, "Here are two scenarios; let's figure out which is the right one" but "Here are two scenarios, and let's think of how many more there might be." What you usually will find is that history has thought of a few that you didn't anticipate.

You may think that it is easy to do better than the Pentagon. My first tour there was in a place called Program Analysis and Evaluation (PA&E), in the late 1970s.[7] In fact, when I got started on Persian Gulf security, to my amazement this initiative was the Pentagon's first serious look at Persian Gulf security, at least in living memory. My colleagues in PA&E said, "Why bother doing that? The Shah will take care of the Gulf for us" (this was in 1977). I did not claim to think the Shah would be gone as quickly as he was, but it did seem to me that such a view was a bit shortsighted.

It wasn't just PA&E where such views prevailed, however; it was the intelligence community. We turned to the intelligence community and asked what was the Soviet threat to the Persian Gulf, and they said, "There is no Soviet threat to the Persian Gulf." Well, what about those 23 divisions in the southern military districts of the Soviet Union? "Oh, those are very low readiness divisions, and besides, the Soviets would never divert to a secondary theater when Europe is the main action." Similarly, we asked them about the Iraqi and Iranian threats to the Gulf. We were told, "One Arab state would never attack another Arab state." So we decided to do away with the intelligence annex that we were going to do for this study and wrote a historical annex instead.

This historical annex examined the three previous Soviet—and I emphasize Soviet, not Russian—invasions of Iran; the first occurred during the 1917 Revolution, and the last one came in 1946. The most interesting invasion turned out to be the 1941 invasion of Iran, which initially was planned as part of the Stalin-Hitler pact when the Soviets were given that area as their sphere of influence. The plan had to be revised because by the time they executed it, Germany was invading Russia and Britain was an ally of the Soviet Union; nevertheless, they invaded Iran to establish a secure route to the Persian Gulf.

We have a German translation of the captured Soviet plan for the invasion of Iran in 1941, and it is almost a blueprint for how they later went into Afghanistan. Those very low readiness divisions are mobilized by bringing in reservists. You send airborne troops in to seize key sites such as bridges, some of them far ahead because the people in between are not terribly good at defending them. It turns out that although mountains can be a big obstacle if they are defended, there is a great advantage to a blitzkrieg kind of offense, as the Russians showed in Iran in 1941 and again in Afghanistan in 1979.

In 1961, when Kuwait declared independence, everyone in the Pentagon seemed to have forgotten this history. The Iraqis challenged this declaration; they said Kuwait was the eighteenth province of Iraq. They mobilized forces on the Kuwaiti border. The

British rejected Iraq's claim and sent a brigade of royal marines, and that was the last we heard of it for quite a few years.

The point is that there really is a lot you can learn from the past, and the most important thing you can learn from the past is the unpredictability of the future. Things happen that we do not plan on, and if you base your policy on a sort of single-point prediction—in this case, either that oil is going to be abundant or that oil is going to be scarce—you are almost certain to make a mistake. What you need as much as possible, although obviously there are limits on how far you can go with this, is the flexibility to adjust to different situations.

It also is worth pointing out that one of the things that has fluctuated over the years has been American military capability in the Persian Gulf. In fact, for the first half of the Cold War, we were not relying on the Shah. We were relying on the British, and they did a pretty good job of it. They pulled out of Aden in 1970, and some people said there would be a power vacuum in the Persian Gulf. I remember that in 1970 we Americans had more or less had our fill of involvement in anything called the Third World. That school of thought prevailed and said, "Vacuum shmacuum; this is old Cold War thinking; people do not fill vacuums."

Three years later, in 1973, we had the first—and I believe only—serious use of Persian Gulf oil as a political weapon in the past 50 years when, during the middle of the Arab-Israeli War, they declared an oil embargo. Although the embargo was short and its effects were limited, its political effects were profound. Secretary of State Kissinger and Secretary of Defense Schlesinger made what I think were empty threats; although they were taken seriously, I am not sure what we would have done about them. This episode drove a wedge between the United States and its European allies, however, on Middle East policy that I would argue lasted almost 20 years—right up until the Gulf War.

As a result of that experience, and partly as a result of those threats made by senior American officials, when I came to the Pentagon in the 1970s it was virtually impossible to talk about Persian Gulf security. Why? Because what it conjured up most immediately was not protecting the countries of the Gulf but invading them to secure

American energy supplies. It is worth remembering that only 25 years ago, that was the main obsession. In fact, the State Department tried to kill our study because they believed that the very idea that we were studying how to protect oil fields would be misunderstood—or perhaps understood—by our Saudi friends; I am not sure which they were more concerned about.

In 1977, the Carter administration proposed to the Soviet Union that we have an Indian Ocean arms control agreement. Frankly, I suspect a lot of people here do not even know, or have forgotten, that what we proposed to the Soviet Union was limiting each side's naval capability in the Indian Ocean to something on the order of five ship-years per year. No one at the time seemed to notice that we needed the Indian Ocean to get to the Persian Gulf and that the Soviets had another way to get there. If the Soviets had not been greedy and tried to get us down to, as I recall, two or three ship-years, we might have had an agreement that would have rendered inconceivable not just operations Desert Shield and Desert Storm but also operation Earnest Will, the 1987–1988 effort to protect Kuwaiti oil tankers and other merchant traffic from Iranian mines and saboteurs in the Gulf, as well as a whole range of other security activities. We really were saved by Soviet greed from an arms control treaty that would have neutralized the Indian Ocean to America's great disadvantage.

Could we ever be so stupid again? Obviously, yes—the question answers itself. How, I cannot quite tell you. Today there seems to be a remarkable consensus on American presence in places that were controversial for 20 years; I include not only the Persian Gulf but Korea, Japan, and Europe. I hope it lasts for another 20 years, but it would not surprise me entirely if we had a Republican president and a Democratic Congress that were once again fighting over U.S. troops in Korea, Europe, and maybe the Persian Gulf.

The 1979 Soviet invasion of Afghanistan and the events surrounding Iran's revolution changed those attitudes in the United States very dramatically and very quickly. However, they did not change so fast in the Gulf, and not because the Gulf countries had a more benign view of the Soviet Union or Iran. In fact, they probably understood better than we did. Nor I do not think it is mainly, as often alleged, because the Arab-Israeli conflict drove a wedge between the Gulf countries and us and made it impossible to cooperate. It did make it costly to cooperate with us, and it continues to make it costly, although fortunately we have made some progress on those issues that has made it easier. I think the main reservation was that they harbored great doubts about whether cooperation with the United States brought any benefits. The costs were obvious to them; the benefits were not so clear.

In 1979, President Carter sent F-15s to Saudi Arabia as a show of force and American resolve in the face of the collapse of the Shah in Iran. While the planes were in the air on the way to Saudi Arabia, we announced that, consistent with the administration's arms control policy, these planes were unarmed. The Saudis were shocked and appalled. We were reminded of this episode a dozen years later, on August 5, 1990, when I went with Secretary Cheney to meet with King Fahd amid the crisis of Iraq's invasion of Kuwait.

After King Fahd had agreed to accept the unprecedented U.S. and coalition force to defend Saudi Arabia, various Saudis took some of us aside, and the message was basically the same. "If this were the same United States that sent unarmed F-15s as a show of force, we would never have said 'yes.' If this were the same United States that left helicopters burning in the Iranian desert after the failure of Desert One,[8] we would have not said 'yes.'" Just as we were starting to get all ginned up in our denunciation of those sniveling, weak, Carter Democrats, they said, "And if this were the United States that left Lebanon under Ronald Reagan after taking 241 dead Marines, and sent what we thought was the first wave of four airplanes in retaliation against Damascus, and then we learned it was the *last* wave of airplanes against Damascus—if *that* were the United States we were dealing with, we would not have said 'yes.'"

In part they were saying, "We are not so convinced you're different;" but they really were saying, "You had damned well better be different." They were expressing skepticism as well as a change of attitude. There had been a change in attitude, however partly because of Earnest Will, in which Rich Armitage played a big role. When the

Iraqis—who we were actually there to protect, although we never actually acknowledged it—took a potshot at the USS Stark and killed 26 American sailors, most of the countries in the Gulf said, "OK, that's it; the Americans are out of here." When we did not leave, it sent a very, very strong, powerful, and important signal.

I have a feeling, although I cannot prove it, that Operation Just Cause—the invasion of Panama in 1989—also contributed to the conviction that when President Bush said he would do something, he did it, and he delivered. It was absolutely crucial to putting that Gulf War coalition together. It was not telephone calls or old friendships. It was the conviction that the United States had not only the capability but the will to deliver.

Even after the Iraqi invasion, there was enormous uncertainty about what our capability was. A lot of that uncertainty had to do with politics; you cannot do an awful lot in the Gulf if you are trying to do it all from offshore because nobody is willing to have you onshore. I remember in those crucial days right after the Iraqi invasion when U.S. policy seemed to "wobble," to use Margaret Thatcher's term. I do not think that it was a lack of resolution on President Bush's part; the British like to think it was Margaret saying, "Don't go all wobbly, George," that decided everything. I think what decided everything was when King Fahd said, "Come along, we're with you," because without the Saudis there was not a whole lot we could do.

In fact, there is a circle that describes how American capability in the Gulf depends on cooperation from the Gulf countries. That cooperation depends on their estimate of our capability, and you end up with a circle—which can be a virtuous circle, when things are going well, or a vicious circle when things are going badly. I think 1991–1992 represented a peak of U.S. power, when U.S. military strength was at a maximum, the coalition was absolutely strong and firm, and potential adversaries in the Gulf were extremely weak. Iran was still on its knees from the war with Iraq, and Iraq was weak because it had just been pummeled so badly.

There has been a considerable decline in America's power in the Gulf since then. It is a decline not only in the strength of the coalition but in the readiness of American forces, although they are still formidable. The decline is important against the backdrop of growth of Iranian and Iraqi capabilities in the area of weapons of mass destruction. We are still a long way from a collapse. We are still at a very high level compared to what we had at any point prior to 1990. This is one of those things like thin ice, however: You really do not know how thin it has gotten until you have fallen through—and at that point you cannot just rebuild your capability by some brief course reversal.

I believe the effects of Desert Storm will be felt for a very long time, not just by countries in the Gulf but also (I hope) by Americans. President Clinton—forgive me if I am partisan in this respect—beat his breast and proclaimed how brave and bold we were because in 1994, when the Iraqis mobilized on the Kuwaiti border, he sent troops there to deter them. It did not take a whole lot of courage after President Bush had demonstrated what could be done. What was remarkable in 1990 was that President Bush took those decisions in the face of enormous doubts about American capability and enormous exaggeration of Iraqi capability. If we got in that situation again where it looked really dangerous to deploy forces because of, for example, Iraqi nuclear weapons, it is not so certain what we would do.

Relating these national security perspectives to the issues of energy and economics, it is important to remember that fuel prices are unpredictable, and threats in the Gulf are extremely unpredictable; hence, the real point to take from history is unpredictability. Second, the U.S. capability to project power fluctuates enormously. Listening to these presentations, I have been thinking that maybe there is a relationship here between oil prices and our capability. When prices go down, we take the whole Gulf region less seriously, and when they go up we start to think about energy scarcity. If there is a relationship, unfortunately it is with a very, very long lag-time—indeed, a very dangerous lag-time. f world prices were to stay at $30 a barrel, perhaps we would get much more serious about Gulf security, but I am not sure we will turn our capability around in time.

Third, the world's excess oil production capacity is still going to come from or through this incredibly unstable part of the world. As the recent OPEC action shows, we can be vulnerable in a regime of low energy prices or in a regime of high energy prices, as long as there is some producer who, for political or economic reasons, is prepared to shut in a lot of that. Bob Manning correctly pointed out that aircraft carriers are not going to do us any good in some scenarios, such as a revolution in Saudi Arabia. It also is worth remembering that if that revolution in Saudi Arabia were to lead to an Iraqi-controlled regime in Saudi Arabia, it would not be just a short-term disruption. It would be long-term control of the Gulf.

Fourth, I think that energy security is still incredibly important. It is not a matter of "jobs, jobs, jobs," as we mistakenly tried to justify it at one point. It is not a matter of the difference between $30 a barrel and $25, or $35; it is the danger of oil being used as a weapon, and it is the danger of all that excess money being used to build extremely dangerous and destabilizing weapons. By 1991, Saddam Hussein had gone as far as he had with weapons of mass destruction because he had all that money.

Fifth, I join my fellow panelists in dropping the term "rogue states" totally. Let me just talk about Iraq and Iran. Saddam remains a megalomaniacal leader with enormous ambitions, not just to control the Gulf but to dominate the Middle East. He could be around for quite a while. As for the Iranians, I think we are seeing very significant and positive changes there, but Iran has regional ambitions. Regional ambitions may be only regional, but the Gulf is a region in which I do not think we can afford to have anyone dominate.

There is yet another factor emerging in this region—namely China, which has been mentioned quite a bit on the panel. It is interesting to think about the fact that the U.S.-Chinese relationship with respect to the Gulf is in the nature of two competitors, both of whom are dependent on the region. Contrast that to the Cold War, when we were both dependent on the region, and the Soviets were not only independent but actually benefited from oil shortages and high prices. On the whole, it would seem that a sort of "competitive dependence," if that is the right term, does appear to introduce some elements of stability. It is particularly reassuring to hear some of the economists say that a real oil shock would do much more damage in

Asia than in the West because that statement suggests to me that China has as much interest as we do in not seeing that happen.

As others have pointed out, it is one thing to say, for example, that the United States and China have an interest in the security of the sea-lanes. Bob Manning is right that you can go around the Straits of Malacca, but you have to get out of the Gulf and get to your own ports. Yet there is a big difference between security provided by the United States to both the United States and China and security provided by China to both the United States and China. Either one of us is going to look at it very, very differently; to those who say, "Well, the Chinese would never think the United States would interfere with sea lanes," just stop and remember how World War II began in the Pacific. We were using control over Japanese sources of oil to try to force a major—and I think correct—political change in Japan's policy toward China, and the Japanese decided that they would rather fight a war to get the oil than drop their ambitions in China.

To those who think that China might not use oil as a political weapon, I just emphasize that this kind of calculation is not made with respect to normal markets or normal energy prices. It has to be judged in the context of a crisis. You could have a crisis over Taiwan, or over the South China Sea and the Spratleys. Unfortunately, Janne Nolan is right that we security types are not interested in the kinds of things that make money or the things that most people are preoccupied with today.

For better or worse, when nations go to war, economic calculations go out the window. The standard may not be how much your country will suffer but how much you can make the other side suffer—which, in fact, is exactly what happened in 1941. It is very important to think about ways of making both major powers—in this case I am referring to the West as a whole and China as an entity—confident in the security of the Gulf. I still prefer a situation in which we are a dominant power that does not abuse that domination to one in which our own supplies are vulnerable.

Finally, I do think that all of this argues the desirability of trying to reduce our dependence on the Gulf in the long term—all the more in light of Yukio Okamoto's statistics on China. As Bob Zoellick pointed out, that is not done in a segmented way. Oil is fungible, and this is an integrated market. It has to mean reducing our dependence on fossil fuels in general. I am very much inclined toward letting markets work. I agree that marginal subsidies to promote inefficient use of ethanol and more efficient use of energy in automobiles is not really where government can help the market.

On the other hand, for those of us who believe that markets are terrific, let us remember that the incredible, revolutionary innovation—the Internet—was a government creation. Let us also remember, however, that the government was not smart enough to take out any options on the Internet. Government really does have a major role in research and development, and maybe more of it would be better. I am persuaded, however, that tinkering with the markets on the margin is a very expensive business—and one we are likely to get wrong.

OPEN DISCUSSION ON FOREIGN POLICY ISSUES

Sheila Heslin, former National Security Council staff member: There may indeed be a gap between the economics of different production areas, causing companies to want to go to the Persian Gulf as a less-cost option. For policymakers, however, what can we do to try to, in essence, hedge against the unpredictability that Ambassador Wolfowitz so eloquently described?

Robert Manning: There are not a lot of good choices. When Willy Sutton was asked why he robbed banks he said, "That's where the money is." Why do you go into the Persian Gulf? Because that's where the oil is. Any way you slice it, two-thirds of the world's oil reserves are in the Persian Gulf. There is just no way to get around it. If you are an oil company, and Saudi Arabia and Kuwait are opening up to foreign investment such that you can get oil out of the ground at $2 per barrel, or offshore West Africa at $4 per barrel, why are you going to go to Kazakhstan or Azerbaijan—where you need $13 or $14 per barrel to make money—and put up with all the corruption and other problems?

I think what you have seen is that the oil companies, certainly in Central Asia, have poked around and have somewhat soured on it.

One oil company executive commented to me that, on reflection, the Russians had not done that bad a job looking for oil in this area, given the limits of their technology. So I may be totally wrong—we might find another giant, double-Tengiz somewhere—but I do not think there are a lot of choices. What choices we do have relate to our own domestic policies—for example, accelerating the movement toward hybrid or fuel cell cars and lowering demand. More efficiencies like that are things we can do, that anyone can do. Deregulation is something the Japanese certainly can do; I would look more to that than to alternative energy sources.

Robert Zoellick: I think the question is who the "we" are when you describe this. From a government-society point of view, it definitely is in our interest to have multiple sources of production, multiple sources of energy, and multiple access routes. The people who are making these decisions, however, have to do it on the basis of some notion of profit; given what we have described about the overall outlook, I can see why it is not in an individual company's interest to expend resources for alternative sources when they have access to a lower-cost producer.

In terms of trying to find a way to minimize exposure to volatility and maximize political reliability, I find it ironic that by having more supply out there, you actually might be increasing volatility because of this dimension relating to quicker market reactions. For society as a whole, I think, this actually is where the conservation and energy-efficiency efforts, as well as reserve stockpiling efforts, are important.

If you think about how we have talked about this, there is the disruption effect and there is the domination of Persian Gulf oil effect. For the disruption effect, you are not going to want to have an alternative Persian Gulf sitting around because that is going to affect the whole supply and demand balance. For that drawback, however, a strategic reserve could be significant and important. For the long-term effect, you cannot get around the fact that most of the supply is in the Persian Gulf; thus, it is a question of the security of the Persian Gulf. I think that is the policy linkage, too.

Paul Wolfowitz: I want to add one last thing on that issue. There is the obvious point that you cannot get around the importance of the

Persian Gulf. If Central Asian oil is going to come out through the Persian Gulf, however, you have compounded the problem. That may be where we are heading if there is not going to be a Turkish pipeline and if things change enough in Iran that we do not object to an Iranian outlet from the Caspian. That is an issue that really ought to be looked at; at the moment, however, we seem to be telling the oil companies to take on a huge added cost that does not bring any economic benefit but is basically for security reasons. If establishment of alternative geographic outlets for energy really has that kind of security benefit, we should be prepared to pay for it—governments should be prepared to pay for it. I am not sure whether it has been thought about that way, but that is how I believe it has to be thought about.

Amy Jaffe: Dr. Wolfowitz correctly points out the huge factor Iraq still represents in the region as a tremendous force of instability, and I would like to hear his ideas of what should be done about it.

Paul Wolfowitz: I could go on at great and controversial length, but basically I think we are missing an incredible opportunity to really change the strategic picture in a way that would redound to our benefit in many, many ways. Saddam Hussein has certain strengths that make him dangerous. He has one enormous weakness, which is that it is reasonable to think that 98 percent of his population, at least, would like to see him hung by the heels. (I don't know the number exactly; they aren't allowed to take public opinion polls in Iraq.) That is not only 100 percent of the Kurds and 100 percent of the Shia—which together make up roughly 75 percent of the population of the country—but most of the Sunnis as well. In fact, it includes most of his close associates, every one of whom realizes that when the wheel turns he may be the next one on the chopping block.

This is not a safe man to be around, and we have done very, very little to support that kind of opposition. It has to be admitted, and I will say right away, that the first mistake was made right at the end of the Gulf War, as I said at the time, in not giving more support to rebellions in the north and the south. It also has to be said in defense of President Bush that, number one, he did heroic work in bringing us that far—for which he never gets enough credit, in my opinion.

Second, the whole situation took us kind of by surprise; nobody saw it coming. Moreover, even I did not think that Saddam would last as long as he has.

Let me also say—and I would like to correct the record because the record in print is appalling on this score—that one of the things you read is that we stopped because the Saudis told us to stop. I can categorically tell you that was not true. I was with Jim Baker on his first trip to the Gulf after the war. His first meeting in Saudi Arabia was with Prince Bandar and Saud Al-Faisal, and they spent about half an hour trying to convince us to support the Shia rebels.[9] They said they were not afraid of the Shia of Iraq, about which you know they were not entirely telling the truth. Their point, however, was, "Saddam is the greater threat. We can deal with the Shia of Iraq; they are not creatures of the Iranians, they fought for Saddam for eight years against the Iranians, they are Arabs, and we can manage."

I think that even today, if they thought the Americans had any resolve to finish the job, they would support us. The fact that they do not support us is hard to measure but is at least in part a reflection of the fact that what they do not want to see is another Desert Fox[10]— four days of pointing out that Saudi Arabia is a base for American planes to bomb Iraq, with Saddam emerging stronger than he was before.

What President Bush said to King Fahd in that phone conversation on August 4, 1990, was that, "If we come, we will finish the job." Yet we keep coming and coming and coming, and we don't finish anything. We have been bombing Iraq two or three times a week, to no effect. So I think there have been many opportunities, and if we were active and serious we could create more opportunities. It seems to me, however, that our policy really has been, "How can we maintain an Iraq policy at minimum political cost that keeps it off the front pages?" It does not matter if we are bombing three times a week as long as it is not a news story.

At some point that country [Iraq] is going to change. It is hard to see how it could get much worse. It could change in a way that would be very ugly and very messy. It seems to me that we have an opportunity to shape it in a way that actually might make it a useful American ally in the Middle East. Just stop for two seconds and think about how we would be viewing the Persian Gulf right now if Iraq were like Egypt.

Question for Robert Manning from representative of the Institute of International Relations in Taipei: Which is a more effective way for the United States to maintain sea lanes of communication in a conflict-prone area such as the Taiwan Straits: to provide more arms sales to keep a balance between both sides or to construct a unique arms control initiative, announced either unilaterally by Taiwan or bilaterally by both sides of the Taiwan Straits, that would declare the Taiwan Straits a zone of peace?

Robert Manning: My starting point is that if there is a military conflict between China and Taiwan, everybody loses. The United States is going to lose, China is going to lose, and Taiwan is going to lose. I think we get carried away because China excels at political theater, so I think it blows it out of proportion often. I am not sure what a "zone of peace" is. It seems to me that this problem has to have a political solution. I do not believe Taiwan is ripe for any kind of solution now, but I have cautious optimism that there still may be the possibility for moving things forward in terms of cross-strait interaction politically. In terms of arms control, however, Taiwan is vulnerable. It has to be able to defend itself. That is what the Taiwan Relations Act says, and I think that we are obliged to help Taiwan do that.

One concern I have is the handling of a potential sale by the United States of AEGIS cruisers to Taiwan. Taiwan's big concern is that China is going to put a deadline on reunification and force the issue before the Taiwanese have these military modernization efforts fully fielded. My question is this, however: Are we not the ones putting the deadline on? If I were a (Chinese) People's Liberation Army military planner and you told me that by 2006–2007, Taiwan is going to have PAC-3 air defense systems and four AEGIS cruisers, my conclusion might be that I have a shrinking window of time in which to deal with this militarily. I am not sure that anybody has thought this through, which is why I do not think there is a military solution in which any side is really going to benefit.

Notes

[1] Securitization is the creation of a tradeable instrument that is based on the value of a good. In this discussion, securitization refers principally to tradeable notes that are based on the current and future price of oil and gas.

[2] The term "moral hazard" refers to the concern among financial policy analysts that actors in the global economy—including governments, private financial entities, and investors—might see fit to incur greater economic risks than they otherwise would be willing to bear if they believed that losses suffered as a result of having taken those excessive risks would be compensated or cushioned in some manner by the international community, such as through the IMF.

[3] The Japanese government initiative, named for Finance Minister Kiichi Miyazawa, to provide financing to distressed Asian economies after the onset of the Asian economic crisis in 1997.

[4] Robert Manning, *The Asian Energy Factor: Myths and Dilemmas of Energy, Security and the Pacific Future* (New York: Palgrave/St. Martins, 2000), see chapter 4.

[5] Under Chapter 7 of the UN Charter, concerning "Action with Respect to Threats to the Peace, Breaches of the Peace, and Acts of Aggression," the Security Council can authorize members to "take such action by air, sea, or land forces as may be necessary to maintain or restore international peace and security" (Article 42).

[6] The "back end" of the nuclear fuel cycle refers to disposal of high-level nuclear waste and long-term storage or reprocessing of spent nuclear fuel.

[7] PA&E is a branch within the Office of the Comptroller, U.S. Department of Defense.

[8] The ill-fated U.S. hostage rescue attempt of April 25, 1980, in which three helicopters malfunctioned and a fourth collided with a C-130 transport plane full of fuel at a rendezvous location in the Iranian desert, killing eight American soldiers. The mission was aborted instead of continuing on to Teheran, where American diplomats and the embassy were held hostage.

[9] Prince Bandar Bin Sultan and Prince Saud Al-Faisal are Saudi Arabia's ambassador to the United States and foreign minister, respectively.

[10] Operation Desert Fox was a four-day U.S.-led bombardment of Iraqi targets in mid-December 1998, explained by President Clinton as a response to Iraq's continued failure to cooperate with the U.N. Security Council and its arms inspection, verification, and monitoring requirements.

PART FIVE

CONCLUSIONS

CHAPTER EIGHT

PRESERVING U.S. AND ALLIED INTERESTS IN A NEW ERA

TOWARD A NATIONAL STRATEGY

Richard L. Armitage,
Lincoln P. Bloomfield Jr., and James A. Kelly

NATIONAL INTERESTS AND NATIONAL STRATEGY

TO CONSIDER GEOPOLITICS IN THE NEW CENTURY IS TO IDENTIFY patterns of power that will define relations between and among states and their peoples. Behind these patterns lie the ambitions and survival imperatives of these actors. Nature and historical fate confer advantages on some peoples and disadvantages on others. Military superiority, economic resiliency, and political influence—and the many component elements that collectively produce such comparative advantages in the international arena—are more likely to be gained by design, however, than by mere providence and happenstance.

The twenty-first century begins with a sense of uncertainty about not only the shape of the "world order," such as it is, but also the global role to which the United States should aspire. The Clinton administration came to office in 1993 evidently hoping that international events would impose minimal claims on its attention and political capital. It left office claiming, in the words of National Security Adviser Samuel Berger, to have "completed the first peacetime expansion of our global reach since the days of Theodore Roosevelt."[1]

Conversely, since 1994 a Republican-led Congress, notwithstanding the Nixon/Ford/Reagan/Bush tradition of promoting American leadership in world affairs, carried its general lack of enthusiasm for President Clinton's executive stewardship into the realm of foreign policy. On a host of initiatives brought forward by the Clinton administration—paying the United States' back dues to the United Nations; ratification of the Comprehensive Test Ban Treaty; pursuit of strategic partnership with Beijing; and responses to situations in Haiti, Bosnia, and North Korea—congressional Republican resistance fed perceptions that the mantle of greater internationalism might have shifted from Republicans to Democrats for the first time since the Vietnam War.

Such impressions, however, may have less to do with core political ideology and more to do with the respective views from the executive and legislative branches during a discrete period of time. Contemporary political antagonisms, as well as the manner with which issues are presented and interbranch consultations conducted, also are factors. We believe that coherence in any U.S. president's approach to international affairs is a key to instilling confidence and that success abroad breeds public and congressional support at home. The recent past, in other words, may not be a reliable guide to the post-millennium American role in the world.

In this study, we have limited our focus to anticipating some of the new ways in which U.S. national interests and the interests of other countries will be affected in coming years. Where interests are considered to be at risk, it is a reasonable assumption that governments will seek to insulate these interests from risk or protect them as the need arises. Less obvious is whether advancement of a country's national interests, on the part of the United States or any other country, must equate to a proactive or interventionist approach to foreign policy.

America's unique status as the world's only superpower since the end of the Cold War has not come without costs in terms of resentment and even resistance, from traditional friends and foes alike.[2] It is one thing for Washington to defend identifiable national interests—and Americans have come to expect at least this much from any administration; it is quite another thing, however, to practice statecraft so effectively as to achieve success in cultivating and retaining preeminent political influence among nations. Credibility and goodwill in the international arena are hard-won and easily lost.

There is general agreement in the United States that wider embrace of worthy principles such as democratization, free market economics and individual rights around the world is to be desired, for a host of reasons. Yet the United States can undermine its interests if its approach purports to advance even the worthiest of principles in a manner that challenges the legitimacy or disrupts the political, social, or economic stability of other countries. Interests asserted with apparently casual arrogance can antagonize others needlessly and engender opposition even where support would be natural. It is possible, in other words, for the world's sole superpower to overreach in foreign policy—to the detriment of American influence and, ultimately, American power. On the other hand, U.S. foreign policy can be too passive if it finds its raison d'etre primarily in reacting to perceived threats as they arise.

Therefore we contend that the United States requires a national strategy to protect America's interests and to continue to foster the most universal possible identification of foreign national, economic, and individual interests with the advancement of American objectives. Updating our concepts of national interests and the potential threats to those interests, as we have sought to do in this book, is only a building block in formulating a policy approach to promote those interests. It is no substitute for clear assertion of, and commitment to, the central idea that U.S. foreign policy should seek to enhance American influence and place the weight of American "power" in the service of principles that are common to most of the world's governments and people. A foreign policy worthy of the term will elaborate the elements of a strategy for doing precisely that.

VIRTUAL REALITIES AND ENDURING REALITIES

If the many contributors to this book agree on one point, it is surely this: To comprehend U.S. national interests in the new century, the traditional foreign policy generalist's grasp of world political and military affairs will no longer suffice, if it ever did. Today's policymakers need a baseline of familiarity with the information-based international economy and its surging capital flows. They should understand key features of the global energy economy today as compared to the fateful and turbulent 1970s. Longstanding security allies and emerging economies alike are vulnerable to new kinds of perturbations as well as traditional threats.

One striking feature of the information revolution, with its increasingly robust global transmission infrastructure, is the shrinkage—if not disappearance—of transaction costs as a burden on the process of global interaction. The speed and facility of researching necessary information; the quality and affordability of desktop publishing; the seemingly limitless "disseminability" of information; and the near-instantaneous ability to authorize fund transfers reliably in a commercial transaction: All are expanding the reach of private actors, multiplying productivity, and driving economic growth.

Yet even as the efficiencies of the information revolution permeate all manner of human endeavors—from farming to law enforcement to garage sales—some tasks cannot so easily shed their physical aspect and take flight into cyberspace. As long as the world depends on crude oil for crucial energy needs, there will be no escape from the need to maintain uninterrupted access to oil reserves and to convey the oil securely from where it is produced to where it will be refined and consumed.

So it is with military operations as well. Although the U.S. armed forces are becoming sophisticated and prolific consumers of information technology, the requirement to bring potent force to bear unavoidably means having soldiers and weapons, sustainable where they are needed, at specified points on the map and at designated times. In other words, for the hydrocarbon-producing industry and for the U.S. military forces on whom much of the world relies to secure its economic lifelines, information technology affords no relief from the dictates imposed by real-world geography—not today and not in 2010.

There surely is some irony in the fact that the much-anticipated global broadband Internet, powered by massive arrays of computers and embedded processors, will add further heavy demands on the world's energy requirements.[3] Even as the information "superhighway" liberates other sectors of activity from the burdens of their inefficient old ways of doing business, it will depend critically on a secure physical supply of energy and the industries and governments that alone can provide it.

GLOBALIZATION'S PATRON SAINT: GOVERNMENT

In thinking about the information revolution, it is normal to focus on what is new about the digital world: empowerment of individuals and private activity and corresponding dilution of government's historically monopolistic influence in society. Yet as we behold the spectacle of private emancipation, it is worth remembering that the only legitimate source of sovereignty in today's world, as in the past half-millennium, is the state. For all the transformation being spawned by information technology, the Westphalian international system is in no danger of being supplanted. "Dot-com" connotes many things, but it does not mean "e-sovereignty."

Looking at the burgeoning global capital flows that are composed, to a significant extent, of the liquid, largely speculative, short-term "portfolio" investment activity of a vast universe of actors, we ought not be surprised that these actors' primary focus is to achieve higher returns on capital while minimizing risk.[4] Recent experience with capital market volatility and extreme energy price trends has shown, however, that these new and better ways to seek rewards and evade risks are only part of the portfolio investment story. There also is a dark side to greater capital mobility.

By nature, many contemporary economic actors are like party-hoppers or fair-weather friends: When the food and drinks start to run out or the storm winds start to blow, the attitude is, "It's time to go—the sooner the better, and let whatever mess is left behind become someone else's problem." When oil prices drop to $10 or rise beyond $30 a barrel, there is pain in different sectors of society. When private investment rushes, herd-like, out of a developing economy such as Thailand or Indonesia, enfeebling the local currency, large segments of society can have their lives disrupted, calamitously so. Yet to the many players exiting with the herd for fairer climes, these consequences are someone else's problem. By default if not design, that "someone else" is government.

We often hear—and did again in the course of this study—that governments should stay out of private economic matters. There is much wisdom to the general admonition against government meddling in markets. However worthy the objectives, government intervention in the workings of a free market runs the risk of unintended consequences. The code of Hippocrates—"first, do no harm"—is appropriately held to be a guiding principle by many government economists, just as it is by physicians.

Yet we feel that it is appropriate to ask unfashionable questions. It is a given that when political and military threats to the free flow of vital energy supplies arise, the United States and other advanced industrial countries will respond; dealing with such threats is a long-recognized domain of foreign policy. Now, however, we find the burden of coping with the damage caused by severe global economic volatility—much of it mainly caused by private economic activity—falling as well to the lender countries of the world. Should these governments—and the voters and taxpayers they represent—not have a voice in the workings of this international economy whose benefits so bountifully accrue to private participants? Indeed, should governments not, as a foreign policy responsibility, try to anticipate, protect against, and be prepared to redress the kinds of liabilities ingrained in the twenty-first-century global economy?

The policymaker's inclination, of course, is to say "yes." The essential issue, however, is how the United States and other governments should think about and configure their roles in relation to the private global economy. To approach that question, we believe that it is important to highlight what is significant about the changing energy and finance sectors of the international economy.

REASSESSING THE STRATEGIC SIGNIFICANCE OF OIL

Oil—a good that until recently was traded within limited, proprietary channels—has become a common commodity, traded globally on the basis of real-time price visibility. Part of this shift is attributable to the broad visibility of oil inventories, which limits the ability to declare false shortages. Notwithstanding high oil prices beginning in mid-1999, partly as a result of withholding of supplies from the world market by leading producers, oil is not likely to become physically scarce for a long time, if ever.[5] It has sharply declined in economic significance to the United States and other advanced economies. Its long-term strategic importance also is in relative decline.

That said, the relative decline in oil's strategic significance must not be exaggerated. Oil remains essential for growth, defense, and most transportation. Its supply and resupply must be assured. Any civil, military, or economic perturbation that might threaten assured oil supplies is certain to bring a strong reaction. As recent high oil prices have demonstrated, oil remains a very important commodity for the time being.

Production from the world's single most important non-OPEC source of oil, the North Sea, has peaked. The North Sea accounted for two-thirds of the Western countries' growth in oil production over the past two decades, but it will start to decline in this decade. There is no comparably large and readily accessible new source of crude oil in prospect, although there are many lesser prospects to be exploited in time.[6]

The oil industry's response to high prices has not been a seamless quest to generate new production, as economic theory might imply. During the 1998–2000 period, during which the industry diverted much of its effort toward mergers and consolidation, priority in its capital expenditures has been to improve recovery from existing oil wells rather than to pursue exploration and new production.

Western oil companies find themselves excluded from many prime production areas because of sanctions restrictions or, in Saudi Arabia, because of a national policy that excludes all foreign companies from its upstream oil sector. Exploration areas that remain for these companies to pursue may be more difficult to access, expensive to exploit, and laden with continuing political or economic risk. These considerations repel investors, who fear the return of low oil prices before they can realize the rewards of underwriting such ventures.

This combination of a shrinking oil industrial base, a preference for depleting current low-cost production sources, and lack of confidence in the profitability of financing new production ventures adds up to a time lag. There is a delayed response in the oil market to higher demand or higher prices. Recent experience shows that even the oil companies themselves see more merit in buying out a competitor or investing in secondary lines of business than in betting their fortunes on "risky" new production activities.

Thus, even if oil prices are abnormally high for a time (e.g., more than $30 a barrel), the risks of investing in new, remotely sited oil that may cost up to $14 a barrel to produce and bring to market cause uncertainty and delays in alleviating the supply shortage. Oil may be losing its significance over the long term, but the present dynamics of exploiting easy oil now and worrying about accessing harder oil later are certain to accentuate the duration, height, and depth of price swings.

Later if not sooner, however, the major Western companies, which for the most part are unable to gain profitable terms of entry into prime OPEC production areas—foremost Saudi Arabia—will go wherever they must to generate new production to maintain adequate global crude oil supplies. Once these companies commit to exploration and production ventures, new technologies will compress the usual time frame for bringing new production on line. It is conceivable that the tight, OPEC-dominated market of 2000–2001 could give way to conditions of global oversupply and lower prices within a matter of a few years.

Regardless of whether this decade brings a supply shortage, a glut, or a balanced market, however, one strategically significant reality is dictated by the decline of the North Sea and the absence of any short-term replacement. Growing global demand will refocus the world's reliance on the Persian/Arabian Gulf to satisfy a greater share of the world's growing appetite for crude oil than in the past two decades.

Therefore, for the near term at least, secure access to the Persian/Arabian Gulf and its hydrocarbon resources will remain a fundamental national interest of the United States and its allies, as well as other oil- and gas-importing countries. Beyond 2010, the world's energy map may assume different characteristics.

FUNGIBLE COMMODITY, GLOBAL MARKET—WHOSE RESPONSIBILITY TO PROTECT IT?

Rising global demand for crude oil, in this decade and beyond, will come predominantly from Asia—namely China, India, and Indonesia, as well as already significant importers such as Japan, the Republic of Korea, and others. In broad terms, it is now possible to foresee a "nexus" of convergent strategic interests between the Pacific region's major oil consumers and the Persian/Arabian Gulf oil suppliers.

This Asia-Gulf nexus will be coalescing at the same time that the U.S. market is more efficiently served by importing crude oil from nearby Western Hemisphere producers such as Canada, Mexico, and Venezuela. Over time, these regional economic convergences of interests—one in the West, one in the East—could also spawn political dimensions.

Would such a trend spell a decline of U.S. policy interest in the security and stability of the Gulf region? Our belief is that the United States will maintain its longstanding commitment to Gulf security for reasons independent of energy considerations. The fact that Saudi Arabia is likely to remain the only producing country with substantial excess production capacity in most market conditions will assure continued American interest in the Gulf on energy grounds as well.

It is less clear how strong a commitment the United States should or will undertake to secure new venues of crude oil production that will come on line with the help of major Western oil companies as North Sea production declines. U.S. policy planners have long grappled with concerns over the internal political stability of key energy producers such as Saudi Arabia, Iran, Algeria, and Indonesia, to say nothing of Iraq. To the extent that energy security remains a first-order national security concern, U.S. policy will have to take a far more proprietary interest in Azerbaijan, Kazakstan, West Africa, and even the internal Russian oil economy. There will be limits to such American interests, however.

In other words, even if the relative strategic importance of oil is on the wane, the level of political risk attending the world's crude oil supply is on the rise, if such a thing is possible after the experiences of the past quarter-century. That is the supply picture.

The demand picture also is fraught with highly significant new trends. First, increasing responsiveness to market principles in the global oil trade has made Western Hemisphere suppliers more price-competitive in the U.S. market than Eurasian producers, given the shorter distances for shipment to U.S. refineries. Yet in any future supply disruption scenario, oil prices will be essentially the same everywhere in the world. Thanks to the integrated global oil market, the effects of a supply interruption in any one place will be felt in greater or lesser measure everywhere.

U.S. officials of an earlier generation could contemplate notions of hemispheric autarky in the oil sector; that concept is now obsolete. There is no longer any realistic near-term option of isolating the U.S. economy from the vicissitudes of the global oil market.[7]

Does this mean that as an essential element of a credible "energy policy" the United States must admit to a role as protector of the world's energy supplies? Although our answer is clearly "yes," such an aspiration must take full account of the other main development in the demand sphere: the rise of China and India as the future economic giants of Asia.

MAJOR NEW OIL CONSUMERS IN ASIA

There are geopolitical implications to China's inevitable surpassing of Japan as Asia's largest consumer of imported crude oil and India's displacement of South Korea as the region's third-ranking oil importer. There is an obvious if intangible quality to the mass and presence of China and India that differentiates them from, for example, a Japan whose nearly 40-year oil concession can so perfunctorily be terminated by Saudi Arabia—as happened in February 2000.

Moreover, although neither China nor India has yet posed any threat, their suppliers in the Persian/Arabian Gulf well know that either is far more predisposed toward and capable of using military means to assert their interests than Japan or South Korea would be.

China's transition from oil exporter to net importer, concurrent with sustained and substantial economic growth, will have several implications. First, China receives growing crude oil supplies via tanker ships out of the Gulf, just as Japan, South Korea, and other East Asian consumers do. As a nation that values self-sufficiency, however, China will plow significant investment into pipeline projects to convey oil internally from its distant west to its populous east.

Second, for the same reasons, China is showing active interest in the stability of the former Soviet Central Asian republics, including the possibility of even more costly west-to-east pipelines. Part of this concern relates to tensions among China's western minority populations, who are ethnically closer to the Central Asian peoples.

Third, China's emphasis on improving relations with Russia under Vladimir Putin has a Central Asian subtext in addition to advancing the potential for connecting pipelines to the great supplies of gas in the Russian far east.

Fourth, China's people and leadership have been struck with the environmental urgency of using cleaner fuels than the powdery coal that continues to generate so much damaging particulate air pollution.

Finally, China's assertion of territorial claims to various South China Sea islands and reefs, which are in conflict with the claims of various close-by Southeast Asian states, has oil security implications. Not only do these claims relate to the vital sea-lanes running from the Gulf to Japan; they also relate to certain but as yet undefined oil and gas reserves under the mostly shallow South China Sea. Japan's foreign policy community understandably sees strategic connections between China's potential quest for influence in Burma/Myanmar, for example, and its growing stake in energy supplies and sea-lanes from the Gulf to northeast Asia.

To these considerations we add the factor of India, which recently has given rise to a more overtly nationalist political tendency, whose population has surpassed one billion, and whose national security ambitions are now underscored by a demonstrated and declared nuclear weapons capability.

The United States carries into this decade a long legacy of service as the protector of the peace in the Pacific—the indispensable political actor to keep regional rivalries and tensions from destabilizing the area. Will the United States adjust its security calculations to account for the rise of two major economic and, over time, military powers in Asia? Is Japan's future energy security assured? Such questions must remain rhetorical for now.

What we can say is that the prospect of China's and India's economic growth in this decade and beyond raises a host of new energy-related considerations that include, but go well beyond, the security of tanker sea-lanes between the Gulf and the Pacific Rim. The rise of two Asian political and economic behemoths in this century with voracious appetites for energy—India as well as China—will alter the region's strategic equation.

THE CHANGING ECONOMICS OF OIL

Not only do the evolving regional patterns of suppliers and their principal markets have political and security implications for the Western Hemisphere, the Persian/Arabian Gulf, and Asia; there is an equally significant overlay of changing interests brought about by the globalization and "securitization" of the oil market. Our study has resulted in several key insights on the economic dimensions of future oil supply and demand.

Although the United States, Japan, and Europe still consume large quantities of imported crude oil, these countries represent the world's "mature" markets. Thus, their projected demand for imported oil will increase only at a modest pace.[8] These economies have evolved steadily from heavy industry into information technology and services, to such an extent that their susceptibility to extreme oil price trends is much reduced.[9]

In the event of sustained very high oil prices, these advanced economies now experience less severe inflation effects;[10] a portion of that effect is indirect—reflecting rising import costs of petroleum-dependent industrial goods whose manufacture in recent years has been increasingly shifted offshore to developing countries. Particularly in the wealthy and prospering economies, oil price increases are manageable.

By contrast, GDP levels of the Persian/Arabian Gulf producers whose economies are dominated by oil, such as Saudi Arabia, are and will remain highly vulnerable to sharp declines in global oil prices. For those countries, sustained very low oil prices would contract the overall economy enough to raise concerns about social and political stability. Nor are very high prices an unambiguous blessing for Gulf producers because they could cause some oil-importing economies to falter, creating downward demand volatility that could send world prices into a deep skid.

Similarly, among oil-importing economies, most developing-country GDP levels are more sensitive to oil price trends than those in advanced economies. This sensitivity will only increase in the key developing economies—many in Asia—that are expected to grow and consume far more imported oil.[11]

Sensitivity to high oil prices among many Asian developing economies is compounded by the fact that oil is dollar denominated. Because higher import costs will create a sudden new demand for dollars, these countries' currencies may weaken against the dollar when oil prices surge, pushing up the real local cost of imported oil even further than the nominal price rise on global oil markets.

Developing countries utilize a smaller share of oil within their overall energy supplies today than they have in the past. These economies tend to be more easily able to cut back consumption in a crunch. In other words, some of these Asian economies have much greater price elasticities for oil than the United States and other Western consuming nations.[12]

Because of the serious impact of this currency-related "double-hit" experienced by Asian oil-importing economies when world prices rise precipitously, OPEC and cooperating non-OPEC producers may find it more difficult in the future to exploit them by maintaining a tight market than it has with the West over the years. As Asia gains status while growing into the most important regional market for oil, OPEC may have to rethink its aggressive price strategies lest it underestimate Asia's price sensitivity. Over time, as the Asian economies develop and become more complex—and particularly as transportation becomes a more robust and vital segment—they will demand an increasing share of the world's oil supply, whether prices are high or low.

What this means is that the leading producers of oil and these significant new consumers of oil are developing comparatively greater stakes in keeping oil prices from trending too low or too high than the advanced postindustrial economies. A sharpening of divergent interests over the desired direction of oil prices between the Gulf's producers and Asia's rising big consumers, with both camps projected to increase their respective shares of global production and consumption, is likely to be reflected in the international political arena sooner or later.

Increasing Asian consumption of imported crude oil will translate into Asian-Gulf economic diplomacy. When prices are high and rising, some Asian governments—China and India immediately come to mind—could rival or even supplant Western countries as leading "demandeurs" for increased production from OPEC. For the oil-producing governments of the Persian/Arabian Gulf, this shift in diplomatic focus from West to East will entail some adjustments in their expectations and political outlook.

SUPPLIER CARTELS AND CONSUMER LEVERAGE

At the mention of energy "diplomacy," it is worth asking how much longer OPEC can expect to maintain sufficient leverage over the world's economies to command their periodic attention. Beyond 2010, we find the oil producers' ability to continue operating in an oligopolistic manner uncertain. Effective consensus among producing country governments in favor of withholding production has been elusive over the years, although effective collaboration ultimately was achieved in support of the price rise beginning in March 1999.

Even when OPEC and other producing countries have acted in concert, the cartel has been an unwieldy and unpredictable actor.

When oil prices have approached high levels in the United States, Europe, and other consuming countries—incurring political backlash, depressed consumption, and encouragement of alternative energy sources—many producing countries have been headstrong in resisting production increases to alleviate the tight market. These "price hawks," whose oil revenue-dependent economies have suffered in very low price periods, fear nothing as much as that oversupply will trigger another collapse of oil prices and revenues.

Indeed, agreement to increase production during high-price periods has proven particularly elusive within OPEC, where only Saudi Arabia and, to a lesser extent, Kuwait and the United Arab Emirates normally have sufficient excess production capability (above their "official" OPEC quotas) to increase global supply quickly. All other producers—when they are at or near peak production—are determined to receive as much revenue as possible for that output. For them, a decline in world prices can only cost them revenues. Hence, Saudi Arabia in particular encounters resistance from OPEC members who already are at peak production when further supplies are needed to stabilize the world market, despite all the risks of inaction.

OPEC's uncertain capacity and reputation for moderating price volatility is becoming more of a liability because the oil market itself is increasingly prone to greater volatility. One reason is that information technology has greatly improved the efficiency of the market, enabling more precise inventory controls in which shipments are timed to meet the production schedules of refiners. As the U.S. market discovered to its discomfort starting in late 2000, refineries no longer carry substantial inventories as they once did; doing so would risk losses if daily product prices fell. In a tight global market, price signals are derived from estimates of available stocks of oil and oil products within producer countries, at sea, or within consumer markets. A condition of low product stocks can set the stage for greater upward price volatility.

Related to this factor is the long-term trend toward "spot" purchasing of oil supplies on the open market by major consuming economies and away from proprietary, long-term relationships tying oilfields on one continent to refineries and distribution networks on another. Oil produced in the Caspian by a major U.S. oil company is likely to be traded onto the market for nearby consumption, rather than being shipped all the way to the United States. The major producers—Saudi Arabia, Kuwait, the United Arab Emirates, and others—have been scrambling to ensure that their products will have buyers in the years ahead by securing ownership shares in the "downstream" refining and distribution networks of key consumer markets, from the United States and Europe to India and China.

The major oil-exporting countries have a well-established tradition of taking the initiative to assure that the global market continues to serve their interests. The clock may be starting to run out on the OPEC cartel, however. As the oil market becomes more transparent and price-driven, it increasingly acquires the aspect of a financial market. Until now, one would not have been inclined to equate oil and finance. The main difference is that for decades, the wealthiest nations of the world, through their central banks, have taken it upon themselves to intervene periodically in the financial markets—albeit not always with the greatest success—in the name of preserving the economic stability on which their societies depend.

In the oil market, by contrast, the main beneficiaries—the consuming countries who pay all the costs of its extraction, shipment, and refining—have neither sought nor exercised a comparable capacity to intervene in their own self-interest. From the time of the 1973 oil embargo, Western consumers and their governments have never seriously contemplated ways to undo the hammerlock the world's leading producers have held over consumers. The reason is that until now, the nature of the world energy market has not offered consumer governments any potential leverage to defend against artificial manipulation of supply and global prices.

We wonder whether the transformation of the energy market by globalization has made such a notion ripe for consideration. Although it cannot be said often enough that market intervention is no panacea, it is hardly a revolutionary concept with respect to financial markets, given the long-established roles of the G-7 Finance Ministerial forum, the international financial institutions (IFIs), and other official entities.

What might a consuming country's "capacity to intervene" in the oil market look like? Presumably it would take the form of crude oil stockpiles maintained by these governments—not to prepare for supply emergencies, as is the case with the U.S. SPR and comparable facilities maintained by IEA member states, but to be available for market interventions to moderate extreme high price conditions. It bears emphasis that in a true market environment, mere capacity to intervene (i.e., ready availability to Western governments of oil stocks to release into the market) can send a sufficient price signal to blunt OPEC's capacity to drive prices upward by curbing production. By making the latter action less attractive, the threat of the former action alone could suffice without requiring actual releases of stocks.

The notion that the governments of major Western oil-importing countries could one day treat benchmark prices of crude oil in much the same manner that their central banks treat the yen or the Euro (i.e., as a market-sensitive index that is subject to potential intervention when it strays outside a desired range) is admittedly fanciful, even today—to say nothing of controversial. It became slightly less fanciful in September 2000, however, when President Clinton authorized the release of as much as 30 million barrels of oil from the SPR even though there was no oil supply emergency.

The Clinton administration was reluctant to state outright that its motive was to moderate high prices; as it turned out, the impact of the release announcement on the markets was neither large nor long-lasting. This action by the U.S. government set a precedent, however, and served as an acknowledgment, witting or otherwise, that the global energy sector is increasingly driven by market economics, with implications for future energy policy.

To point this out is not to predict, much less advocate, a new ethos of government interventionism in world energy markets. In the broader context of a sound, comprehensive energy strategy grounded in respect for market principles, however, the possibility of supply intervention as a potential arrow in the policy quiver is now on the table.

CAPITAL MARKET VOLATILITY—
A MODERN STRATEGIC CONCERN

In much the same manner that energy, long considered a strategic good, gradually is coming to be understood more as a standard market commodity, the global financial marketplace itself—by dint of its sheer mass and influence—gradually is acquiring a more strategic character.

Measured by the numbers, oil commands nowhere near the relative importance within the international economy of 2001 that it did in the fateful 1970s; this decline in its importance will continue through 2010 and beyond. Increased financing potentially required by extreme high oil prices in 2010—estimated by our study in the range of $100–150 billion worldwide—is a small fraction even of today's multitrillion-dollar capital markets.

Thus, although severe disruptions and extreme trends in the international oil economy of the future certainly can affect important interests, their impact in terms of capital flows simply will not be a major driver in the international financial system, as was the case a quarter-century ago. Even the world's developing economies are becoming less vulnerable to sudden oil price shocks. Our study has found that in many of these countries, extreme oil price trends— high or low—are not regarded as having as much impact on their own financing requirements as previously. The multiplicity of capital flow mechanisms that are available to developing economies today have spurred sufficient financial activity, inward and outward, to handle capital needs generated by oil market disruptions or price-related discontinuities in those markets.

That said, in the event of a true oil shock—such as a very large-scale cutoff of supply or a sudden, sustained price jump to unprecedented levels—financial markets probably would not handle the crisis smoothly. Instead, they could be expected to react reflexively to rapid movements in asset prices, creating serious risks for banks and potentially for some national economies.

We are concerned that new kinds of vulnerabilities are infecting developing-country capital markets by virtue of these very intermediation mechanisms.[13] Access to short-term portfolio investment can bring many advantages, but the tendency of investors and speculators to react en masse to rumor and political uncertainty—whether related to possible oil price spikes or other key economic indicators—can create a herd effect of capital flight, with adverse consequences. "Contagion" is the term used, reflecting parallels in historic experience with disease pathogens.

When the oil price shock is downward, the proliferation of financial instruments relating to the energy sector—what has been termed the "securitization" of hard energy assets—means that a precipitous decrease in oil prices would be felt, as never before, within the broader financial markets. Although energy consumers and workers in advanced economies may be said to have a declining level of interest, compared to previous decades, in oil as a strategic good that can severely affect their jobs or household budgets, investors are increasing their interest in oil as a driver of related market investments.[14]

Overall, as oil declines in relative economic significance, the global capital economy itself becomes a key locus of concern about sudden instability. To economic policymakers, the uncertain record of developing countries trying to conform their markets and institutions to advanced Western norms suggests that we have yet to perfect the formula for transitioning an autarkic or developing economy into the charmed circle of global capitalist nations. To foreign policy and national security planners, however, the message is more urgent: Developing economies that are newly exposed to modern global capitalism carry risks of sudden and potentially serious instability.

Nor does this cautionary point suggest that it is preferable for a country to forgo market-enhancing initiatives. The insight here is that modernizing these developing economies trades one set of risks for another. For example, although most economies in the developed and developing worlds are far better suited to handle inflows and outflows of capital than in previous decades, in most economies of Asia—notably China and Japan—banks remain the predominant mechanism for intermediation of capital flows. Banks alone—irrespective of the quality of their assets—are ill equipped to handle conditions of financial market volatility. As long as alternative chan-nels and instruments for inward and outward investment are not permitted to flourish, this overreliance on banks also must be con-sidered a continuing risk factor in Asian countries.

In other words, there is no going back to a less sophisticated, less connected economic world. Globalization is eroding the traditional "home bias" of developing-country institutional investors, so they are increasingly looking to expand and diversify their holdings in foreign markets. During the 1997 Asian financial crisis, local rather than foreign institutions were the first to pull their investments out of these markets. The twenty-first-century world is marked by an expansion of equities, bonds, and portfolio investments in many de-veloping-country markets—which are far more leveraged than pre-viously, when banks were the predominant mechanism for intermediation of cross-border capital flows.

The fundamental new challenge for policymakers to address here is volatility. Volatility of capital flows has greater potential to dis-rupt the internal order of developing countries than the price of oil itself. Although the robust and ever-growing network of capital flow channels worldwide is an efficient mechanism to facilitate many as-pects of growth, it does not promise to smooth these flows; if any-thing, it promises to accelerate and magnify disruptions.

CALIBRATING OLD AND NEW IN A POLICY FRAMEWORK

Thus, the new century has begun with several familiar features of the "old" geopolitics still intact. Advanced economies continue to con-sume large quantities of crude oil, even as promising fuel alternatives are making their debut at the retail level. The world's oil producers at the end of the twentieth century found that they still have the abil-ity to tighten global supply and push up prices, even though chang-ing conditions in the energy sector point to a day—perhaps not very far off—when OPEC will be much less able to exercise such market power to its advantage.

Most important, however, the Persian/Arabian Gulf retains its strategic importance as the world's primary source of crude oil as well as an important source of liquified natural gas. Global dependence on this area's resources is increasing in the short run, at a time when the future character and stability of regimes from Baghdad to Teheran to the Arabian peninsula are an open question. Uncertain political prospects in energy-producing countries in the Caspian basin, North Africa, and West Africa only add weight to the conclusion that the governments of key energy-importing economies will need to pay close attention to the internal politics of major oil producers for at least another decade.

That said, traditional notions of energy supply security should be updated. It is still true that a hostile action to close, or threaten to close, the Straits of Hormuz at the mouth of the Persian/Arabian Gulf would constitute a threat to U.S. and allied interests. The global oil market of today introduces vulnerabilities, however, that previous national security planners would not have been required to anticipate.

For example, the concept of "transit risk" must be broadened to include disruption or penetration of information networks that control the transportation or conveyance of oil from the exporting country to the importing country. Threats of force, including missile tests and movements of military forces, could be intended as much to influence oil prices as to achieve strictly political objectives.

Just as U.S. national security interests will remain linked to the availability and affordability of oil in the Persian/Arabian Gulf for at least the coming decade, the longer-term outlook is for an international environment in which oil may lose much of its strategic importance.[15] The U.S. military services are engaged in elaborate planning and wargaming studies to anticipate the battlefield environment 15–25 years hence. Policy planners need to begin weighing the implications of a world—perhaps not so far into the future—in which oil may no longer be a *casus belli* to the United States or its principal security allies.

Policymakers can begin by looking at the global economy and recognizing its manifold capacity to import risks and injure U.S.

interests. A propensity to think nationally in a "globalized" world can be a hindrance in considering U.S. national interest vulnerabilities in the international capital market system.

When the Asian financial crisis broke in 1997, one had the sense that Washington believed it already was too late to take meaningful, much less decisive, governmental action to ward off a potential contagion. The United States seemed to have concluded that whatever economic damage was about to occur around the world—in Japan, Brazil, or even the United States— could not be stopped.

Fortunately for Americans, the worst did not occur beyond Asia. Having ridden out that storm, the United States did not appear to believe that there were any significant lessons to learn from this episode. President Clinton declined to attend the APEC summit meeting after the crisis hit Asia.[16]

Yet the Asian crisis set in motion and helped underscore sweeping structural changes throughout the global economy that are bringing more benefit and risk to the developing and developed worlds alike. What remains for U.S. policy planners—ideally in conjunction with other governments—is to recognize that the volatility in Southeast Asia in 1997 was not an anomaly but a harbinger.

With the pace of global capital flow activity already approaching $20 trillion per year and no evident limit to its future growth, it is imperative to begin assessing in earnest the nature of this new force and its potential adverse impacts on national and international interests. Only then can efficacious preventative and remedial measures be devised and multilateral coordinating mechanisms beneficially employed.

The concept of "interdependence" among the nations of the world, popularized in academia as transnational patterns of activity grew in the 1970s, seems incomplete as a description of the globalization phenomenon even in its present form. There is an "independence" of markets and their innumerable participants, encompassing ever more of the world's public as well as private economic interests, that follows no flag and owes no formal allegiance to any national interest or policy priority.

These free markets exhibit an unparalleled capacity to create value and fuel prosperity—benefits for which governments are rightly grateful—but they assume no burdens of responsibility for the negative side of the ledger. Governments remain the only viable—and certainly the only willing—agents of action to address needs for which no compensating economic reward exists. It is time for U.S. foreign policy analysis to incorporate into its assumed core competency a serious appreciation of the nature, influence, and potential for sudden and large-scale harm inherent in the international capital flow economy.

DIPLOMATIC CHALLENGES

Our study has showed that although some aspects of "energy security" have not changed in the past three decades, others clearly have. It is natural and appropriate that the United States expand the focus of its political dialogue with European and Asian security allies, notably Japan, to address nontraditional as well as traditional concerns about energy supplies and global market stability generally.

Beyond Europe and Japan, however, it can reasonably be asked whether U.S. foreign policy takes enough cognizance of the foregoing factors. Regardless of all of the major issues outstanding between Russia and the United States, the former is a major energy producer with the potential to exploit large new reserves and help supply European and north Asian energy needs. Its economy is critically sensitive to world energy prices. Any U.S. policy strategy aimed at promoting compatible Russian policies backed by domestic economic progress and social stability must recognize Russia's own vulnerabilities to global market trends—specifically to low oil prices.

U.S. relations with China, which is expected to become a voracious consumer of imported crude oil as its economy grows, have struggled in recent years to accommodate a chaotic agenda ranging from positive engagement to a negative and cold posture. Expanding trade relations coexist alongside U.S. concerns about China's nuclear espionage, threats against Taiwan, proliferation activities, human rights record, and Tibet, among others. The U.S.-China relationship may be the world's most consequential bilateral relationship in coming years. China's economic growth could become the central reality driving numerous important trends and ultimately defining the security landscape from the Gulf through the Pacific Rim.

Similar points could be made about India—the world's other major future claimant for Gulf energy exports. Only recently have leading American politicians begun to accord India the attention it merits as a developing major power in the world. Much obviously remains to be done in cultivating U.S.-Indian dialogue to address old and new potential sources of tension and crisis. India needs electric energy, which is constraining even slow levels of growth. Of course, despite its signaled intentions, we cannot yet say whether India will seek its economic potential with foreign participation or continue to accommodate domestic constituencies at the expense of more rapid economic progress.

The traditional U.S. role as a stabilizing presence in Asia will have to account for the new dynamics of economic growth in China and India, their expanding economic interplay with the Gulf, and a marked increase in the sensitivity of transit routes from the Gulf to both countries. Contemplating China's and India's rising strategic stakes in the Gulf, one might conclude that, by comparison, the U.S. economic connection to the region's oilfields is declining and may be less "vital" today than it was at the end of the 1970s, at the height of the Carter Doctrine era.

Such a conclusion would overlook the implications of globalization in the energy sector, including the proliferation of tradable market instruments based on global supply and demand for oil. Arguably, U.S. national interests are becoming more rather than less tied to the stability of the Gulf, all the more so as a consequence of these nascent—and potentially competing—Chinese and Indian strategic interests in the vicinity of this traditional "arc of crisis."

Such factors only serve to complicate a very challenging geopolitical backdrop for the U.S.-Japan relationship. The flow of oil from the Middle East to the Far East, as well as the flow of capital in the other direction, will stimulate competitive tensions among the countries of Asia. At the very end of the long logistical route from troubled political environs such as Iraq, Kuwait, Saudi Arabia, and

Iran—via the Indian Ocean, the South China Sea, and the Taiwan Straits—lies the most dependent major consumer of their oil: Japan. The evolving strategic complexion of this West Asia-to-East Asia energy economy raises a host of security concerns for Tokyo as well as Washington.

Of these issues, only the military concerns—unimpeded access to the Gulf and security of sea-lanes to East Asia—have been well anticipated by the United States and discussed (and only occasionally, at that) with Japan over the years. In truth, the Strait of Malacca piracy problem probably has received more attention. Much room remains for bilateral discussion of common energy policy responses during periods of economic crisis, strategies to promote political stability and moderation in oil-producing countries, and defenses against nontraditional forms of risk to energy supplies.

Risk management lies at the heart of strategies pursued by private actors in the global economy. As this economy gains mass, compelling governments and international organizations to respond to any adverse consequences of its volatile and apolitical impulses, a role clearly exists for the United States and other like-minded governments—at the level of foreign policy planning and bilateral political diplomacy—to do some serious risk mitigation and risk management of their own.

A good start would be an unapologetic recognition that "national interests"—public as well as private—are at play in the global economy. This strategy requires that governments study and assess these modern risks and cooperate where possible to contain them. How skillfully and energetically the United States grasps this challenge will bear on its future security, prosperity, and standing as a leader among nations.

CONCLUSION

We conclude by offering three basic recommendations, with the expectation—which we hope is not misguided—that the lines of analysis in this study will spur others to pursue further inquiry and develop productive courses of action.

1. *Articulate a national U.S. energy strategy that contemplates the availability of effective leverage to deter or alleviate oil price extremes—high and low; prepare possible measures, to be authorized by Congress and exercised by the president, to counter extreme price trends and, when necessary, mitigate their adverse impacts on U.S. citizens.*

Such a policy position need not create the expectation that the U.S. government will act in every instance of an unbalanced market, even though the goal of having the means to respond to extreme high or low price trends would be embraced explicitly. This policy is not an abandonment of free market philosophy—only a recognition that price extremes can adversely affect the public good, in the United States and abroad, and that the international oil market already is overlaid with the political agendas of other state actors.

Why should the U.S. government assume any burden of action? Participants in our study have argued—reasonably, in our view—that government ought to avoid meddling in the workings of the free market if at all possible. There are legitimate reasons for concern that governments do not act as rationally in the economic sense as private parties and that their level of concern about the adverse consequences of high prices might not be matched by a similar level of concern for the adverse consequences of low prices. We see merit in these perspectives.

The oil sector cannot be said to be an altogether free market, however. Not only do the key producing countries operate as a cartel, albeit a loose one, with the intent to control supply and manipulate prices; the U.S. government itself already is profoundly implicated in the world supply situation, with an impact on global price trends. How so? U.S. officials over the years have routinely lobbied friendly producing countries to increase or decrease supply, depending on the prevailing circumstances.[17]

In addition, the many sanctions restrictions, imposed unilaterally or through the United Nations on oil-producing states in the 1980s and 1990s have directly impeded—by design in many instances—these producers' oil export potential. Considering all of these political influences by producing and consuming countries alike, the upward oil price movement that began in March 1999 was a by-product of many factors; the rationality of an unfettered free market was not foremost among them.

Before authorizing or legislating new sanctions against foreign countries with a significant role in the production or conveyance of the world's energy supply, the executive and legislative branches should examine the likely impact of these measures on the global economy. At a minimum, U.S. policy could then anticipate and consciously avoid unintended "boomerang" effects that harm its own interests.

The administration and Congress also should revisit the mandate governing use of the SPR, which needs to be filled and probably enlarged. The SPR should continue to serve its intended purpose, in line with IEA policy, which is to provide relief in the event of emergency supply disruptions. We believe, however, that there also should be a separate component or stand-alone reserve available to increase supplies when tight global market conditions drive prices to levels that cause harm to segments of the population and sectors of industry.

The SPR and this proposed separate "price stabilization reserve" need to be supported with an annual appropriation of funds. The SPR's funding has been irregular, aimed at achieving a kind of market-timing. We believe that a consistent and regularized approach to these reserves would send an important message that oil, cheap or dear, is never far from U.S. strategic planning. An annual appropriation also would have the merit of a kind of dollar-cost averaging, with more oil acquired when prices are lower, and less when prices are higher.[18]

A declaratory U.S. policy backed by such tools would be even more potent if other major energy-importing countries developed parallel policies along with price stabilization reserves and pledged to coordinate their actions relative to the global energy market. The net effect of such an initiative could be to influence the calculus of key producers, which we hope would discourage them from overly assertive cartel behavior that is deemed to be damaging to the interests of consuming countries. In other words, what we are suggesting here is effecting a historic global shift of leverage away from the principal oil-exporting countries and toward the principal oil-consuming countries.

RICHARD L. ARMITAGE, LINCOLN P. BLOOMFIELD JR., AND JAMES A. KELLY   229

Thus, we argue that U.S. energy policy should go beyond planning emergency assistance measures for qualified individuals and entities that are severely affected by prices that move above or below specified parameters. It should take a comprehensive approach to guarding against international dangers posed by extreme price distortions, whatever the cause. The time when a passive and ad hoc posture might suffice has passed.

> 2. *Recognize the vulnerability of U.S. interests to unanticipated extreme volatility in international capital markets and engage other governments in a structured dialogue on ways to minimize risks and cooperate in effective responses when destructive episodes occur.*

Economists have studied the 1997 Asian economic crisis and drawn lessons pertaining to the adequacy of institutional mechanisms within developing economies and the appropriate role for international financial institutions in those countries. Economic policy offices in the U.S. government have provided input to the reform agendas recommended to the affected Asian countries.

As a matter of foreign policy, however, the United States has not sufficiently acknowledged the early lesson of globalization that developing-country markets carry the ever-present risks of economic reversal, crisis, and contagion. Confidence in a country's economy can evaporate unexpectedly, spurring the panicked flight of local and foreign capital alike and potentially leaving social and political unrest in its wake. Do adequate policy mechanisms—unilateral U.S. measures, tools available to other states, or those of the IFIs—exist to anticipate and try to prevent such a crisis or to respond effectively enough to mitigate its adverse effects?

Again, posing such questions might appear insensitive to the presumption that government intervention in private markets is inherently undesirable and to be avoided. Indeed, there is a compelling argument that governmental intervention aimed at mitigating private risk in the marketplace induces recklessness on the part of economic actors—the moral hazard" concern.

Adhering to a "hands-off" philosophy would not necessarily mean that the U.S. government is indifferent to the impact of an economically devastating flight of capital on the overall well-being of friendly countries such as Thailand or the Philippines (each, it bears mentioning, a treaty ally of the United States). Viewed through a broader foreign policy and national security lens, however, the problem posed by the prospect of ruinous capital flight in developing economies ought to be susceptible to policy safeguards that do not incur the "moral hazard" disadvantage. In this regard, we commend for further study the utility of credit risk derivatives (see chapter 6) as a brake on capital flight if these markets face sudden destabilizing pressures.

In any case, it is evident that at the level of national policy—as understood by the State Department, the Defense Department, the National Security Council staff, U.S. ambassadors posted abroad, the intelligence community, and Congress in its foreign affairs oversight function—the fact of an $800 billion and growing daily global capital economy has not yet fully registered as a defining feature of the new geopolitical environment.

That is why we argue that the foreign policy community as a whole should take more seriously the need to anticipate the political and social liabilities attending global capital participation in many developing-country economies, large and small. The global financial "ecosystem" will experience chronic volatility; when that volatility surges to extremes, however, like El Niño it can inflict harm on U.S. interests writ large, international as well as domestic. We urge official Washington to engage foreign policy and finance officials of other countries in a cross-disciplinary dialogue on the geopolitical implications of this new fact of life.

> 3. *The United States and the world's leading economies—above all, Japan—must engage in a broad, candid, and far-reaching dialogue about the implications of the transforming international environment and explore ways of harmonizing their policy efforts on several fronts.*

One could derive from these pages an exhaustive list of bilateral and international policy issues that the United States might pursue fruitfully with various key nations of the world. Here we address the U.S.-Japan dimension because it amply illustrates the possibilities for worthwhile U.S. engagement with others on such matters. Indeed, to identify concerns that could seriously impinge only on the shared interests of the United States and Japan is to recognize that these two allies and global partners alone have a large agenda of shared critical concerns.

It is evident that Japan's long-standing efforts to secure proprietary access to crude oil reserves in the world has not—and in fact cannot—totally immunize the Japanese economy from a disruption of energy supplies from the Persian/Arabian Gulf region or a period of extreme high energy prices. Moreover, the growth of China, India, and other Asian economies with their own rising energy needs is diluting the influence that Japan has sought to cultivate since the 1970s as a major energy producer.

Japan already has made more substantial conservation gains than other advanced economies; there is not much more to be gained by greater efforts in that area. Because of feasibility considerations, overambitious nuclear energy expansion plans dictated by the country's needs have been scaled back. The promising idea of piping Japanese-developed natural gas from Sakhalin Island southward has been regarded by some Japanese policymakers as requiring prior resolution of the Northern Territories dispute with Russia. That is not a goal that Japan can be confident of reaching with President Putin any time soon, however, given the sensitive territorial issues he confronts in other parts of Russia.

It is time for the United States and Japan to explore collaboration on long-range energy strategies, including short-term responses to potentially harmful extreme trends. In 2000 Japan conducted two important national energy strategy reviews—one sponsored by the Ministry of Economy, Trade, and Industry (METI) and the other by the Liberal Democratic Party. At a minimum, these efforts signaled that new policy directions in energy policy are possible in Tokyo.

As U.S. officials develop their own comprehensive energy policy, they should engage Japanese officials regarding Japan's challenge in meeting its future energy needs in a secure and affordable manner. A central component of this dialogue must be joint strategic assessment of the rise of major new Asian energy competitors—including China, India, and, over time, Indonesia—as well as an updated common understanding of energy "transit risk" in the information age.

As Yukio Okamoto compellingly explains, the prospective dimensions and implications of China's economic growth in the next quarter- to half-century are certain to be a prime strategic focus for Japan—and likely for the United States as well. If Chinese economic growth proceeds anywhere close to the path very credibly suggested by Mr. Okamoto, its energy consumption one day could become the overriding geopolitical driver of the Asian security environment.

China has not yet shown much recognition of changes in its own strategic outlook regarding the value of stability in the oil-producing countries of the Gulf or secure sea-lanes between the Gulf and Pacific Rim. How those new priorities will be reflected in future Chinese political and military policy is of direct interest to the United States and Japan. Discussions between the United States and Japan are needed, the better to inform each country's dialogue with China.

Beyond these steps, the United States and Japan should coordinate strategies to anticipate and manage the consequences of financial crisis conditions brought on by extreme global or regional market volatility. The experience of the 1997 Asian economic crisis showed that the United States and Japan perceived their respective interests and gauged their responses very differently. Persistent weakness in Japan's economy—to which Asia's troubles subsequently became a contributing factor—has frustrated U.S. economic policy as Japanese trade surpluses and U.S. trade deficits alike have continued to increase.

If only out of concern that periodic bilateral frictions in the trade and finance policy arena not impede sensible and far-reaching strategic cooperation between the two governments, the U.S.-Japan foreign policy dialogue should now extend explicitly to global economics. It no longer makes sense to maintain mutually isolated, parallel tracks of bilateral dialogue involving momentous alliance commitments on one side and politically debilitating economic discordancy on the other—as often has been the case during the past decade or more.

The path Japan follows to revivify its economy will have direct implications for U.S. economic equities, and vice versa. As the two governments address shared risks and vulnerabilities emanating from the emerging global economy, they must speak more candidly and aspire to forge more comprehensive understandings of the best ways for the world's two leading economies to prosper together 'without detracting from one another's interests. Comparable U.S. efforts with other governments around the world can flow from this example of global partnership.

Throughout the 1990s, one sometimes heard the complaint in Washington that U.S. policymakers reached too readily for the military option in responding to crises other than war. The military, the complaint went, is a "hammer," but not every crisis is a "nail." That criticism applied to a world adjusting to the sudden fall of communism and the rise of localized ethnic conflict and festering situations of humanitarian duress. Now these nettlesome features of the international landscape have carried over the millennial dateline, engaging the machinery of government to adapt and become more responsive to contingencies of many descriptions.

Our thesis is that a new geopolitics is upon us—the progeny of an era featuring the enabling and empowerment of a limitless number of the world's private entities and individuals, interacting with a speed, efficiency, and capacity unimaginable in the industrial era. With that positive potential comes an inherent fragility, as well as a shared vulnerability to disruptions and distortions resulting from deliberate malign acts or random systemic irregularities.

Political and societal interests are at stake in this system; when global economic circumstances inflict misfortune on these interests, people who are harmed look to political institutions for redress and relief. Notwithstanding the rise of potent, nonsovereign forces in the new international environment, governments alone possess the legitimacy and capacity to assert controlling influences where necessary and appropriate. The task of shaping a policy framework to address the challenges of the new era must begin now.

Notes

[1] Samuel Berger, "A Foreign Policy for the Global Age," *Foreign Affairs* 79, no. 6 (November/December 2000): 23.

[2] See, for example, Peter W. Rodman, *Uneasy Giant—The Challenges to American Predominance* (Washington, D.C.: Nixon Center, 2000).

[3] See George Gilder, "Internet in the Balance," *Wall Street Journal*, October 20, 2000, p. A18.

[4] We draw a distinction here between portfolio investors, with their short-term profitability focus, and direct investors, with a more than 10 percent stake (see chapter 4) in tangible assets, who are inherently less mobile and more committed to a longer view within a particular market.

[5] The point is that by the time depletion of potentially accessible supplies could create real scarcity, conservation and alternative energy sources are expected to mitigate the imbalance of supply and demand for oil.

[6] Some regard the Caspian Basin as a potential equivalent to the North Sea.

[7] This comment could apply to legislative initiatives floated in the U.S. Congress during 2000 that purported to reduce imported oil as a share of the total crude oil consumed in the United States, on a percentage basis. Because the U.S. government does not own or control private-sector oil reserves, production facilities, and trading entities, the owners of that production are free to sell their oil wherever in the world it will fetch the highest price. Indeed, much of the government-owned SPR oil released to the market in the fall of 2000 by President Clinton was sold to refiners in Europe, where demand was greater at the time. To be successful, any effort to ensure a secure, affordable energy supply for the American people must include strategies to boost worldwide supplies and curb worldwide consumption of energy, given the increasingly borderless nature of the twenty-first-century energy market.

[8] Even though oil consumption as a percentage of GDP is in decline in the United States, absolute levels of oil consumption and imports have been rising in recent years and are contributing factors to the millennial oil price surge. Still, the United States is seen as a "mature" market for imported energy because, as a well-developed economy, its potential rate of increase in energy consumption is much less than comparable rates for major developing economies of Asia.

[9] Measured in terms of oil as a percentage of GDP.

[10] Indeed, on October 19, 2000—a full year into the global high oil price rally—Federal Reserve Board Chairman Alan Greenspan, in remarks at the Cato Institute, said, "To date, the spillover [i.e., the influence on the prices of other goods in the economy] from the surge in oil prices has been modest. Any effect on inflation expectations...has been virtually nil."

[11] China, with its heavy reliance on coal for energy, is somewhat of an exception, with a net financing requirement for oil of perhaps 0.05 percent of GDP—a level comparable to that of the United States.

[12] In September 2000, consumers in some European countries waged street protests against high fuel prices; the retail prices charged to these consumers, however, consisted primarily of government taxes added onto the cost of the commodity and the profit margin.

[13] Economics correspondent Joseph Kahn, reporting on sudden financial market reverses in Turkey and Argentina despite these countries' excellent level of compliance with the IMF's suggested reform agenda, commented as follows: "The lesson seems clear: Nations that aggressively rebuild their financial systems in the first-world mold are just as vulnerable to shocks—perhaps in some cases more so—than nations that make such changes halfheartedly. The more foreign investment they attract, the greater the risk that a sentiment shift will wound their economies." Joseph Kahn, "When Nations Are Punished For Fiscal Discipline," *New York Times*, December 10, 2000, p. BU4.

[14] With the spread of retail investing, these different categories—"consumer" and "investor"—can refer to the same people. Within advanced economies, as the potential impact on household budgets or job security of a sharp rise in oil prices is in decline, the growing pool of investors is increasingly likely to view with concern the possible impact of a plunge in oil prices on their retirement savings.

[15] See, for example, Amy Myers Jaffe and Robert A. Manning, "The Shocks of a World of Cheap Oil," *Foreign Affairs* 79, no. 1 (January/February 2000).

[16] Vice President Al Gore, addressing the assembled APEC heads of state in President Clinton's place, chose not to focus on the devastation that had just befallen many of their economies but on the alleged mistreatment in jail, weeks earlier, of the summit host's political rival. He then departed the Kuala Lumpur summit prior to the opening dinner.

[17] See, for example, Andrew Hamilton, "How the White House Helped Pump Up the Price," *Washington Post*, April 30, 2000, p. B3.

[18] Dollar-cost averaging is an investment approach that commits funds according to a predictable calendar rather than speculating on cyclical price movements. Under this approach, acquisitions made when asset prices are low will compensate for those made at high prices. Thus, in return for sacrificing the potential for maximum speculative rewards, the investor will face lowered risk over time.

INDEX

Page numbers followed by the letters n *and* t *refer to endnotes and tables.*

Credit risk derivatives, 161, 166n10
Currencies, 82–83, 122, 157–159, 215
Current accounts, 101n23, 123–131

Debt securities, 77
Deepwater oil production, 43, 164
Defense industry, 7, 162, 177–178, 179
Department of Energy, 32, 45
Derivative financial instruments, 72, 100n5
Deutsche Bank, 139
Developing countries: capital flight from, 207–208, 220–221, 230–231; capital flows in, 73–79, 105t; direct investments in, 73–74, 77, 104t; economic instability of, 220–221, 236n13; official finance to, 75–76, 105t; OPEC exports to, 36–37; portfolio investments in, 73–74, 76, 77, 79–81, 104t; private finance to, 75–76, 79–81, 106t
Direct investments, 100n3; in developing countries, 73–74, 77, 104t; historical changes in, 73–74, 76, 104t; mobility of, 235n4; stability of, 83
Distributive generation, 165n1
Dollar(s), 122–131; future crisis of, 130–131, 156; historical strength of, 124–125; Japan and, 123–125, 126–131; oil shocks and, 157, 215; OPEC and, 124, 125–126, 130–131
Dollar-cost averaging, 229, 236n18
Downstream investments, 31–32
Drilling technologies, 38–39

E-commerce, 20–21
East Asia/Pacific region, 103t, 106t, 121t
Ebel, Robert E., 145, 165n4
Economic value-creation, 70–71, 93–94
Electricity Directive on Competition, 25
Emissions trading, 24
Energy conservation, 35, 41, 174

Energy consumption, 15–16, 21–22
Energy demand, 27, 206–207
Energy efficiency, 15–16, 97
Energy futures, 18–19, 20, 50–51n3
Energy industry, 14, 22–23, 135–137
Energy Information Administration (EIA), 32, 45
Energy intensity, 71, 93–94, 96–97, 120t–121t
Energy markets, 13–50; changing characteristics of, 13–28; energy trading and, 17–22; environmental protection and, 16, 23–25; government intervention in, 218–219, 228–230; natural gas and, 25–26; oil commoditization and, 17–19; projections for, 27–28; technology and, 14–17, 22–23
Energy security: in Asia, 31, 172, 183–184, 185, 194; and global security, 180; in 1984 presidential election, 179; reality *vs.* perception of, 181–186; U. S. role in, 172, 179, 183–184, 211–212; during war, 194. *See also* Oil supply security
Energy trading, 18–22, 50n2
Environmental protection, 16, 23–25, 136
Equity finance, 78–79
Euro(s), 131
Eurobonds, 84, 101n20
Europe: banks of, 76–77; capital flows in, 104t; direct investments in, 104t; energy intensity of, 121t; GDP of, 109t, 110t; natural gas in, 53t, 54t; net exports of, 110t, 117t, 118t; in oil price scenarios, 90, 112t, 114t, 116t, 117t, 118t; oil reserves in, 53t; portfolio investments in, 104t. *See also* *specific countries*
European Union (EU), 25, 37, 41, 119t, 120t
Exchange rates, 82–83
Exxon Mobil, 22

Fahd, King, 190, 191, 198
Finelli, Francis A., 162
Foreign direct investment (FDI). *See* Direct investments
Foreign Policy (journal), 5–6
Franssen, Herman T., 58–65, 155, 171
Fuel, transportation, 66n3, 143, 154
Fuel cells, 181
Fuel reformulation, 23, 136
Fuel riots (2000), 66n3, 236n12
Fusaro, Peter C., 13–50, 126, 130, 133, 135–137, 138, 141, 147, 154, 155, 159, 163, 167, 177, 181

Gas. *See* Natural gas
Gas Research Institute, 25
Gasoline, leaded, 23
Germany, 81, 103t, 123, 161, 162
Goldstein, Larry, 137–138, 142, 144–145, 156–157, 158, 165n3
Gore, Al, 236n16
Government(s): and capital flows, 207–208, 230–231; and energy markets, 218–219, 228–230; information technology and, 207; and oil industry, 141–142; and oil prices, 144–145, 151, 208; and technology, 177–178, 179
Greenhouse gases, 23–24, 51n11, 165n2
Greenspan, Alan, 138, 235n10
Gulf Cooperation Council (GCC), 60, 66n4
Gulf region. *See* Middle East; Persian Gulf

Hedge funds, 19, 20, 51n7, 157, 158
Heslin, Sheila, 195
High oil price scenario, 38–44, 57t; economic implications of, 86–87, 94–95, 111t–112t, 113t–114t; net export change in, 88–92, 117t; stay-at-home capital in, 94–96
Home bias, 80–81, 148–149
Houston Street, 20
Hussein, Saddam, 6, 193, 197–198

Hybrid cars, 181

Ikle, Fred, 186
Index trading, 20, 51n8
India: capital flows in, 75, 76, 105t, 106t; downstream investments in, 32; energy efficiency in, 97; energy intensity of, 96, 120t; GDP of, 109t, 110t; in high oil price scenario, 44, 57t, 112t, 114t, 117t; in low oil price scenario, 37, 56t, 91, 112t, 116t, 118t, 150; Middle East and, 45; net exports of, 110t, 117t, 118t; in normal oil price scenario, 55t, 112t; oil imports to, 139, 212–214; poverty reduction in, 75; private finance in, 106t; stock market turnover in, 78; trade with, 93, 119t; U. S. and, 93, 119t, 226
Indian Ocean, 189
Indonesia: banks of, 162; capital flows in, 75, 76, 105t, 106t, 107t; energy intensity of, 120t; GDP of, 109t; in oil price scenarios, 44; private finance in, 106t; stock market turnover in, 78; trade with, 119t
Industrial countries: capital flows in, 73–74; direct investments and, 73–74, 104t; portfolio investments and, 73–74, 104t
Inflation, 4, 123, 131n3, 214, 235n10
Information technology: and derivative financial instruments, 72; and energy intensity, 71, 93–94; and energy markets, 22–23; and exchange rates, 82–83; and military operations, 206; and national interests, 205–207; and oil stocks, 39–40; and transit risks, 223; in value-creation, 70–71, 93. *See also* Internet
Interest, open, 19, 51n6
Intermediation: by banks, 72, 76, 148, 160, 221–222; and capital flows, 72, 148, 150; historical changes in, 69–70, 148; risks of, 220–221
International Energy Agency (IEA), 50,

52n17, 59, 61–62, 65
International oil companies (IOCs), 37
International Organization of Securities
    Commissions (IOSCO), 161, 166n9
International Petroleum Exchange (IPE),
    19
Internationalism, 204
Internet, 16–17, 20–22, 51n9, 206–207
Intifada, 61, 63, 66n5
Iran: competition and, 42; GDP of, 110t;
    in high oil price scenario, 57t, 111t,
    113t, 117t; in low oil price scenario,
    37, 56t, 111t, 115t, 118t; natural gas in,
    25; net exports of, 110t, 117t, 118t; in
    normal oil price scenario, 55t, 111t; oil
    production potential of, 41, 46; oil
    reserves in, 54t; political change in,
    181; regional ambitions of, 193; 1979
    revolution in, 5, 18, 58, 189–190;
    sanctions against, 8, 142; Saudi Arabia
    and, 145–146; Soviet invasions of, 187
Iraq: competition and, 42; GDP of, 110t;
    in high oil price scenario, 57t, 111t,
    113t, 117t; Kuwait invaded by, 6, 187–
    188, 190–191; in low oil price sce-
    nario, 37, 56t, 111t, 115t, 118t; net
    exports of, 110t, 117t, 118t; in normal
    oil price scenario, 55t, 111t; oil-for-
    food program in, 60, 61; oil produc-
    tion in, 45, 60–61; oil production
    potential of, 41, 45, 46, 140; oil re-
    serves in, 54t; political stability of,
    197–199; regional ambitions of, 171,
    193; sanctions against, 8, 45; weapons
    of, 6, 192, 193
Israel, 7, 63, 190

Jaffe, Amy Myers, 142–143, 159, 163–
    164, 181, 197
Japan: alternative energy in, 175; banks
    of, 76–77, 160, 161, 162; and Bretton
    Woods, 123; bubble economy of, 127–
    128; capital flows in, 103t, 104t; China
    and, 233; consolidation in, 14; current
    account of, 123–124, 126–131; direct

investments in, 104t; and dollar
    crisis, 122–131; energy conservation
    in, 174; energy intensity of, 120t;
    energy policies of, 173–177; energy
    security in, 31, 172, 185; environ-
    mental compliance in, 24; GDP of,
    109t, 110t, 174; in high oil price
    scenario, 44, 57t, 90, 112t, 113t, 117t;
    in low oil price scenario, 35, 37, 56t,
    112t, 115t, 118t; Middle East and, 45,
    175; net exports of, 110t, 117t, 118t;
    in normal oil price scenario, 55t,
    112t; nuclear power in, 175, 176,
    185; oil consumption in, 138; oil
    imports to, 138; oil stockpiling by,
    41; OPEC price hikes and, 131n4–
    132n4; portfolio investments in, 81,
    104t; Russia and, 232; trade with U.
    S., 119t; U. S. alliance with, 156, 175–
    176, 226–227, 231–234
Japan National Oil Corporation
    (JNOC), 185
Jiang Zemin, 182, 186
Joint Forum, 161, 166n9
Jordan, 7

Kahn, Joseph, 236n13
Kazakhstan, 47, 48, 52n16, 75
Keegan, Don, 186
Kelly, James A., vii–x, 133, 203–234
Khobar Towers bombing, 8
Kissinger, Henry, 188
Korea, 14, 66n6, 107t, 119t, 120t. *See
    also* South Korea
Kuwait: competition and, 42; down-
    stream investments by, 31–32; GDP
    of, 110t; in high oil price scenario,
    57t, 111t, 113t, 117t; Iraqi invasion
    of, 6, 187–188, 190–191; in low oil
    price scenario, 37, 56t, 111t, 115t,
    118t; net exports of, 110t, 117t, 118t;
    in normal oil price scenario, 55t,
    111t; oil production potential of, 41,
    64, 138; oil reserves in, 54t
Kyoto Protocol, 23, 51n11, 165n2

Middle East

Persian Gulf War, 6, 18, 64, 198

Petrobonds, 19

Petrodollars, 4

Philippines, 32

Plaza Accord, 127

Pollution, 23–24

Portfolio investments, 100n3; in developing countries, 73–74, 76, 77, 79–81, 104t; goal of, 207; historical changes in, 73–74, 76, 104t, 152; home bias in, 80–81, 148–149; mobility of, 207–208, 220–221; by oil-producing countries, 152–153; regulation of, 95

Poverty reduction, 75

Presidential election of 1984, 179

Price assessments, 20, 51n8

Private finance, 100n2, 100n3; composition of, 76; to developing countries, 75–76, 79–81, 106t; sources of, 79–84. *See also* Direct investments; Portfolio investments

Program Analysis and Evaluation (PA&E), 186, 200n7

Putin, Vladimir, 213, 232

Qatar, 25, 26

Rapid deployment force, 5

Rationing, 158

Reagan Revolution, 127

Recessions, economic, 18, 35

Recommendations, 227–234

Regulatory reform: and capital flows, 71, 95, 155; and energy trading, 20

Renewable energy, 43–44

«Rogue» states, 145, 180, 193

Rueff, Jacques, 125

Russia: capital flows in, 75, 76, 105t, 106t; China and, 213; economy of, 225; energy intensity of, 120t; GDP of, 109t, 110t; Japan and, 232; net exports of, 110t; in oil price scenarios, 38; oil production potential

of, 140, 145; and oil supply security, 62; poverty reduction in, 75; private finance in, 106t; trade with U. S., 119t. *See also* Soviet Union

Sanctions: under Clinton, 7–8; against Iran, 8, 142; against Iraq, 8, 45; oil industry on, 142; and oil prices, 143, 228–229; against OPEC, 60, 142–143; and spare productive capacity, 142–143, 145

Saud Al-Faisal, Prince, 198, 200n9

Saudi Arabia: China and, 37, 182; competition and, 42; downstream investments by, 31–32; environmental protection and, 24; foreign exchange income in, 4; GDP of, 110t; in high oil price scenario, 42, 45–46, 57t, 111t, 113t, 117t; Iran and, 145–146; Japan and, 176; in low oil price scenario, 35, 37, 44, 45–46, 56t, 111t, 115t, 118t; natural gas in, 25; net exports of, 102n28, 110t, 117t, 118t; in normal oil price scenario, 55t, 111t; oil production potential of, 41, 64, 138; oil reserves in, 54t; and oil supply security, 138; and OPEC supply management, 217; political stability of, 63, 176, 180, 183; terrorism in, 8; U. S. and, 190–191

Schlesinger, Arthur, 188

Scholes, Myron, 101n19

Securities, debt, 77

Securitization, 167, 200n1, 214

Seismic technologies, 26

Self-generation of energy, 165n1

Shell, 164

Sieminski, Adam, 133, 137–140, 141–142, 146, 162–163, 173

South America. *See* Latin America

South Asia, 103t, 121t

South China Sea, 43, 213

South Korea: capital flows in, 105t, 106t; currency of, 158; direct investments by, 77; downstream invest-

ABOUT THE CONTRIBUTORS

RICHARD L. ARMITAGE is currently U.S. deputy secretary of state. At the time of this study, he was president of Armitage Associates L.C. He previously served as U.S. coordinator for assistance to the newly independent states of the former Soviet Union, presidential negotiator for the Philippine Bases Agreement, special mediator of the Maqarin Dam water rights issue between Israel and Jordan, and assistant secretary of defense for international security affairs, among other positions.

LINCOLN P. BLOOMFIELD JR. is currently U.S. assistant secretary of state for political military affairs. At the time of this study, he was a partner at Armitage Associates L.C. He previously served as deputy assistant secretary of state for Near Eastern affairs, deputy assistant to the vice president for national security affairs, and principal deputy assistant secretary of defense for international security affairs, among other policy positions.

HERMAN T. FRANSSEN is president of International Energy Associates, Inc. and a director of Petroleum Economics, Ltd. He previously was senior economic adviser to the minister of petroleum of the Sultanate of Oman for about a decade and, before that, chief economist of the International Energy Agency in Paris. He has served both the U.S. executive and legislative branches.

PETER C. FUSARO is president of Global Change Associates, an energy-strategy consulting firm based in New York. His previous affiliations include service as senior vice president for energy consulting at ABB Financial Services. He has also worked for Petroleos de Venezuela, the U.S. Department of Energy, and the New York City Mayor's Energy and Telecommunications Office.

JAMES A. KELLY is currently U.S. assistant secretary of state for East Asian and Pacific affairs. At the time of this study, he was president of the Pacific Forum CSIS, based in Honolulu. He previously served in the U.S. government as special assistant to the president for national security affairs and deputy assistant secretary of defense for Asian affairs, among other positions.

CATHERINE L. MANN is senior fellow at the Institute for International Economics in Washington, D.C., and currently teaching at the Johns Hopkins University Paul Nitze School of Advanced International Studies. She is an adjunct professor at the Owen School of Management at Vanderbilt University. She has held several posts at the Federal Reserve Board of Governors and at the World Bank, and she has served as a senior economist on the staff of the President's Council of Economic Advisors.

ROBERT A. MANNING is currently senior counselor for energy, technology, and science policy at the U.S. Department of State. At the time of this study, he was the C.V. Starr Fellow and director of Asian Studies at the Council on Foreign Relations and a consultant to the U.S. Institute of Peace. He has previously served as policy adviser to the assistant secretary of state for East Asian and Pacific affairs.

R. TAGGART MURPHY is professor, College of International Relations, Tsukuba University, Japan, and senior nonresident visiting fellow at the Brookings Institution in Washington, D.C. He is author of *The Weight of the Yen* (Norton, 1996) and, with Akio Mikuni, of *Japan's Policy Trap* (Brookings, 2002).

KEVIN G. NEALER is a principal at the Scowcroft Group, a Washington-based international business advisory firm. A former Fulbright professor and current adjunct professor at Georgetown University's McDonough School of Business, he has lead responsibility for the firm's financial services practice.

Janne E. Nolan is the international program director at the Eisenhower Institute in Washington, D.C. She also teaches in the National Security Studies Program at Georgetown University and serves on a number of U.S. government policy advisory panels. She previously served as a policy official in the U.S. Department of State and has held policy portfolios at the Brookings Institution and on the U.S. Senate Armed Services Committee staff.

Yukio Okamoto is currently senior adviser to the prime minister of Japan. At the time of this study, he was president of Okamoto Associates in Tokyo. A well-known expert commentator on U.S.-Japan relations, he had served previously in several policy positions in Japan's Ministry of Foreign Affairs.

Adam Sieminski is a director and global oil strategist at Deutsche Bank Securities in Baltimore. He previously served as the senior energy analyst at NatWest Securities and as a partner at Washington Analysis Corporation.

Paul D. Wolfowitz is currently U.S. deputy secretary of defense. At the time of this study, he was dean of the Paul Nitze School of Advanced International Studies at the Johns Hopkins University. His many previous policy positions in the U.S. government include undersecretary of defense for policy, assistant secretary of state for East Asian and Pacific affairs, U.S. ambassador to Indonesia, and director of policy planning at the U.S. Department of State.

Robert B. Zoellick is currently the U.S. Trade Representative and a member of the president's cabinet. At the time of this study, he was a research scholar at the Belfer Center for Science and International Affairs at Harvard University, resident fellow at the German Marshall Fund of the United States, and a senior international adviser to Goldman Sachs. His previous U.S. government policy positions include undersecretary of state for economic affairs, deputy White House chief of staff, and counselor to the secretary of the treasury.